LANGUAGE, SELF AND LOVE

Language, Self and Love

Hermeneutics in the Writings of Richard Rolle
and the Commentaries on the Song of Songs

DENIS RENEVEY

UNIVERSITY OF WALES PRESS
CARDIFF
2001

© Denis Renevey, 2001

British Library Cataloguing-in-Publication Data.
A catalogue record for this book is available from the British Library.

ISBN 0-7083-1696-4

All rights reserved. No part of this book may be reproduced, stored in a retrieval system, or transmitted, in any form or by any means, electronic, mechanical, photocopying, recording or otherwise, without clearance from the University of Wales Press, 6 Gwennyth Street, Cardiff, CF24 4YD. Website: www.wales.ac.uk/press

Typeset at University of Wales Press
Printed in Great Britain by Dinefwr Press, Llandybïe

In memory of my mother, Regina Renevey (1929–1979), and my father, Jean Renevey (1924–2001)

Contents

Acknowledgements ix
Abbreviations xii

Introduction 1

PART ONE *Hermeneutics and Language of Love in the Twelfth Century* 7

1 Language Theory in the Twelfth Century 9

2 Hermeneutics and Degrees of Love 22

3 Discovering the Self through Love in the Writings of William of St Thierry 41

PART TWO *Self and Tradition: Richard Rolle and the Commentary Tradition of the Song of Songs* 61

Prologue 63

4 From *Interpres* to *Auctor*: New Contexts for the Vocabulary of Love 66

5 Love of God and Lovers of the World: Self and Audience in *Contra amatores mundi* 103

6 Hermeneutics and Degrees of Love in the Epistles 122

Afterword	151
Notes	155
Bibliography	212
Index	223

Acknowledgements

This book is an offshoot of the dissertation that I submitted for a doctorate at the University of Oxford. My initial stay at Lincoln College, Oxford, was made possible thanks to a generous scholarship from the Berrow Foundation. I would like to thank very warmly its benefactor, the Marquis de Amodio, for his generosity. Without his support, my stay at Oxford simply would not have been possible. I was the recipient of a Junior Research Fellowship from the Swiss National Science Foundation to complete doctoral work there. The SNSF has also financed two and half years of postdoctoral research at Oxford. Dr Vincent Gillespie, from St Anne's College, provided support and encouragement throughout. Although much pruning and revision work have taken place in the preparation of this book, what remains and can be considered valuable owes a lot to him. Douglas Gray and Stanley Hussey who examined the thesis provided critical comments which have led to some of the revisions.

Much time has elapsed since the inception of this project and its present completion. This allowed for earlier versions of the book or some of its parts to fall into several helpful hands, and it is a pleasure for me to record here my debts to friends and colleagues. Derek Brewer saw a description of the project and made suggestions which led to the present title for the book. His pointing to Charles Taylor's *Sources of the Self* has had an important impact on the way the book has taken final shape. Roger Ellis read a draft of chapter 1 and made very useful comments. As organizer of the Medieval Translator Conference, he also provided the platform where some of the ideas for this book took initial shape. I am grateful to him for having been so lavish of advice and care to the young and immature scholar that I was. Ralph Hanna III read an early version of this book and made suggestions for change, some of which have been taken into consideration. Nicholas Watson has read a draft of this version and has kindly lent his support, offering many useful suggestions which I have taken into account in the final preparation of this version. I also would like to thank the anonymous reader for the University of Wales Press who offered very professional advice on how to set out revisions for the final version. I hope to have been able to live up at least in part to his/her high expectations. If the book finds a more general audience than those specializing in the mystics, it is in great part due to the alterations which were triggered by his/her careful suggestions. It goes without saying that I am entirely responsible for errors and infelicities which may still remain.

Christiania Whitehead provided much support in the final stages of the work, and the collaborative editing project which we embarked upon together was instrumental in leading to the strong desire to complete this one as well. Anne Mc Govern-Mouron has been an academic companion from the start of my graduate studies at Oxford. François Amberg has proved a great help during IT crises, gracefully providing replacement equipment during cases of emergency. Thanks to him and to Marlène Zwygart for their kindness. Some other friends and colleagues have provided support in more ways than one. I would like to thank John Sykes, Frank McGovern and Joel Simon for reading papers which have been shaped to make parts of this work, as well as discussing the mystics with me. The post-Oxford experience in Geneva would not have been as pleasurable and academically stimulating without the companionship of Anne-France Morand and Gregory Rowe. My friends Sandra and Volker Wenk were kind enough to offer me the use of their house as a solitary retreat in the village of Reppaz, where much of the writing for this book took place from one summer to another. The village, overlooking some of the most overwhelming views of the Alps, stands above the road leading to the St Bernard Pass, an important medieval alpine road to northern Italy and Rome. No other place could have been as inspiring as that. Susan Jenkins, Duncan Campbell and Ceinwen Jones from the University of Wales Press have been the editors that every author would dream of. They have turned administrative tasks into joyful and constructive exchange. My colleagues in Fribourg and Lausanne have provided the stimulating environment for the completion of this project.

My wife Patricia has been my companion long before I even considered writing on the mystics. She has watched me embark on this project while pursuing her own musical interests, but at the same time showing a great amount of tolerance and grace to see me through with it. It would not have been completed without her support and her inspiring piano-playing.

This book is dedicated to my late parents, Regina and Jean Renevey. Sometimes with great surprise and wonder, they watched me indulge in what was then a passion and has now become my profession. I am immensely grateful to them for having let me develop my own professional aspirations when in their youth the cultural and economic context did not always make possible the development of their own.

Denis Renevey
August 2001

Abbreviations

CCist	*Collectanea Cisterciensia*
CSt	*Cistercian Studies*
DR	*Downside Review*
DS	*Dictionnaire de spiritualité: ascétique et mystique, doctrine et histoire*, ed. M. Viller *et al.* (Paris, 1937–95)
DTC	*Dictionnaire de théologie catholique: contenant l'exposé des doctrines de la théologie catholique, leurs preuves et leur histoire, commencé sous la direction de A. Vacant, E. Mangenot, continué sous celle de E. Amann* (Paris, 1903 (1899–1972))
EETS	Early English Text Society; volume numbers in the Original Series are prefixed OS, those in the Extra Series are prefixed ES, those in the Supplementary Series are prefixed SS
ELH	*English Literary History*
JWCI	*Journal of the Warburg and Courtauld Institute*
MA	*Medium Aevum*
MED	*Middle English Dictionary*, ed. H. Kurath *et al.* (Ann Arbor, Mich., 1952–)
MMTE	M. Glasscoe (ed.), T*he Medieval Mystical Tradition in England. Exeter Symposium*, 6 vols. (Exeter, 1980, 1982; Cambridge, 1984, 1987, 1992, 1999)
MQ	*Mystics Quarterly*
MSR	*Mélanges de science religieuse*
OED	*Oxford English Dictionary*
OLD	*Oxford Latin Dictionary*, ed. R. G. W. Glare (1968; repr. Oxford, 1992)
PL	*Patrologia latina*, ed. J.-P. Migne (Paris, 1841– 64)
RAM	*Revue d'ascétique et de mystique*
RMAL	*Revue du moyen age latin*
RSR	*Revue des sciences religieuses*
RTAM	*Revue de théologie ancienne et médiévale*
SC	Sources chrétiennes (Paris, 1941–).
Super cant.	E. M. Murray, 'Richard Rolle's Comment on the Canticles: Edited from MS Trinity College, Dublin, 153' (Ph.D. thesis, Fordham University, 1958)
VHCE	*The Victoria History of the Counties of England*

Introduction

The late medieval period has received insufficient attention with regard to its contribution towards a language of interiority.[1] More often than not, the account of Augustine's immense impact on the language of inwardness for the Western tradition of thought is followed by accounts of the ways authors of the Enlightenment accommodated the Augustinian model to their new preoccupations.[2] The aim of this volume is partly to fill in the gap between Augustine and Rousseau by considering a range of texts which align themselves to the Augustinian model of the inwardness of radical reflexivity while delving into the complexities of a specific biblical text, the Song of Songs. It is also with the appeal to the first-person standpoint that, from the twelfth century onwards, commentators of the Song of Songs engage with this highly performative book in their search for truth.[3]

Language, Self and Love demonstrates the importance of the commentary tradition for the shaping of the medieval self which personally engages with the writing of commentaries in particular, and medieval subjectivity in general. It participates in uncovering this medieval sense of inwardness not by looking at the popular penitential literature which followed the implementations of the 1215 Fourth Lateran Council decisions on the need for the laity to receive confession annually, but by looking at a highly specialized body of Latin and vernacular theologies where the self is described in its attempts at establishing a direct relationship with the deity.[4] That relationship is negotiated with the mediation of the amorous discourse of love of the Song of Songs.

However, before discussing at greater length the case of the commentary tradition of the Song of Songs as textual space from which notions of the self and the language of inwardness developed, let us consider for a moment the Augustinian contribution.[5] The most significant contributions to the language of interiority by

Augustine of Hippo (354–430) are found in the *Confessions*, *On the Trinity* and *On Free Will*. Augustine develops in those texts a language which places the first-person standpoint as central to the search for truth. Although strongly influenced by Neo-Platonism, especially as conveyed by Plotinus (*c*.205–70), Augustine nevertheless argues that the passage from a lower to a higher order has to pass through a consideration of inwardness. In linking Platonic thought to Christian mystical aspirations, Augustine creates a paradigm which places the self and the language of inwardness at the core of all serious spiritual investigation. This paradigm will have an impact on all subsequent spiritual investigations in the medieval West. However, the language of interiority, which Augustine uses to construct his method of introspection and to describe the soul in its quest for the beatific vision, is indebted to Plotinian imagery, with its strong sexual overtones. Sexual imagery also contributes importantly to the making of the medieval self in a series of texts that feed on the Augustinian concept of the self while emerging from a significantly different textual tradition in which sexual language plays an even more important role than in the Augustinian one. As Taylor's *Sources of the Self* aims to explain the making of the modern identity, this particular medieval tradition is passed over silently. One of the aims of *Language, Self and Love* is to make good such an omission by considering the role played by the commentary tradition of the Song of Songs both in the way it shapes Western medieval mysticism in general and participates in developing further the language of interiority for the delineation of the medieval self in particular.

After the magisterial work of Beryl Smalley on the Bible and its commentaries, interest in this tradition has received new impetus with the writings of Minnis, Scott and Wallace, who have put special emphasis on the development of a medieval literary theory within that corpus, which is based on perceptions of the nature and role of the divine and human authors.[6] The commentary genre forms the core material of the present volume in an approach which feeds on the evidence provided by previous scholars, but which is given a different bearing here. Indeed, less than the making of authorship, it is the making of the self that informs my reading of those biblical commentaries. For that reason, I have chosen to limit my investigation to one specific book of the Bible, the Song of Songs.

The Song of Songs belongs to the group of the wisdom books of the Old Testament.[7] It has received more attention from biblical scholars than any other book of the Bible. One can possibly account for this attention by the fact that the Song of Songs is in form and content a difficult text that defies and invites a multiplicity of interpretations.[8] The question whether it has a proper place in the Bible has been answered in Jewish and Christian exegesis by the provision of a spiritual interpretation. For, indeed, the Song of Songs is most often regarded as a series of love poems describing various moments of a particular love relationship with a rich, sophisticated and sexually daring imagery, where God is not mentioned. In short, a literal explanation cannot justify the place of the Song of Songs in the biblical canon. Worse, if not offered a spiritual meaning, verses like 'Let him kiss me with the kiss of his mouth/For your breasts are better than wine', for example, are at best nonsensical, at worst subversive, therefore challenging God's authority over the Word. It is my contention that the challenging textual task of making sense of the language of the Song of Songs within the biblical context created a space from which further advances in the discovery of the self were made. However, as there were several interpretative streams for the Song of Songs, not all commentators chose to describe the book as one which put emphasis on the relationship between the redeemed soul and God (mystical treatment), but instead used it to talk about either the relationship of the Church and God (ecclesiastical treatment), or that of Mary and Jesus (Marian interpretation).[9] Most of the commentaries considered below belong to the mystical stream.[10]

It is indeed the process of accommodation of some of the terms belonging to the semantic field of carnal love, present in the Song of Songs, for the definition and conceptualization of the relationship between the soul and God, which is the object of my investigation. If commentaries belonging to the mystical stream do not place discussions on the human *auctor* at the centre of their concerns, they facilitate instead active penetration into the textual layers of scripture on the part of the narrative voice.[11] This process allows for the making of metaphorical meaning from the erotic terms of love of the Song of Songs.

Metaphorical meaning and affective involvement are paramount in the most celebrated twelfth-century mystical commentaries on the Song of Songs. The intimate engagement of the narrative voice with the text engenders questions on the nature of language and its role in conveying the reality of spiritual experience. Thus, spiritual and literary concerns often merge together in the commentaries whose narrative voices perform in the affective mode. Rather than expounding different medieval theories on affectivity, I have selected a number of late medieval texts in which the affective mode is integral to their commentaries and mystical writings. I thus offer case studies in which the Song of Songs stands as material for the experimental uses of the language of love by commentators in expressing their mystical experiences and the discovery of their own selves. The preponderance of the mystical interpretation in hermeneutics allows appropriation of the original text on the part of the interpreter.[12] This mode of appropriation, which signally departs from the original intention grounded on the biblical context, confers on the authorial voice of the commentary a substantial ability to manœuvre the lexical terms into contexts more closely related to its inner experiences.

One of the characteristics of mystical affective writings is that of narrative performance. The narrative voice in commentaries by William of St Thierry (c.1075–1147/1148), St Bernard of Clairvaux (1090–1153), Richard of St Victor (d. 1173) and Richard Rolle (1300–49) enters into, and interacts affectively with material from the Song of Songs. Rather than explicating and expounding possible meanings, the narrative voice exploits the material as a conduit for mystical experience. Following Matter on this issue, I acknowledge the commentary as a literary genre, as all the treatises 'display a clear consciousness of belonging to a type, a method, a mode of literature'.[13] Within the larger definition of commentary as genre, Matter considers Song of Songs commentaries as forming a special category. The pervasive accommodation of verses and images of the Song of Songs within the liturgy, sermons, postils, anchoritic and mystical treatises, epistles, lyrics, tales, fables and other secular genres took place in parallel to, and possibly as a result of, the development of the commentary of the Song of Songs as a literary category. After a careful appraisal of some significant treatises belonging to this category, *Language, Self and Love* considers its impact on other derivative medieval religious writings.

A great number of twelfth-century exegetical works on the Song of Songs point to discussions on affective intention and language of love. Moreover, works like the *Benjamin minor* and *Benjamin major* of Richard of St Victor contribute to this analytic study of the function and role of images and symbols within a contemplative system by demonstrating an acute degree of awareness of the link between contemplative practice and literary theory. Working within the commentary framework, William of St Thierry, a less well-known figure than his friend Bernard of Clairvaux, provides a complex, refined and ambitious mystical system by adopting a self-referential attitude in his approach to the language of love.

The corpus of Richard Rolle, the fourteenth-century hermit of Hampole, provides us with important materials where the transference of the metaphorical discourse of love from one context to another can be carefully surveyed. Although *Incendium amoris* and *Super psalmum vicesimum*, composed before *Super canticum canticorum*, contain some love imagery, I would contend that Rolle's own commentary on some of the verses of the Song of Songs is the cornerstone for the expression of his later mystical utterances. *Super canticum canticorum* offers interesting insights into Rolle's treatment of the commentary genre, used in his case as a means of translating his personal experience. Moreover, I would contend that it constitutes a fundamental work for our understanding of his mysticism, as well as the source for his elaboration of the didactic three degrees of love, knowledge of which is vital to the decoding of the most elevated passages of his Middle English writings. Rolle profits from the malleability of the commentary genre by making *Melos amoris*, another treatise closely dependent on the Song of Songs, the locus for the deployment of his most arresting account on his life as a contemplative. Here again, the metaphorical discourse of love acts best in reviving for the reader the feelings associated with the contemplative state. Unlike the previous works by Rolle discussed in this study, *Contra amatores mundi* unveils the importance of the language of love for a potential, possibly imaginary, audience. As we will see, Rolle employs a strategy which stresses the multiple meanings, carnal and/or spiritual, of the language of love, according to both the new contextualization and the degree of spiritual preparation of the potential audience of this treatise. The Latin and Middle English epistles, written for specific recipients, nuns or recluses in the case of the Middle English ones, are evidence of further contextualization for the language of love, in a manner not dissimilar to that offered in the thirteenth-century literature of guidance for women, such as the pieces which form the Wooing Group.[14] In those texts which address an audience known to Rolle, he offers meaningful insights which point to the interdependence between religious experience and linguistic competence. For, indeed, Rolle is going to explicate to his readers that their ability at decoding the written signs found in the epistles will have an impact on the development of their spiritual sophistication. Climbing the spiritual ladder marked by Rolle's three degrees of love implies a growth in love which depends on a process whereby the reader must decipher, make meaning of and then perform the written signs.

Language, Self and Love accounts for the development and transformation from a self-reflexive to an altruistic discourse which allows the reader to take possession of the text and to perform it. The writing process, which is usually essential to mystical performance, is here replaced by a text which makes of reading an active performance. By constructing an audience alongside a discourse whose main characteristic is the inwardness of radical reflexivity, Rolle posits a compromise in the form of the epistolary genre which allows for greater accessibility and performative possibilities on the part of his audience. The latter is only distantly aware of the sources for the rich love imagery which pervade the epistles. Hence, rather than providing an account of the authorial roles played out by Richard of St Victor, William of St Thierry and Richard Rolle, among others, *Language, Self and Love* contributes instead to inform our understanding of the making of their selves in particular, and the medieval self in general, on the basis of information drawn from their writings.

Part One

Hermeneutics and Language of Love in the Twelfth Century

1
Language Theory in the Twelfth Century

The Twelve Patriarchs and *The Mystical Ark* of Richard of St Victor (d. 1173), also called respectively *Benjamin minor* and *Benjamin major*, present the most comprehensive twelfth-century study of the role of the imagination in the making of figurative language. My specific aim in this chapter is to look particularly at the ways Richard of St Victor, heir to the Augustinian tradition through the writings of Hugh of St Victor, discusses the making and the roles of metaphorical language within his mystical system.[1] Although his immediate concern is not with language theory as such, his sharp focus on the ways language operates in the work of contemplation leads him to an attentive consideration of language use and theory.

An examination of the textual evidence provided in the Ricardian corpus requires a brief prior discussion of the place of his two major treatises on contemplation in the larger context of the Victorine scholastic and mystical tradition.[2] Hugh of St Victor (end 11th cent.–1141) came to the abbey of Saint-Victor in Paris at an early age, soon after 1115. From 1127 onwards, he became very active as a teacher and became the founder of the school of Saint-Victor. It was during this period that Hugh wrote one of his masterpieces, the *Didascalicon*.[3]

This monumental didactic work, described in its subtitle as a medieval guide to the arts, stands as the cornerstone for the entire Victorine scholastic tradition. It is a guide to the process of reading as well as being a teaching guide. It approaches all aspects of learning by a detailed consideration of the *trivium* and the *quadrivium*. The *Didascalicon* praises instruction as a means of achieving restoration of one's own true nature. In true Augustinian fashion, its concern is with radical reflexivity. In book 1 of the *Didascalicon*, Hugh of St Victor discusses the threefold power of the soul which consists in providing: (1) life to the body, (2) judgement of sense perception and

(3) the power of mind and reason.[4] According to Hugh of St Victor, judgement of sense perception relies on the ability to remember and memorize when the sensible object has been removed from the eye. Memory and the ability to name partake in the making of the inner geography of the self:

> Moreover, such beings as possess sense perception not only apprehend the forms of things that affect them while the sensible body is present, but even after the sense perception has ceased and the sensible objects are removed, they retain images of the sense-perceived forms and build up memory of them.[5]

Considerations on language, sense perceptions, imagination and memory are discussed further in the treatise. The *Didascalicon*, as the next passage quoted clearly bears witness, is imbued with the same Neo-Platonic ideology as some of the Augustinian treatises. The incorporeal nature of spirits and souls, which stands beyond the world of the sensible, is apprehended by reason through imagination:

> In different respects, therefore, the same thing is at the same time intellectible and intelligible – intellectible in being by nature incorporeal and imperceptible to any of the senses; intelligible in being a likeness of sensible things, but not itself a sensible thing. For the intellectible is neither a sensible thing nor a likeness of sensible things. The intelligible, however, is itself perceived by intellect alone, yet does not itself perceive only by means of intellect. It has imagination and the senses, and by these lays hold upon all things subject to sense. Through contact with physical objects it degenerates, because, while through sense impressions it rushes out toward the visible forms of bodies and, having made contact with them, draws them into itself through imagination, it is cut away from its simplicity each time it is penetrated by any qualities entering through hostile sense experience. But when, mounting from such distraction toward pure understanding, it gathers itself into one, it becomes more blessed through participating in intellectible substance.[6]

While Hugh of St Victor traces the soul's way down into corporeal entities, Richard of St Victor works on the reversal phenomenon, that is the soul's attempt at regaining its original simplicity in order to achieve its journey back to its state of primary intellectible substance.[7] It is the work of contemplation, final step in the practice of proper living, which provides the tools for the completion of that task.[8]

The Twelve Patriarchs, composed between 1153 and 1162 by Richard of St Victor, and its sequel, *The Mystical Ark*, expand on the work of contemplation as described by Hugh of St Victor by considering the roles given to imagination and the making of metaphorical utterances in contemplative activity. The two treatises stand together as the first systematic account offering a discipline for preparation of the self in the work of contemplation.

In the form of personification allegory, Richard of St Victor paints a magisterial portrait of the rational soul under the image of Jacob. Soul's pursuit of truth and virtue requires the support of all its faculties, described by Richard as Jacob's two wives and their handmaidens by whom he had thirteen children, allegorized as aspects of the spiritual life. Bala, the handmaiden of Rachel, represents imagination, and divides into two: the animal imagination, which wanders randomly without any purpose, and the reasoned imagination, servant to reason.[9] Reasoned imagination, essentially described as a faculty operating in its creative linguistic role as producer of metaphors, functions as a messenger between the physical world and reason. The reasoned imagination operates at two levels. First, it makes literal use of images to convey fear of future damnation; the personification adopted for this level is Bala's first child, Dan.[10] Secondly, it makes comparisons, analogies and metaphors to convey future heavenly joys and contemplation in ecstasy; Naphtali, Bala's second child, personifies that second level. The perception of spiritual realities, facilitated by imagination, can be acquired only if affections grow into virtues. The unions of Jacob both to Leah, which stands for the affective part of the soul, and to her handmaiden Zelpha, which stands for the five bodily senses, result in the birth of those virtues. Thus, abstinence (Gad) and patience (Asher) are born from the union of Jacob to Zelpha, while fear of God (Ruben), grief (Simeon), hope of forgiveness (Levi), love of God (Judah), joy of interior sweetness (Issachar), hatred of vices (Zabulon) and shame (Dina) are born from the union of Jacob with Leah herself. The birth and the subsequent practice of those virtues by the self eventually lead to a state of full self-realization, possibly followed by contemplation in ecstasy. These two states are characterized by self-knowledge and ecstasy, represented respectively by Joseph and Benjamin, the two sons of Jacob and Rachel. They bring about the death of discursive reason, figured by the death of Rachel in giving birth to Benjamin (contemplation). It is to this latter aspect, contemplation, that Richard devotes his whole attention in *The Mystical Ark*.

In this work, most likely written after *The Twelve Patriarchs*, Richard defines six degrees of contemplation with regard to the nature of the objects used to prompt contemplative activity.[11] In the first kind of contemplation, the soul wonders at the objects of the world perceived as a manifestation of the divine. It is the imaginative faculty which is solely responsible for this process. Imagination plays another important role in the second degree of contemplation. From the objects of the world, brought to reason by imagination, the former draws analytical and abstract knowledge. This kind of contemplation is further removed from the external world. The third degree of contemplation – most important to our investigation – makes use of the external world only to provide reason with images as a means of access to invisible things. It is at this level that metaphorical utterances play an active role in the Ricardian system. Imagination is left out from the fourth degree onwards, as reason in this degree goes beyond image to have, through pure *intelligentia* (understanding), knowledge of things above sense and reason itself. In the fifth and sixth degrees, understanding takes over from reason to present objects of contemplation which, once presented to reason, are not beyond comprehension in the fifth degree. The objects of contemplation in the sixth degree on the other hand consist of subtle intellectual and theological concepts which are both beyond and contrary to reason: for example, the concept of the Trinity of three persons in one God is such an object of contemplation.

Moreover, following St Paul, but also influenced by Platonic philosophy, Richard of St Victor describes three heavens according to the tripartite division of mental faculties such as the imaginative, the rational and the intellectual: accordingly these are the imaginative, the rational and the intellectual heavens.[12] Additional information on the internal processes by which the soul experiences contemplation is given by the definition of three modes of contemplation. The first mode, *dilatatio mentis* (enlarging of the mind), is reached through the effect of meditation, and gives the soul insight into the objects of the world. The second mode, *sublevatio mentis* (elevation of the mind), defines the state whereby the soul, with the gift of special grace, reaches and gains access to realities which are beyond itself. The *alienatio* (alienation), or *excessus mentis*, constitutes the third mode. At this stage, the soul forfeits its faculties and is totally seized by the object it contemplates. The soul loses consciousness of itself and the world.[13] In the first three degrees of contemplation – incidentally those where imagination plays an active role – experience is achieved mainly by *dilatatio* and *sublevatio*.

I would like now to turn to the consideration of the role of imagination, more especially to the activity of *translatio*, which stands for the making of metaphorical language. The remaining part of this chapter considers, first, the didactic role of metaphorical language in the contemplative process. It then turns to another function of metaphorical language by giving attention to its descriptive qualities to express the ineffable.

THE DIDACTIC ROLE OF METAPHORICAL LANGUAGE

Book 2, chapter 18, of *The Mystical Ark* offers a Platonically influenced definition of the kind of contemplation where imagination creates metaphorical utterances:[14] 'there are invisible things that we perceive mentally and yet we form them in us out of a similitude of visible things'.[15] Through the subordination of imagination to reason, the rational soul perceives the links between visible objects and the invisible world. They are expressed with symbols, allegories and metaphors. Those literary devices best encapsulate any spiritual experience, and form, within literary language, a species of their own. The Platonic world of ideas is equated to the first heaven, where imagination works under the guidance of reason:[16]

> And so imagination takes a place in the first heaven, reason in the second, and understanding in the third. And of these, the first is gross and fleshy in comparison with the others, and in its own certain way it is touchable and corporeal since it is imaginary and phantastical, drawing after itself and retaining in itself forms and similitudes of corporeal things.[17]

The two highest heavens have no need of imagination. Moreover, the fifth and sixth kinds of contemplation, he asserts, are beyond the Platonic system.

It is therefore only in the first three degrees of contemplation that metaphorical language is effective as an active element in the work of contemplation. To return to *The Twelve Patriarchs*, Naphtali, second son of Bala and Jacob, relishes the invention of metaphorical language.[18] This process of invention is explained in simple, but telling terms:

However, that imagination is rational when from those things which we know by means of bodily sense we fabricate something else in the imagination. For instance: We have seen gold, we have seen a house, but we have never seen a gold house. Nevertheless, if we wish we are able to picture to ourselves a gold house. In any case a beast cannot do this.[19]

Richard has already stressed earlier the importance of the subordinate role of imagination, and now gives a series of warnings, exemplified by means of allegories, to prevent imagination from cutting its tie with reason. Richard draws the foundation of his system from Romans 1: 20, probably under the influence of Augustine's *De doctrina christiana*: 'For the invisible things of him form the creation of the world are clearly seen, being understood by means of those things that are made.'[20] Reason, unable on its own to rise to an understanding of invisible things, needs imagination to represent to itself celestial things through the form of similitudes between corporeal things and celestial things. This feature constitutes the core of the third degree of contemplative activity. At those stages, linguistic competence decides importantly the success of contemplation, as the soul, since the Fall, has had no other means to gain access to higher realities. The role of imagination is therefore vital, as it links the exterior world to the inner world, sensation to reason:

> Therefore the imagination (inasmuch as she is handmaid) runs between mistress and servant, between reason and sense. And whatever it imbibes from outside through the sense of the flesh, it represents inwardly for the service of reason. Thus imagination always assists reason, never in fact withdrawing itself from her service for a single moment. For even when sense fails, imagination does not cease to provide. For when I am placed in darkness, I see nothing, but if I wish I am able to imagine anything. So always and in all things, imagination is ready, and reason can employ her service everywhere.[21]

Richard demonstrates the importance of the reasoned imagination for the expression and understanding of spiritual truth. The beauty of visible things uplifts the soul to spiritual realities: 'It describes invisible things through the forms of visible things and impresses the memory of them upon our minds through the beauty of certain very desirable appearances'. [22]

When Richard reconsiders these matters in *The Mystical Ark,* he teaches that the third degree of contemplation divides into five stages, delineated according to the five different ways the imaginative principle uses objects in metaphorical utterances to represent invisible spiritual realities.

From biblical examples, Richard lists five kinds of metaphors according to the quality and nature of the object used for the transference from a literal to a metaphorical meaning. A metaphor can be made from the particular nature of an object, such as in the following example: 'His legs are marble columns, which have been set upon golden bases' (Song of Songs 5: 15). The external quality of an object, which Richard limits to colour or figure, may also serve as vehicle for a metaphorical utterance. It is through the visual sense that the imagination sends the message decoded by reason. Richard illustrates the point with the following example: 'My beloved is dazzling white and ruddy' (Song of Songs 5: 10). Metaphors are drawn also from the internal quality of an object. All the other senses may be active for the making of such an utterance. It is hearing which is called forth in the following example: 'And the sound which I heard was, as it were, the sound of harpers harping on their harps' (Rev. 14: 2). The natural use of an object – rain and snow in the case given by Richard – may also become vehicle for a metaphorical utterance: 'Built upon the foundation of the apostles and prophets, with Jesus Christ Himself the chief cornerstone' (Eph. 2: 20). That such sophisticated discussions on language theory took place during the flowering period of the commentary tradition is certainly not coincidental.

The metaphorical language of scripture, both imaginary and intellectual, conveys truths which must be decoded in the light of the anagogical sense. Pleasurable corporeal objects, used as similitudes or vehicles for metaphorical utterances, create desires which, although originating from the carnal world, lead the contemplative to focus on God.[23] The stories of Jacob, Moses and Aaron provide a skeleton for *The Twelve Patriarchs* and *The Mystical Ark*, from which Richard shapes spiritual riddles that provide access to divine wisdom: 'For what do we call sacred Scripture except the bedchamber of Rachel, in which we do not doubt that divine wisdom is hidden beneath the veil of attractive allegories?'[24]

The reader gains individual experience and psychological insight when he searches for the spiritual kernel infused (if the mixed metaphor can be allowed) in the biblical stories.[25] Richard's distinctive relationship with scripture relies on the ways he uses it to make sense of his own self in order to surpass himself.[26] Unlike Thomas Gallus (d. 1246), whose cosmological mysticism depends on the Dionysian metaphysical approach to God,[27] Richard describes, perhaps under the influence of St Bernard, passionate affective states.[28]

Chapters 11 to 13 of *The Twelve Patriarchs* contribute to a better understanding of the use of metaphorical discourse in the Ricardian system. The soul, repentant for its past sins, has been consoled by the Holy Spirit, and, its affections now restored, feels that an intimacy is developing between itself and God. Friendship, and the frequent visits of God to the soul, bring an ineffable joy, expressed in the discourse of the bride and bridegroom.[29] As a causal factor in the pursuit of spiritual knowledge, love replaces fear, grief and hope.[30] Before seeking union with its Creator, the rational spirit must first love his justice.[31] Love, the fourth son of Jacob (rational spirit) and Leah (affection), is called Judah, which at this stage embodies confession. When the soul realizes that it exists because of God's love, it is then ready to pursue its spiritual inquiries. Divine intelligence, the fusion of intelligence and love, called Rachel by Richard, facilitates inquiries and investigation:[32]

> Where there is love, there is seeing. We gladly look at one whom we greatly love. No one doubts that since he can love invisible goods, he will want immediately to know and to see them through the understanding. So the more Judah grows (that is, the affection called loving), the greater there burns in Rachel the desire to give birth, which is the pursuit of knowing.[33]

The love of invisible goods leads the soul to desire to know and see through understanding.[34] The Trinity demonstrates this state of perfect stability, where the order of being, the order of knowledge and the order of love dwell in harmony.[35]

Richard of St Victor eases the reading and memorization of the technical language of *The Twelve Patriarchs* and *The Mystical Ark* with the provision of a set of images and personifications. The use of the ark as *locus*, where each different degree of contemplation finds a specific niche, allows progressive access to the work of contemplation.[36] Parts of the fabric of the ark also play a role in the mnemonic function of this image borrowed from the Old Testament. Richard maintains however that the book, the *locus* and even metaphorical language are temporary: '[the soul] thinks by means of imagination because it does not yet have the power to see by means of purity of understanding'.[37] In the first degrees of contemplation, and more especially in the third degree, spiritual beauty is reached by means of metaphorical discourse. It is an important tool in leading reason to perceive and experience invisible realities. Beyond the third degree however, the soul enters a domain of pure substance, formless and shadowless, for which no contingent tool can provide access.

METAPHORS AS DESCRIPTIVE TOOLS

Richard stresses imagination's powerlessness to help the soul in the higher experiences of contemplation:

> What would imagination do there, where there is no changing and no shadow of vicissitude; where the part is not less than its whole, nor the whole is more universal than its individual parts; indeed, where the part is not lessening the whole, and the whole is not made up from parts, since that is simple which is set forth universally, and that is universal which is brought forth in the particular as it were; where the whole is single; where all is one and one is all? Certainly without doubt human reason fails in these things. And what can imagination do there? Without doubt in such kind of manifestation imagination can hinder it and is completely unable to assist.[38]

The soul does not need the support of literary metaphors in the final stages of its mystical ascension, because it has become pure enough to identify itself as image and resemblance of God.[39] But if imagination fumbles as a working tool in the higher degrees of contemplation, it still provides the fallen soul with the most efficient language, metaphorical discourse, for their description. The receiving of grace for instance is one of the most lyrical passages of *The Mystical Ark*. While Pseudo-Dionysius ceases his descriptions before reaching the unknowing, Richard resorts to the language of love to describe worlds beyond the cloud:[40]

> A moment in the garden, a moment in the hall, a moment in the chamber until at last finally after much waiting and great weariness He enters the

bedchamber and occupies the most intimate and secret place. A moment in the garden while the whole crowd of those making a disturbance is dispersed. A moment in the hall while the chamber is decorated. A moment in the chamber when the bridal bed is prepared. And the Beloved is forced to wait a moment and a moment in all of these places: a moment here and a moment there. He is heard from the garden. He is seen in the hall. He is kissed affectionately in the chamber. He is embraced in the bed-chamber.[41]

The recollection of ecstasy (*alienatio*, or *excessus mentis*), hidden by the veils of forgetting, can in part be articulated by metaphorical language.[42] On a razor's edge with the ineffable, and limited by spatio-temporal contingencies, metaphorical discourse translates the *alienatio* better than any other mode. It seems that, in the eyes of Richard, the ability to read in the carnal imagery self-evident truths about the spiritual union is an aspect of synderesis, that is, a natural habit impressed on the cognitive faculty of individuals.[43] The bride and bridegroom imagery facilitates only a fractional understanding of the *unio*. Metaphorical discourse at this level of the contemplative life attempts to capture and express glimpses of the summit of contemplation.[44]

By means of the *virtus imaginativa* the authors of scripture succeeded in expressing with carnal imagery the divine wisdom which was communicated to them.[45] The religious writer becomes himself *auctor* by making metaphors gesture towards spiritual reality. It is at this singular moment that literal language, transposed beyond its initial domain, captures the ineffable.[46] The role of the creative imagination in capturing the inexpressible is momentous.[47]

As the soul progresses on its journey back to God, it develops elaborate techniques to express spiritual realities. Language, rather than making use of abstract terms, resorts to corporeal and carnal objects encapsulated in an array of rhetorical devices.

The prophetic voice of Naphtali fashions the future joys within literary discourse by means of comparison (*comparatio*) and transference (*translatio*).[48] The latter, literary mechanism for the making of metaphorical discourse, works towards expressing spiritual beauty. Richard of St Victor explicates Genesis 49: 21, 'Naphtali is a hind sent forth, giving words of beauty', with the sensual vocabulary of the Song of Songs:[49]

> But how is he 'giving words of beauty'? Perhaps the more evidently we show this by an example, the more completely we can persuade. You wish

to hear words of beauty, words of pleasantness, full of beauty, full of sweetness, such as Naphtali is accustomed to form, or such as he agrees to form. 'Let him kiss me with the kiss of his mouth' (Song of Songs 1: 1). 'Stay me with flowers, comfort me with apples, for I am sick with love (ibid. 2: 5). 'Your lips, O my spouse drip like honeycomb; honey and milk are under your tongue; and the smell of your garments is like an aromatic odor' (ibid. 4: 11). What is heard more gladly or more avidly than such words? What, I ask, is found sweeter or more joyful than such words? These words seem to sound like something carnal, but nevertheless spiritual things are described by means of them. Thus Naphtali knew to mix carnal things with spiritual things and to describe incorporeal things by means of corporeal things so that the twofold nature of man finds in his words that from which he who consists of both corporeal and incorporeal nature might marvelously refresh himself. Perhaps it is for this reason that they taste so pleasantly to man because in a way, as has been said, they refresh his twofold nature.[50]

Metaphors of love please and restore the twofold nature of man. They lead to exultation (*exsultatio*) and joy (*jucunditas*), which, besides devotion and admiration, lead also to ecstasy (*excessus*).[51] Richard envisions the complete man, both carnal and spiritual, and envisages a co-operative interrelationship between the inner and the outer bodies, partaking of the divine mysteries. The theme surfaces again in the more detailed chapters of *The Mystical Ark*. Richard emphasizes the interrelationship between body and soul, and shows how, apart from the sexual member, all the body's parts may become subservient to the will of the soul. The will and the action it implements become undifferentiated.[52] The reasoned imagination, responsible for the making of metaphors of love, rather than nourishing the carnal impulses by fabricating fantasies, entices the senses to submit to the will of the inner person. Metaphors of love allow the carnal desires of the outer body to become subservient to the will of the inner body. Their transference into a context devoid of carnal connotations forces a mutation of their nature within this new domain. The carnal element remains however instrumental to the growth and purification of desire when it focuses on the higher degrees. The Ricardian spiritual quest shares the same positive and unitive approach of the Bernardine system. The outer person does not need to be resented: the process of spiritualization focuses intensely on the psyche, on the surrendering of the will to the inner person.

Richard ends his literary investigation of the role played by figurative language with an *apologia*, pointing to the need for the development of tools of inquiry to make religious literary theory self-sufficient:

> But to explain this topic fully and sufficiently would require a tract of its own. The more the reason of this speculation pays attention to this reasoning, the more this topic needs a more careful and greater inquiry. However, it is evident that in our times the greatest and almost the chief consolation of spiritual men is in this and subsequent speculations. For there are very few who are able to rise up to the two highest kinds of contemplation.[53]

Alongside Bernard of Clairvaux, Aelred of Rievaulx and William of St Thierry, some of the most prominent twelfth-century spiritual writers, Richard of St Victor has been recognized as a very important figure in the Western spiritual tradition. I hope I have demonstrated that, within this tradition, his prominence is owed in no small part to his subtle and masterly discussions on the nature and role of figurative language. He is in my view the finest religio-literary theorist of the twelfth century. His studies on the effect and meaning of the figurative language of scripture, and more especially his interest in the metaphorical discourse of love, stand as witness to twelfth-century awareness of the role of figurative language in the field of contemplation.

His influence, among others, on the fourteenth-century Middle English mystics has been recognized:[54] Richard Rolle, Walter Hilton, the Cloud-author, William Langland, and possibly Julian of Norwich, were directly, or indirectly, influenced by his work. Together with a Middle English translation/adaptation of the *Twelve Patriarchs*, which exists in thirteen manuscripts, those works are testimony of the high regard later medieval writers had for his spiritual discussions which gave a prominent place to language and the role of imagination.[55]

In his cataphatic approach to the divinity, Richard of St Victor discusses at length the role of imagination in the first three states of contemplation. With the *virtus imaginativa*, the authors of scripture succeeded in expressing in the physical language the divine wisdom which was communicated to them. For the religious writer, the making of a metaphor gestures towards spiritual activity. At this singular moment, literal language, beyond its domain, captures the ineffable: 'And so we are brought back again sharply to metaphor as essential expression of that which cannot be soberly stated in words – or, rather, the creative imagination which "sees" directly the reality.'[56]

Mystical language evidences the close association that exists between the spiritual experience and its formulation. Explicating the technicalities of the spiritual quest has led Richard to focus on its *ars docendi* rather than its *doctrina*.

Studies such as Richard's on the effect and meaning of the figural language of scripture, and more especially interest in the metaphorical discourse of love, stand as witness to the medieval awareness of the importance of literary competence for the work of contemplation. Richard of St Victor proposes an elaborate and systematic account to which a long line of biblical commentators contributed, in the wake of the pioneering work of Pseudo-Denys, Augustine and his followers. With the contemplative treatises of Richard, the Victorine tradition offers the medieval West the most systematic account yet of the role of discourse and the work of imagination in the contemplative field. It also situates the self in its quest for union with the deity as an entity whose very construct the discourse of love and contemplation encloses, while at the same time this discourse is seen as fashioning itself out of the utterances of the writing self.

2
Hermeneutics and Degrees of Love

THE SONG OF SONGS

If not all spiritual writings in the Middle Ages express similar theoretical concerns for the power of language in its claim for accessing divine truth, a great number of them nevertheless express an awareness for language's possibilities and limitations in the articulations of the relationship which individuals claim with the divine. All religious literary genres, such as commentaries, postils, meditations, odes and prayers, express a stage in the preparation for the future spiritual vision of God, the 'face to face', which stands as the common image for the expression of the beatific vision. My concern here is not with considering the religious literature set up within a liturgical framework and performed as part of a communal ritual, however fruitful such an endeavour may be. In its first part, this chapter explores a limited segment of this religious literature, the genre of the biblical commentaries, more especially commentaries on the Song of Songs. Within that category, it searches evidence for the manifestation of the emergence of the self, perceived as a participant in a direct exchange with the divine.

> Before the flesh has been tamed and the spirit set free by zeal for truth, before the world's glamour and entanglements have been firmly repudiated, it is a rash enterprise on any man's part to presume to study spiritual doctrines . . . How can there be harmony between the wisdom that comes down from above and the wisdom of the world, which is foolishness to God, or the wisdom of the flesh which is at enmity with God?[1]

No one was better informed than Bernard of Clairvaux (1090–1153) about the dangers of inviting an audience, be it a monastic one, to read the Song of Songs. For, even the monks of Clairvaux, trained in the new spiritual discipline of the Cistercian order, could be led by the carnal and sometimes cryptic imagery of the Song of Songs to dangerous misunderstandings. For the problematic features of this biblical book were many to a medieval reader. A brief consideration of the imagery of the Song shows the daring use of a sexually explicit vocabulary. Kisses, breasts, cheeks, embraces, lips, wounded heart, drunkenness, enclosed gardens, doves: those words, some of which are recurrent in the book, seem to refer to a secular love context. Indeed, the Song of Songs is an account of a love relationship between a lover and his beloved. Although the commentator's task is to explicate the terminology chosen by the divine author, by doing so he may awaken the carnal impulses of his audience and therefore lead them to a totally opposite consideration than the spiritual one, which was the only one the divine author could have intended. Moreover, this terminology is often set next to an imagery that is often exotic, if not cryptic. For instance, despite the undeniable poetic quality of some of those images, lines like 'your hair like a flock of goats which have come up from Mount Galaad' (Sg. 4: 1) or 'your nose like a tower of Lebanon which looks toward Damascus' (Sg. 8: 4) ask for a creative mind for the decoding of the meaning of the comparisons. In addition to the difficulties linked to the content of this book, commentators also worked at clarifying the structure of the book by attributing parts to different characters in order to make sense of its dialogic and performative dimensions.

The statement by Bernard of Clairvaux offered above shows how aware he is of the dangers of offering such an audacious text to one who would still hesitate between the wisdom of the flesh against divine wisdom. For that reason, Bernard of Clairvaux advises that reading of the Song should be limited to a spiritual élite:

> The novices, the immature, those but recently converted from a worldly life, do not normally sing this song or hear it sung. Only the mind disciplined by persevering study, only the man whose efforts have borne fruit under God's inspiration, the man whose years, as it were, make him ripe for marriage – years measured out not in time but in merits – only he is truly prepared for nuptial union with the divine partner, a union we shall describe more fully in due course.[2]

This passage makes direct allusion to the way the reader should impersonate the role of the beloved in order to perform partnership with the divine lover. Bernard, like his twelfth-century contemporaries, points to the way the medieval self has to engage with the text and its imagery. Providing guidance for a proper performance of the Song is one of the tasks that commentators are set.

Recent historical and theological scholarship has assessed further the role of the biblical commentary in general, and the commentaries on the Song of Songs in particular, in medieval culture. Among this new research, Ann Matter's *The Voice of my Beloved* has the ambitious aim of covering the whole of the medieval period, from the fourth to the fourteenth century. Because of her wide-ranging, but careful, account of the evolution of the exegesis of the Song of Songs, she can only pay a cursory look at individual texts, and only to mark the most important tendencies within that tradition. Thanks to this ground-clearing work, of which Matter's is only a part, it is now possible to pay more detailed attention to some of the issues raised by some exegetes.[3]

The Song of Songs had an immense appeal to medieval commentators.[4] Together with the Psalms, it received the greatest attention, with at least eighty Latin commentaries written between the fourth and the fourteenth century. One of the most influential pre-medieval commentaries was that of Origen of Alexandria (*c*.185–*c*.253/254), the third-century exegete, who developed the three levels of biblical interpretations.[5] It is very likely that Bernard of Clairvaux had read Origen, since the library of Clairvaux owned an exemplar of his commentary on the Song.[6] The importance of Origen for the making of the commentary as a sophisticated literary tool for the explication of the Bible is well known. His style of biblical exegesis found support from Ambrose, bishop of Milan, who transmitted it to Augustine. The importance given by Origen to the mystical sense of scripture, via the allegorical method, has a shaping influence on the mystical commentaries which are at the heart of my study in Part 1. John Cassian (*c*.360–*c*.435) developed Origen's allegorical methods in his *Collationes* into a system based on four levels of meaning: the literal, the allegorical, the anagogical and the tropological levels.[7] *Lectio divina* which pervaded Western monasticism made ample use of Cassian's four scriptural senses in order to extract from the Bible knowledge, sacred and profane, which had been offered to man by God. A literal reading of the Bible delivered historical information. The allegorical exposition of the Bible, which in fact consisted of the allegorical, tropological and anagogical levels, not always clearly distinguishable, yielded information belonging to the faith for the first one, to morality and self-discipline for the second, and to spiritual progress in the afterlife for the last one. Cassian exemplified his theory of the four scriptural levels with the test case of the word 'Jerusalem', which was used by Guibert de Nogent who wrote shortly before 1084, and found its way into the prolegomena to Genesis in the *Glossa ordinaria*:

> There are four ways of interpreting Scripture ... The first is history, which speaks of actual events as they occurred; the second is allegory, in which one thing stands for something else; the third is tropology, or moral instruction, which treats of the ordering and arranging of one's life; and the last is ascetics, or spiritual enlightenment, through which we who are about to treat of lofty and heavenly topics are led to a higher way of life. For example, the word Jerusalem: historically, it represents a specific city; in allegory it represents holy Church; tropologically or morally, it is the soul of every faithful man who longs for the vision of eternal peace; and anagogically it refers to the life of the heavenly citizens, who already see the God of Gods, revealed in all His glory in Sion.[8]

Of course, not all levels were systematically considered by commentators of the Bible. Authors often deliberately chose to concentrate on one or two levels in their commentaries of certain of the books of the Bible. The tropological level appealed most to the writers of mystical commentaries, that is, commentaries whose main aim is to explicate the relationship between a Christian soul and God. The multi-vocality of scripture claimed also by Augustine found a fertile ground for justification in the Song of Songs, a biblical book rich in erotic imagery and hence a rather difficult read at the literal level in the context of sacred scripture.

The sophisticated Victorine theoretical account of the work of imagination and language in the sphere of the spiritual life is seen at work in the commentaries on the Song of Songs. This long poem of fourteen songs, probably the work of a single author, is characterized by a sensuous language, claimed by some scholars to be borrowed from Old Egyptian love poetry.[9] Such flourishing sensuous imagery made the inclusion of this book in the Bible rather awkward. There is no explicit reference to God in its eight parts. If any text required a commentary to justify its place in the biblical canon, the Song of Songs was the outstanding candidate.[10] The very nature of this book gave birth to an enormous commentary tradition which went beyond the original function of the genre as explication.[11] Because of the fuzzy literal meaning of this text, commentators could easily appropriate it to satisfy their immediate religious and political concerns. For Origen, Bede and others, the bride and the bridegroom described in the Song become the Church and Jesus, Mary and Jesus, or the soul and Jesus. Bede (673–735) offers a solid allegorical interpretation against the *Libellum de amore* by Julian of Eclanum, which is influenced by Pelagianism. The *liber primus* of Bede's *Allegoria expositio* sets a context for the Song of Songs by arguing against the view of Julian, who believed that the love described in the Song of Songs was born out of the physical body.[12] But Bede's position does not allow for a mystical interpretation of the Song. Each verse is attributed to either the Church or Jesus. According to Bede, Julian of Eclanum negates the divine nature of the love instilled in the Song of Songs by refusing to read its allegorical sense. Bede decides to decipher the Song in the light of *caritas*. The privileged *lector catholicus*, Bede argues, cannot fail to read blasphemous sentences in the *Libellum de amore* of Julian. Bede provides us with a few examples of Julian's own interpretation of some of the verses of the canticle.[13] Bede responds to Julian's adherence to the literal meaning of the text by claiming a Christian allegorical interpretation of this difficult book.[14] Through the sacrament of baptism, grace pours into the *homo catholicus*, which enables him to seize the higher allegorical meaning, beyond the literal sense. Bede first copies the verses of the Song of Songs (*ad litteram sic habent*) and follows in *liber secundus* with the allegory of the bride and the bridegroom representing the Church or Jesus.[15] He disentangles the mysteries of the allegorical sense, introducing his exegesis with expressions such as *quod est aperte dicere, id est,* etc. Because of his political intention, that is, to counter heretical views propagated by Julian, Bede makes use of the Song of Songs and the allegorical interpretation to offer space for orthodox theology. Bede presents thus the view of the orthodoxy without using the Song as a means of exploring the self. Bede's exegetical approach breaks down the highly poetical narrative to make it a detailed and accurate account of the relationship between Christ and the Church.[16]

It was only in the twelfth century that the Song of Songs came to be considered as a site for the development of a more personal encounter with the divinity. Lubac rightly points out that modern scholars assign too great a place to the masterpiece of Bernard of

Clairvaux when defining or talking about the mystical commentary and suggests the commentary of Pseudo-Richard of St Victor as being representative of the spiritual commentary.[17]

Bernard's *Sermones super cantica canticorum*, started in 1135 and left incomplete at his death in 1153, nevertheless exercised a great influence on other writers engaging with the biblical book. The writing of a commentary on the Song of Songs stands as a high and risky literary and theological enterprise. Most writers note their awareness of the dangers of such a task in their prologues. As there is no real prologue to this series of sermons, evidence for the caution with which Bernard begins this enterprise is found in a letter addressed to the Carthusian Bernard of Portes:

> It is not as though you were asking me to do some little thing that would be quite easy and ordinary. You would not be so insistent were it only a small matter. Your many letters, and the vehemence which animates them, are a clear enough indication of how serious you are in the matter and what great store you lay by it. And the more anxious I feel you to be, the more diffident do I become. Why so? Simply because I do not want to bring forth an absurd mouse in return for your great hopes.[18]

Although the humble tone of this letter perhaps serves partly as the rhetorical device characteristic of most of the epistolary exchanges of that time, the same anxiety on Bernard's part finds a more genuine voice in a second letter addressed to the same recipient:

> My vexation gnaws at me like a worm, and my grief is ever with me. I am troubled enough on other accounts but, I must confess, on none so much as on this. It vexes me more than all the labours of my journey, than the discomfort of the heat, than the anxieties of my responsibilities.[19]

Those two letters are revealing of the *causa scribendi* of the *Sermones*.[20] Bernard of Portes may not be the sole reason for the writing of such a piece, as Bernard, in his first sermon, introduces in his *explanatio* the *Sermones* as the concluding book of his monastic programme. According to him, the spiritually enlightened monks need a more nourishing diet than milk. The Book of Ecclesiastes and the Book of Proverbs provided the first two loaves of bread, antidotes to the misguided love of the world and the excessive love of self. The third loaf, result of the first two, can only be masticated by the experienced contemplative.²¹ Bernard continues by defining the *causa divina* of the Song and stressing the importance of experience over learning: 'Only the touch of the Spirit can inspire a song like this, and only personal experience can unfold its meaning. Let those who are versed in the mystery revel in it; let all others burn with desire rather to attain to this experience than merely to learn about it.'²² In many other instances, Bernard shows great reverence for this biblical book and shows awareness of fulfilling a difficult but ambitious spiritual task by considering several levels of meaning for the Song.

William of St Thierry (*c*.1075/80–1147/8), friend of Bernard, instead offers to talk only about the tropological level, a task which he considers inferior to the allegorical exposition which considers the Church in the guise of the similes pervading this poetic book. William offers a detailed 'type C' prologue with a consideration of the *inscriptio*, *materia* and *modus agendi* of the work.²³ What is striking about William is the sustained attention he promises to give to the tropological sense of scripture in this commentary, thus making this work the most remarkable exploration of the self in its relation to God:

> We do not presume to treat of those deeper mysteries the *Song of Songs* contains with regard to Christ and the Church; but restraining ourselves within ourselves and measuring ourselves by ourselves, in the poverty of our understanding we shall (as anyone may venture to do) touch lightly on a certain moral sense apropos of Bridegroom and Bride, Christ and the Christian soul. And we ask for our labor no other reward than one like to our subject, namely love itself.²⁴

William's caution has more to do with the *modus agendi* than with the *materia*, although it gestures to Bernard's attempt which William regards most highly. By placing his claims below those of Bernard, he is able thus to partake in the same anxiety which Bernard expressed when considering such enterprise. If Bernard's commentary does not give evidence as to his personal involvement with the material of the Song, its superb exposition of the other levels of meaning made it possible for William to delve into the tropological sense.

Pseudo-Richard of St Victor uses the prologue of Gregory the Great's own commentary on the Song of Songs as a way of introducing his own. Gregory's prologue abounds with literary issues.²⁵ Its *accessus* informs the reader about the allegories and enigmas of the *sermo divinus* used to lift up the soul of fallen man. In similar fashion to Bede, Pseudo-Richard borrows the voice of Gregory to suggest how the physical love of the Song suggests a higher kind of love:

> In this book entitled the Song of Songs, words of carnal love are placed so that from its own body the soul, renewed, regains its heat through speeches of its own customary usage, and is stirred to a love that is above through the words of a love that is below. For in this book kisses are named, breasts are named, cheeks are named, thighs are named – in which words the sacred Scriptures are not to be mocked, but the mercy of God is all the more to be considered, because while he names the members of the body, he thus calls the soul to love.[26]

Gregory's prologue, here appropriated by Pseudo-Richard, encapsulates in a few words the complex theories on language and imagination which Richard of St Victor developed in his two magisterial treatises. To Pseudo-Richard, the elevated language of the Song requires a particular preparation on the part of the audience, conditioned by a *digna intelligentia charitatis*. It is the latter, that is, the proper understanding of love, which allows an unveiling of the mysteries contained in the tropological sense. The understanding of the Song of Songs presupposes a particular awareness on the part of its reader. We have indications here that, far from being a scholastic and rhetorical exercise, the writing of the commentary on the Song of Songs is the expression of a devotional attitude. One of the writer's tasks is to convey to his readers the attitude which made the tropological reading possible.

If the commentary of Pseudo-Richard of St Victor cannot be attributed to Richard with certainty, the least one can state is that this author made use of Richard of St Victor's theoretical system about language for the writing of his treatise. The author of the commentary makes abundant use of metaphors as an affective response to the Song. As an example, for *In lectulo meo per noctem quaesivi quem diligit anima mea* (Sg. 3: 12) the author provides the following hermeneutical instruction: 'The soul which seeks God and desires to reach to the love and knowledge of God must seek them in a bed, that is in the repose of the soul.'[27] Pseudo-Richard expands the metaphorical utterance with a commentary which encourages the deployment of further metaphors. Juxtaposition of the terms *quies mentis* and *lectulus* throughout chapter 1 increases each term's cognitive capacity. The metaphorical discourse relies on several vehicles (*lectulus, quies mentis*) at the same time: 'So the peace and quietness of the soul is the bed in which the spouse rests. In this bed she seeks the beloved during the night, when the desires of the flesh have sobered, and victory follows after struggle and hardships, and repose is granted.'[28]

Later, Pseudo-Richard introduces the Virgin Mary as an *exemplum* for spiritual and immaculate beauty.[29] One of her breasts represents corporal compassion, the other, spiritual compassion. In the course of his commentary on this verse, the image of the breast is followed by that of the vine, followed in its turn by images of honey and milk. Filigrees of *figurae* support a spiritual reading of the text and capture within their framework the transcendental dimension of each object.

By tracing the theories and concerns expressed by Richard of St Victor and most commentators of the Song, one comes to see the importance the carnal literal sense plays in mystical commentaries on the Song. No appreciation of the love of the soul for God could be conveyed without the support of carnal imagery, which functions as a bearer of affective and cognitive force in moving the soul to love. Twelfth-century writers were aware of the creative power of tropes, or metaphors, and made abundant use of their power to convey their own understanding of the nature of the relationship between the individual soul and God. But even at a lower level, Bernard, for instance, uses terms which, because of their association with the common activities of his audience, are most effective in touching their consciousness, while metaphorically these terms articulate an aspect of the relationship of the soul with God. When addressing *milites*, he uses warfare imagery and notions of service and faithfulness to entice them to serve God by entering the monastery as soldiers of Christ.[30] Bernard's mystical theology depends very much on the progressive interiorization of love imagery as a means of undergoing a spiritual process of refinement, a move from a carnal to a spiritual love. His *De diligendo Deo*, which will be discussed later, is based on such an assumption.

Even if, as we shall see later, William of St Thierry differs significantly from his friend Bernard of Clairvaux, with a much more psychologizing reading of the Song, he nevertheless also delineates clearly the function of the carnal vocabulary of love within his own spiritual system:

Therefore the Holy Spirit, when he was about to deliver over to men the canticle of spiritual love, took the story which inwardly is all spiritual and divine and clothed it outwardly in images borrowed from the love of the flesh. Love alone fully understands divine things; therefore the love of the flesh must be led along and transformed into the love of the spirit so that it may quickly comprehend things like to itself. Since it is impossible that true love, pining for truth, should long rest content with images, it very quickly passes, by a path known to itself, into that which was imagined. Even after a man becomes spiritual, he still shares in the delights of fleshly love which are natural to him; but when they have come into the possession of the Holy Spirit, he devotes them all to the service of spiritual love. This is why, without telling her name or whence she comes or to who, she is speaking, as if brazenly bursting forth from a hiding place, the heroine proclaims: 'Let him kiss me with the kiss of his mouth!'[31]

There is humanism and a healthy apprehension of the sexual impulse in these lines. As this passage attests, William makes use of the delights of fleshly love to explain the use of sensuous erotic imagery by the languishing soul. He further encompasses carnal love in his incantation to Love:

O Love, from all love, even that which is fleshly and degenerate takes its name! O Love, holy and sanctifying, pure and purifying! You, Life who are life-giving! Show us the meaning of your holy canticle, reveal the mystery of your kiss and the inner pulsing of your murmured song wherewith, to the hearts of your sons, you chant your power and the delights of your sweetness.[32]

This form of prayer does not exclude fleshly love, even though it is recognized as a minor expression of spiritual love. There is thus a shared assumption about the value of fleshly love and the power it generates when it finds expression with inspired writers like Bernard or William. God himself had to make recourse to the language of fleshly love and lower himself in order to make his voice understandable to human beings. Hence the use of a similar fleshly language in the Bible itself.

If we return to Bernard, we notice how in his mystical theology the figure of Christ in his humanity serves as a focal point for the purification of carnal love. Within this context, the vocabulary of love bears important cognitive functions. Several stages of conversion mark the life of the contemplative monk. Carnal imagery serves in the first instance to purify fleshly desires. From a love of the flesh, Bernard will guide his monks to the exclusive love of the flesh of Christ. His commentary addresses an audience which has at least partially demonstrated its eagerness for the desire for God, the *quaerere Deum*, one of the ideals of the Benedictine rule.[33] In the *De diligendo Deo*, Bernard expresses his view on the idea that desire is part of the rational man's nature. While seeking comfort in the luxuries of the earthly world, the rational man will want what he does not possess, or want better than he already possesses. According to Bernard, the will ultimately realizes that only the desire for God can be fulfilled: 'How much more the soul that loves God seeks no other reward than God whom it loves. Were the soul to demand anything else, then it would certainly love that other thing and not God.'[34] Bernard has a positive outlook on the nature of man. The latter, disappointed and failing in his covetousness for temporal objects, eventually opts for a more elevated goal. Experience, guided by reason, teaches him to move from a love of the world to the love of God.[35] Such a transitory state is best encapsulated by the vocabulary of love and courtship. It participates as well in converting the *affectio* of the aspirant contemplative to the spiritual life by 'exciting him to heavenly desire'.[36] Thus the erotic vocabulary serves not only to express contemplative experiences, but participates in important ways in the experiential process which fashions the writing and the reading/hearing of the treatises. The affective engagement of the commentators with the Song led in part to the development of the theory of the degrees of love, not displacing, but supplementing the theory of the four levels of scripture.

However significant Bernard's contribution, a brief look at his exegesis reveals limitations in his understanding of the soul. Bernard interprets the Song of Songs according to the allegorical and the anagogical levels. The edifying mystery of the incarnation of God into the person of Jesus constitutes the core of St Bernard's mystical theology. The *Sermones* shift freely from an interpretation of the bride as the soul to that of the bride as the Church. However virtuosic such a juxtaposition, it seems to limit the range of individuality accorded to the soul. Bernard always foresees the soul as a member of the Church. When the soul converses with the bridegroom, it is under the jurisdiction of the Church, and as part of its body. The Bernardine mystical theology never credits the soul with an individual entity. Rather it serves a social role within the body of the

Church. The anagogical level is therefore the allegorical level in disguise, personified through the depiction of one of the elements constituting the whole social body. When dealing with the *modus scribendi* of this work, Bernard affirms his allegorical interpretation, with emphasis on the humanity of Jesus:

> With good reason then I avoid trucking with visions and dreams; I want no part with parables and figures of speech; even the very beauty of the angels can only leave me wearied. For my Jesus utterly surpasses these in his majesty and splendor. Therefore I ask of him what I ask of neither man nor angel: that he kiss me with the kiss of his mouth.[37]

Bernard speaks further about the necessity of unveiling the mysteries hidden in the bodily language of the Song:

> The words that describe these visions or images seem to refer to bodies or bodily substances, yet they are means of conveying spiritual truths to us, and hence there must be a spiritual character to our inquiry into their causes and meaning. And who is qualified to investigate and comprehend those countless affective movements of the soul caused by the presence of the Bridegroom dispensing his multiform graces? Yet if we turn our gaze into our interior, and if the Holy Spirit will be pleased to give us his light to see the fruits that by his action he constantly produces within us, I think we shall not remain entirely devoid of understanding about those mysteries.[38]

If the commentator must delve in the deepest recesses of his own self to make meaning, it is more often than not a meaning which makes sense of the role of the Church and mediates its position with God.

Although such is the planned strategy of Bernard, he is often seduced by the emotive power of the Song.[39] At times Bernard moves away from the allegorical frame and into effusive passages inspired by images of the Song. The literal force of the imagery soon asks, then, for an emotive involvement best expressed via metaphorical discourse. Bernard then becomes imitator rather than *interpres*. His decoding of the meaning of the highly charged words of the Song becomes a hymn of praise to the poetic beauty of the Song, equally abounding with sensual imagery:

> On all these occasions he is kind and gentle, full of merciful love. In his kisses he shows that he is both loving and charming; with the oil and the

ointments that he is boundlessly considerate and compassionate and forgiving; on the journey he is gay, courteous, ever gracious and ready to help; in the display of his riches and possessions he reveals a kingly liberality, a munificent generosity in the bestowal of rewards.[40]

The effusive quality of this passage does not necessarily match the intention expressed in his second sermon. An affective response sometimes supersedes the overall allegorical strategy, thus allowing Bernard to become more personally involved with the imagery of the Song.

William offers instead an interpretation entirely focused on the bride as representing the individual soul. The relationship described is an intimate one, between the individual soul and God, outside any framework limiting its potential meaning:

> He also offers this same kiss to the faithful soul, his Bride, and imprints it upon her, when from the remembrance of the benefits common to all men, he gives her own special and personal joy and pours forth within her the grace of his love, drawing her spirit to himself and infusing into her his spirit, that both may be one spirit.[41]

Such interpretation is more forcefully deployed in the first song of the same book which summarizes the plot of the poem. William interprets the narration with the soul and Christ as the main characters of the drama. However, the poem contains several layers of meaning: it is both a historical drama and the story of soul's conversion to God and espousal to his Word.[42] Like Origen, William, in his preface, considers the literary form of the song and describes the essence of the dramatic performance:

> Now this song is written in the manner of a drama and in dialogue style, as if to be recited by characters and with action. Just as various characters and various actions appear in the recitation of dramas, so in this song characters and affections seem to combine to carry through this trafficking of love and the mystical contract of the union of God and man. The characters or groups of characters here are four: the Bridegroom and his companions, and the Bride and the chorus of young maidens.[43]

The whole setting of the Song, even the minor characters, point together to the drama taking place between the bride and the bridegroom. The dialogic quality of the poem allows William to commune with the concerns of the bride in her quest for her beloved. William, as we will see further in the next chapter, makes the Song and the writing of the commentary a performative act – to be more precise a mystical performative act – in which William re-enacts the affective movements of the characters. As Déchanet pointed out, William offers a moral commentary, that is, a commentary which, rather than providing allegorical figures to explain the mysteries of the Church, is going instead to provide a textual space for the self to enter into an intimate exchange with God.[44] However, if William appropriates the Song to encode his own experience, it is also to describe in more general terms the spiritual journey, the sublimation of love, marked by a rite of passage, from a carnal to a spiritual state.

To sum up, the few medieval commentators I have considered display various attitudes to their task. If all of them show a certain self-restraint, they each express it with a different voice. When considering the mystical commentaries of the Song, we notice how Bernard eschews the tropological level in most of his sermons. However, on several occasions, he displays an awareness of the enormous metaphoric potential for the poetic utterances of the Song. Bernard at no time negates the existence and the worth of the carnal imagery for a mystical interpretation. His eclectic mind leads him to use the Song to cover a prolific number of topics, from contemplation to general political issues of his day. On the interpretation of 'The fig tree has put forth its green figs' (Sg. 2: 13), Bernard offers an acerbic criticism of the Jews, thus reflecting contemporary negative feelings:

> Perhaps a Jew will complain that I have gone to excess in insulting him by calling his understanding cow-like. But let him read Isaiah and he will hear something even less flattering: *'The ox knows its owner, and the ass its master's crib; but Israel does not know me, my people does not understand.'* See, Jew, I am kinder to you than your own prophet. I have put you on a level with beasts, he sets you below them.[45]

However, one notices among most twelfth-century commentators the emergence of sustained concerns about the power of language in relation to the spiritual life. William of St Thierry and Pseudo-Richard of St Victor mark a new development in this respect. Their association of the discovery of the self through the writing or the reading of commentaries on the Song make the genre the repository of the Western mystical tradition. The tropological level allows the writer a deep engagement with the material, the more so if, as in the case of the Song, it is of a performative nature. The rich sensuous imagery of this biblical book and its performative qualities gave rise to an affective response which the commentators will have to contain by way of categorization. It should be no surprise to us that two of the authors discussed so far wrote affective treatises on the degrees of love.

THE FOUR DEGREES OF LOVE

The emotive power of the Song contributed to a growth in awareness by twelfth-century commentators of the *affectus*. Blanpain defines the *affectus* in the following manner:

> Let us say that, in the psychology of the twelfth-century spiritual authors, the *affectus* is like an 'urge' which incites, which creates the desire. The subject is influenced by an attraction, he is 'affected' by a value which entices him. The desire is put into movement, it turns towards, focuses upon, one direction, one object.[46]

Such definition is corroborated by Richard of St Victor who, in *The Four Degrees of Violent Charity*, uses the term *affectus* to define the way by which the soul is touched:[47]

> Doesn't thy heart seem to be deeply touched when the inflamed arrow of love penetrates the human soul in its last recess and pierces so completely its affective power that the soul has no more strength to contain or dissimulate the ardour of its desire?'[48]

Affectus, ratio and *memoria* are the three parts of the soul. The *affectus* can give birth to four different *affectiones*: *amor, timor, gaudium* and *tristitia*.[49] Aelred of Rievaulx (*c.*1109–66) provides the following information on the sentiment of *affectus* in his *Speculum caritatis*: 'The sentiment of *affectus* is then a spontaneous and sweet inclination of the heart itself towards someone.'[50] Elsewhere in one of his sermons, he makes clear that what he defined as the sentiment of the *affectus* is the *affectio*: 'The *affectio* is, it seems to me, a spontaneous inclination of the soul towards someone, associated with pleasure.'[51] In the context of this sermon, Aelred has in mind here the first of the four *affectiones*, *amor*. It is however clear that the concept of the *affectus* and its four *affectiones* was part and parcel of the psychology of twelfth-century authors.

Like Aelred, most spiritual authors put emphasis on *amor* in their discussions. *Amor carnalis*, also called *affectio carnalis*, plays a pivotal role in their presentations of the early stages of the spiritual life. Bernard makes the transfer of the *affectio carnalis* from the world to Jesus an essential element of his mystical doctrine. The humanity of Jesus stands in part as a translation by God of his cryptic message. Jesus is the Word, he is the parchment which God has chosen to present himself to his people. Thus the love for Jesus is still an *affectio carnalis*, since God as the second person of the Trinity has chosen a human form. The inclination towards carnal pleasures, resulting in lustful acts, changes into a growing awareness of the bodily sufferings of Christ, accompanied with a desire to want to share them, generated by a feeling of *caritas* and *compassio*. Devotion to the humanity of Christ partakes in the first steps of Cistercian mysticism.[52] Affective identification with the crucified body of Christ permeates one of Bernard's most influential passages of his *Sermones*:[53]

> While gazing on the Lord's wounds he will indeed not feel his own. The martyr remains jubilant and triumphant though his whole body is mangled; even while the steel is gashing his sides he looks around with courage and elation at the holy blood pouring from his flesh. Where then is the soul of the martyr? In a safe place, of course; in the rock, of course; in the heart of Jesus, of course, in wounds open for it to enter. Left to its own strength it would surely have felt the penetrating steel; it would not endure the pain; it would be overpowered and reject the faith. But now that it dwells in the rock is it any wonder if it endures as rock does? Nor should we wonder if, exiled from the body, it does not feel bodily pains. Insensibility does not bring this about, love does.[54]

Sermon 61, based on Song of Songs 2: 14, 'My dove in the clefts of the rock', delineates the body of Jesus as safe haven for the soul. The emotive appeal of this verse leads Bernard to direct the *affectiones* of his audience to such an object. The Christian soul should be led to desire entrance into the body of Christ through the open wound. Such aim is conveyed with highly affective and sensual language. The narrative voice seduces its audience into such a concept by means of lexical terms whose literal meaning is carnally seductive. Such strategy depends on a highly sophisticated theology of love, ranging from a vicious self-love to an absolute and pure love of God.[55] In the second stage of the textual game, the audience deciphers the text in accordance with its capacity for exploring the mystery of the metaphorical meaning in a spiritual context. The text initially incites the reader to check and reshape his affective landscape in order to align it with the expectations of the commentator. Each reading forcefully challenges the contemplative on the orthodoxy of his beliefs and experiences, ideally regulated by the first of the *affectiones*, *amor*, which creates the desire for *caritas*.[56]

In the Bernardine categorization of four degrees of love, explicated in the *De diligendo deo*, the purification of this *affectio* involves four successive stages.[57] In the first degree, man loves himself for himself (*homo diligit propter se*). This state is defined as an *affectio carnalis*, which Bernard sees as non-purified love, and which constitutes the essential but raw material for the progression to the fourth degree. In the second degree of love, man loves God for himself (*homo diligit Deum propter se*).[58] At this stage, the love is still selfish, as man understands that loving God brings forth advantages for himself. Yet the perception and love of God evolves into a love of God for himself (*homo diligit Deum propter ipsum*).[59] The third degree of love corresponds to an awareness of the nature of God, rather than his attributes. At this stage man desires to experience the sweetness of his encounter:

> Whoever loves this way, loves the way he is loved, seeking in turn not what is his but what belongs to Christ, the same way Christ sought not what was his, but what was ours, or rather, ourselves. He so loves who says: 'Confess to the Lord for he is good.' Who confesses to the Lord, not because he is good to him but because the Lord is good, truly loves God for God's sake and not for his own benefit.[60]

The third degree is the highest stage man can possibly attain while he lives in the physical body. His *affectio* cannot reach a state of purification whereby he forgets himself absolutely for the sake of the love of God. The fourth degree, not to love oneself except for the love of God (*nec seipsum diligat homo nisi propter Deum*), is the apex of *caritas*, defined by the full and absolute melting of the will of man into the will of God.[61] It is a state of total surrender, of which only a few contemplatives have a glimpse while they live in their physical body:

> I would say that man is blessed and holy to whom it is given to experience something of this sort, so rare in life, even if it be but once and for the space of a moment. To lose yourself, as if you no longer existed, to cease completely to experience yourself, to reduce yourself to nothing is not a human sentiment but a divine experience.[62]

This fourth degree of love, described as nuptial love, is translated into, and expressed by, the vocabulary of love and courtship of the Song of Songs and its mystical commentaries.

In *The Four Degrees of Violent Charity*, Richard of St Victor offers a detailed and systematic study of *caritas*.[63] The metaphor of love as fire, with its strong physical basis, as well as the four degrees of love, called *insuperabilis*, *inseparabilis*, *singularis* and *insatiabilis* stand at the core of the Victorine treatise.[64] Moreover, Richard of St Victor defines further his four degrees as (1) the love of the heart, (2) the love of the whole heart, (3) the love of the soul and (4) the love of all the virtues.[65] For each degree, the articulation of the relationship of the individual with God is couched in a distinct affective mould:

> Maybe David was still in this first degree, while ruminating with full confidence about the second, when he was saying in his psalm: *I will praise the Lord with my whole heart*. The one who is at the second degree can sing confidently: *With my whole heart have I sought you*. The one who touches the third can already say: *My soul breaks for the longing of your ordinances at all times*. The one who has ascended to the fourth degree and who loves God with all his strength can say in all security: *I will not fear what man can do unto me*, because *his heart is disposed to trust in the Lord*. His *heart is strengthened, he shall not be moved until he looks over his enemies*.[66]

Richard of St Victor also qualifies the degrees of charity according to the model of natural love. The first degree celebrates the betrothal, the second the wedding, the third the consummation of the marriage and the fourth the childbirth.[67] It is likely that the Victorine presentation of the contemplative life by means of the fusion of the carnal and spiritual senses had an immediate appeal to Rolle, even if he did not possibly grasp the complexity of the psychological system offered by his namesake.[68] For, indeed, Richard of St Victor, in contradistinction to the spiritually based categorization of Bernard, delves more deeply into the abysmal recesses of human emotions, trying to make sense of the whole range of psychological urges. In the case of his study Richard describes *caritas* as embracing the feelings of humanity, friendship, affinity, blood-ties and brotherhood. However, the feeling of love which penetrates the core of the soul and which is regarded as the highest form of love, finds expression in 'I am wounded by love'.[69] *Caritas* can be felt with different degrees of strength, whatever its desire. It is this broader approach which contributes additional information to the psychology of the self. His study of *caritas* is not immediately preoccupied by the spiritual desire for God. Indeed, in all its degrees, *caritas* is shown to affect the inner self, whatever its object of attention. Hence, in the first degree, it enters into the affective power; in the second degree it paralyses cognitive thinking; in the third it annihilates action. The fourth degree is reached when nothing can satisfy the desire of the soul.[70] Richard of St Victor shows the devastating effects of the higher degrees of love when they are directed at a carnal object. If the first degree of love is to be wished in a matrimonial relationship, all the others are negative and are a prefiguration of future damnation. On the other hand, when God is loved, the higher degrees should be the aim, as they bring the soul closer to the future joys of the beatific vision. In the first degree, God is loved with the heart, the soul and the mind, even though those faculties or powers are not completely involved. In the second degree, one loves with one's whole heart; in the third, with one's whole soul; in the fourth, with one's whole strength.

In addition to his awareness of the importance of metaphoric language for the construction of a psychological landscape, Richard demonstrates here the ambiguity and paradox of human emotions in its dealings with carnal or spiritual objects. One will have to wait for the writings of Rolle to witness the anxiety which such ambiguity can cause when one's own affective input is still in the process of delineating its spiritual aim. On the other hand, William of St Thierry's contribution, discussed in Chapter 3, provides the best account of the making of a self through the language and the tradition of the commentaries of the Song of Songs.

3
Discovering the Self through Love in the Writings of William of St Thierry

While Lubac regards the commentary of Pseudo-Richard of St Victor as one of the best mystical commentaries, my own investigation contends that the relationship between hermeneutic practice and the discovery of the self is more explicit in the spiritual writings of William of St Thierry. William's personal engagement with the Song is made possible thanks to the performative nature of the Song and his knowledge of Bernard's own project with this text.

In order to grasp the extent of William's hermeneutical practice and the impact of its results on the psychology and literature of the twelfth century, it is appropriate to consider the effect of the language of the Song of Songs on some key terms in the spirituality of that period. My aim is to demonstrate how the contextualization of the term 'face to face' within the erotic and potentially emotive language of the Song broadens the semantic meaning of the term. It is therefore necessary to look at the use of this term in other writings of William. This chapter looks at the ways William applies the nuptial imagery of the Song of Songs to the concept and image of the 'face to face', the most common image to express the beatific vision, in three important works, namely the *De contemplando Deo*, the *Meditativae orationes* and the *Expositio super canticum canticorum*.[1] The metaphorical discourse of love plays five important roles in William's hermeneutics, corresponding to five levels or degrees in which the soul places itself when it actively looks for the spiritual union.

DE CONTEMPLANDO DEO AND THE MEDITATIONS

Although the 'face to face' expression has no amorous or sensual connotation in any of the biblical books in which it is set, commentators of the Song of Songs and mystics appropriate it as a metaphorical expression to make it the climax of the spiritual union.[2] William of St Thierry, whose most prominent works circulated under the attribution of his close friend Bernard of Clairvaux during the medieval period and later, uses the 'face to face' to express the ultimate union between the soul and God. In the *De contemplando Deo*, probably written between 1119 and 1120, William refers several times to the face of God.[3] Although this treatise aims to touch the *affectus*, it is nevertheless devoid of nuptial vocabulary and the soul is never personified as the bride. The reason for the absence of the amorous discourse of the Song of Songs in this treatise must be found in the fact that it was written while William was in charge of the monastic house of Saint-Thierry, that is before he delved with Bernard into the spiritual significance of the biblical book during his stay at Clairvaux. The tone of the *De contemplando* suggests oral delivery, even though its content speaks more for an intimate and private meditation. The treatise is divided in two parts, one describing the journey of the soul towards God, and the second focusing attention on the Holy Trinity, which is considered as the source of love.[4]

The desire for the vision of the face of God is central to the first part of the treatise. However, the narrative voice finds much presumptuousness in the desire for this vision.[5] The postlapsarian soul has first to focus on the humanity of Jesus, and then enter into his wounds in order to have access to his heart. Hence, the discourse on the beatific vision in this treatise remains patently hypothetical:

> And yet that slight experience has sufficed to kindle my longing afresh, so that I can scarcely now contain myself for hoping that one day you will remove your covering hand and pour out your illuminating grace, so that at last, dead to myself and alive to you, according to the answer of your truth with unveiled face I shall begin to see your face, and by that seeing shall be united to you. O face, face, happy face that merits thus to be united to yourself through seeing you! It builds in its heart a tabernacle for the God of Jacob and does everything according to the pattern shown it in the mount! Here with truth and fittingly it sings: 'My heart has said to you, "My face has sought you; your face, Lord will I seek." '[6]

The 'face to face' expression speaks only of the narrator's potential experiences in the afterlife.[7] It is likely the negative theology of the sixth-century author Pseudo-Dionysius and the austere and somewhat restrictive spirituality of Anselm of Canterbury (1033–1109) may account for the discretion William demonstrates when describing the summit of contemplation. Some of the phrases show him sorting out the effects of those mystical doctrines on his Augustinian precepts: 'For, faint with longing, I say to myself: "Who loves what he does not see? How can anything be lovable which is not in some way visible?"'[8] Other passages of this nature show the extent of the influence of Pseudo-Dionysius via one of his medieval commentators, the ninth-century theologian John Scot Erigena. His Neo-Platonic system of emanation from and return to God has an impact on William's own history of the individual soul.[9]

The *Meditativae orationes* were probably composed by William in 1128, at a time when he was still abbot of the Benedictine house of Saint-Thierry. There is a certain unity between the twelve meditations, as each may be considered as describing a step in the soul's search for God. One moves from a consideration of the soul's choice between good and evil in the first meditation, to an attempt on the part of the soul to represent the Trinity in the second. The third meditation, dealing with expression of joyful and peaceful contemplation, is followed in the next three meditations by prayers for instruction. The seventh meditation asks for the contemplation of the face of God, and the eighth expresses the desire of divine union. The ninth meditation, Anselmian in tone, considers with shame the soul's numerous failures. It brings the narrative voice in the next two meditations to ponder on the incarnation and passion of Christ. Meditation on the humanity of Jesus is a necessary requirement for the development of love towards God.[10]

Five of the thirteen *Meditativae orationes* use the 'face' expression, either in the context of 'the face of God', 'the face of man' or 'the face to face'. According to Monique Simon, who has studied in detail this aspect of the *Meditativae orationes*, rather than describing a spiritual itinerary in the sense that each text represents a step on the part of the soul towards God, those texts on the contrary evolve around a certain number of key images and ideas appearing recurrently and cyclically.[11] *Facies* appears ninety-three times and *vultus* forty times in the whole collection.[12] The *facies ad faciem* or *facies et facies* appear eight times in four different meditations.[13]

The semantic field in which *facies* is contextualized is extremely varied. As the 'face of man', William designates the interior man, that part of the soul which will meet God in its essence in the other world. The 'face of Christ' is the face which our own face must imitate to conform to, in order to be able to see God 'face to face'. The 'face of God' has a twofold meaning: it is our understanding of him in this life, but it is also our ignorance of him, as he will be revealed to us as he is in the other life. William also uses *facies* to designate proper persons, or to build up an allegorical construction.[14] The semantic fields in which *facies* is used are springboards for the 'face to face'. Each semantic field attempts a discovery of God through his creation, and more especially through man. However, in contrast to the *De contemplando Deo*, William uses the *facies ad faciem* in the Meditations, although he does allude to presumptuousness again:

> Forgive, O Lord, forgive. The love of your love drives me; you know, you see how things are with me. I am no scrutinizer of your majesty; a pauper is what I am, seeking your grace. I beg you by the sweetness of your sweetest tenderness, do not let me be crushed by your majesty, rather let me be supported by your grace. Forgive me, I say, for to see God – here in a riddle only but hereafter face to face – is faith's proper desire.[15]

William insists on the fact that our knowledge of God is obtained through riddles, and however obscure they may be, they suffice in conveying a feeling of the presence of God in the soul.

This feeling of presence is explored elsewhere by William. Meditation X pays attention to the humanity of Christ and the effects of its representations in painted images. The re-enactment of the passion impresses on the mind the semblance of the 'face to face':

> And as the river of joy floods that soul more completely, she seems to see you as you are. In sweet meditation on the wonderful sacrament of your passion she muses on the good that you have wrought on our behalf, the good that is as great as you yourself are great, the good that is yourself. She seems to herself to see you face to face when you thus show her, in the cross and in the work of your salvation, the face of the ultimate Good. The cross itself becomes for her the face of a mind that is well-disposed toward God.[16]

If the humanity of Jesus and the symbols that recall it portend the majesty of God, a broader understanding of his essence comprises the apophatic stripping of all his attributes.[17] Hence, following Origen, one must also look for the influence of apophatic spirituality in some passages. For instance, Meditation III, a sort of gloss on Exodus

33: 20, blends cataphatic and apophatic approaches. The being, the essence of God, leads William to ponder on the non-being. The answer which God gives to Moses in Exodus 3: 14, 'Ego sum qui sum', is, according to William, beyond the realm of rational understanding. In other words, the surest approach to God consists of a process of elimination and annihilation:

> This sort of understanding makes neither division nor conjunction in the Trinity. But, when and how and as far as the Holy Spirit wills, it controls the believing mind, so that something of what you are may be seen by those who in their prayer and contemplation have got past all that you are not, although they do not see you as you are. Nevertheless this understanding serves to soothe the loving spirit, for there is clearly nothing in it of that which you are not and, although it is not wholly what you are, it is not different from that Reality.[18]

William continues by considering the mystical union as participation in the trinitarian life itself. The mystical union between the soul and God, operated by the Holy Spirit, is similar in nature to the union of the Trinity. The expression of the soul's apprehension of the Trinity-unity concept asks for a strong self-negating apophatic statement:

> Neither the onlyness nor the plurality disturbs him, but the oneness of the Trinity and the three-foldness of the Unity so avail for him, that with a loving and sober understanding he comprehends the majesty of the divine incomprehensibility by the very fact that he does not comprehend it.[19]

Reason, by means of its discursive language, fails to perceive the mystery of the Trinity and the *unitas spiritus*. Meditation VIII instead demonstrates how affective language and bridal imagery come to terms with the 'face to face'. *Ostende mihi faciem tuam, soror mea*, a composite of Sg. 2: 14 and Sg. 4: 9 appropriated by the son of justice and addressing his spouse, underlies a positive strategy encompassing the multi-layered faces of the imperfect soul, which stand as reflections of the yet impure *affectiones*. The infinite bounty of God makes possible the exchange of the truth of human justice which inhabits the humble soul, against the truth of God's infinite justice.[20] William selects the *osculum* metaphor to mark the special nature of this interaction: 'And when she thus proffers the kiss of a righteous confession, you receive her with the kiss of peace.'[21] The sufferings of the Word made flesh are forcefully recalled to demonstrate their absolute necessity for the salvation of man. Through the image of the kiss, applied in a very original way to the passion, William exploits the bond which he has built upon the kiss image of the bride and the bridegroom. The spitting, the slapping, the beating reeds and the bath of blood have redeemed man and made possible the exchange of kisses. The list of sufferings endured by Christ proceeds with the nailed hands, the nailed feet, the dying ears, the eyes and the open side from which the blood pours out. William juxtaposes to this list a parallel catalogue of his own limbs which, and he makes this point very clearly, are responsible for the pains endured by the Saviour.[22] The positive tone, devoid of exaggerated exclamations or affective outbursts, describes the generosity of God towards mankind. The *osculum* cluster circumscribes the whole passion episode, as well as the gift of love which gave the passion its meaning.

William broadens the field of meaning of this metaphor by associating the kiss with the breathing in of the *spiritus*.[23] The exchange of breath takes place in the partaking of the Eucharist, when the body and blood of Christ are literally eaten. The materiality of the sacramental ritual reinforces the recollection of the passion incidents in the mind. Rumination does not denote here a reflection upon words or images: eating the Eucharist becomes rumination, full experiential re-enactment of the Passion:[24]

> we there regurgitate the sweet things stored within our memory, and chew them in our mouths like cud for the renewed and ceaseless work of our salvation. That done, we put away again in that same memory what you have done, what you have suffered for our sake.[25]

The kiss imagery provides William with rich avenues to express the process by which the soul, redeemed by the passion and gaining experience through the Eucharist, regains access to and favour before God. Confession and exchange of peace mark the initial steps of the development of this love relationship.

THE COMMENTARY ON THE SONG OF SONGS: BOOK 1

The *Expositio super canticum canticorum* was written after William had given up responsibilities as abbot of Saint-Thierry and had entered the newly founded Cistercian abbey of Signy in 1135. During one of his visits at Clairvaux, while both Bernard and William were kept sick in the infirmary of the monastery, they discussed the spiritual meaning of the Song of Songs, and William set to write his own commentary on the Song of Songs. Although the importance of the exchanges between Bernard and William must be stressed, the new conditions offered to William in the Cistercian context, devoid of political, administrative and didactic involvement, also shaped the commentary. For, indeed, the commentary by William does not address and does not aim to instruct a particular audience. It describes a self eager to engage with the Augustinian language of radical reflexivity, a self discovering its inner dimensions as it enters into an amorous relationship with the divine being. The account by William is a highly reflexive and personal one, in which the language of love plays a portentous role.

Indeed, the desire for the vision of the face of God, a pervading theme in the whole of his corpus, expresses the climax of the love relationship between the soul and God. The 'face to face' metaphor is used ten times in *Expositio super canticum canticorum*, four times in Song of Songs 1, six times in Song of Songs 2, the latter representing about a third of the entire work.[26] Meditation VIII and the exposition on the first strophe of the Song of Songs share identical thematic concerns. The exchange of breaths, the face and the kiss define the union between the lover and his bride. Although William has stated in his prologue his desire to offer a moral reading of the biblical book, he nevertheless offers a magisterial demonstration of his exegetical skills by providing several levels of meaning for the 'kiss' expression. At the literal level, the kiss is the union through the mouth of two bodies: it is a sign and incentive to the union of the souls. The kiss stands also at the allegorical level as the gift of the Word made flesh to the Church. The anagogical level yields a somewhat similar meaning, with a more narrowed focus at the infusion of joy and grace of his love on each individual soul.[27] To William, the fulfilment of the mystical experience which is encapsulated in the kiss metaphor corresponds to an absolute participation on the part of the soul in the trinitarian experience. As God is in reason of the Son, and as the Son is in reason of God, so is the soul a partaker of this unity and fusion through the grace of the Holy Spirit.[28]

Experience plays a vital role in William's system. It is the former which is going to decide the degree of intimacy the soul will develop with God.[29] In addition to his statement about the performative nature of the spiritual life, William connects hermeneutic practice to performance:

> This is why, as we set about the task of pondering the epithalamium – the nuptial canticle, the song of bridegroom and bride – and examining your work, we beseech you, O Holy Spirit, that we may be filled, O Love, with your love, in order to understand the canticle of love. Thus may we also become in some measure participants in the holy conversation of Bridegroom and Bride, that what we read may take effect within us. For where affections are concerned, only persons possessing like affections can readily understand what is said. Draw us therefore unto yourself, O Holy Spirit; O Holy Paraclete, O Holy Comforter, comfort the poverty of our solitude which seeks no solace apart from you. Enlighten and quicken the desire of him who tends toward you, that it may become the love of one having fruition of you. Come to us that we may truly love you, that whatever we think and say may flow from the fountainhead of your love. May the canticle of your love be read by us in such wise as to kindle in us love itself. Yes, may love itself show us the meaning of its own canticle.[30]

This passage encapsulates a central tenet of twelfth-century spiritual practice. Participation in the drama of the Song of Songs goes hand in hand with the writing of the commentary. What William intimates is that literary production depends on the quality of the affective involvement which accompanies the reading of the text by its commentator. Hermeneutic production of the kind advocated here is possible only if its interpreter is imbued with spiritual love while reading and meditating. The process by which such mystical commentary is conceived affects also its maker. William's textual practice shapes and challenges his own status as *interpres* and mystic. The implausible literal sense of the Song of Songs in its biblical context contributes to the making of a system which includes man as body and soul in his relationship to God. If the most noble and excellent book of the Old Testament is couched in such erotic and sensual vocabulary, if God has inspired this vocabulary to facilitate our understanding of the spiritual life and move us to desire the vision of the face of God, then man, made in the image and likeness of God, can accept it as it is, and use it for its noble purpose, as a tool to restore man's *affectiones*.[31] Awareness of linguistic issues, manifested for instance by the word-play on *affectus* and *effectus*, clearly demonstrates the role of the writing process when operating such restoration.

The *affectio* called *amor* receives a more detailed treatment as it is informed by William's personal involvement with the Song. Three aspects of love, according to three specific terms, emerge out of his interaction with the text:

> For this canticle deals with the love of God – the love whereby God is loved, or the love whereby God himself is called Love. Whether we call it love or charity or dilection matters not, except that the word 'love' seems to indicate a certain tender affection on the part of the lover with the implication of striving or soliciting; 'charity,' a certain spiritual affection or the joy of one who has fruition; and 'dilection,' a natural desire for an object which gives delight. But all these things one and the same Spirit works in the love of Bridegroom and Bride. To sing the new canticle, the movements of all the holy virtues are indeed so useful to the love of Bridegroom and Bride that (granted due and orderly progress of the said virtues) they are all transformed finally into acts of love. Other things shall certainly be made void, but 'charity never fails.'[32]

The viewpoint adopted by William allows for a vision of this love affair as a translation of the relationship between God and a soul whose *affectiones* are completely bent to him. In order to recreate this situation in the new textual setting of the commentary, William has to perform the role of the soul/bride described in the Song. One must regard the text as an offer by God to perform the drama which ultimately leads to the beatific vision. The writing of the commentary requires a transference of the plot within the consciousness of its author: 'But the action always takes place in the consciousness and heart of the Bride, whoever she is, as she pours out her soul before the Lord her God and hears with joy what the Lord God speaks in her.'[33] *Quaecumque illa est*, says William, thus opening an opportunity for the commentator to endorse this role and act it out in his consciousness.

The particular sensibility which one can see blooming out of William's commentary has its roots in the writings of Origen. According to the latter, contact with the divine mystery takes place in the depth of the soul and from there guides all the active faculties. The description of the spiritual life as an amorous adventure finds also a developing ground in Origen. According to Verdeyen, the Cistercians, and William in particular, depart from the scriptural terminology to become more personal and subjective.[34] The emergence of this sensibility is made possible because of William's personal response to the metaphorical discourse of love of the Song. By setting the plot within the consciousness and heart of the bride, William partakes in the exploration of the self by means of metaphorical language. Preoccupations about language's role in the spiritual experience echo or parallel those discussed more systematically in the treatises of Richard of St Victor. In the higher reaches of the contemplative life, metaphorical language lacks cognitive force to express the nature of that particular experience. William nevertheless expresses this departure into a level of consciousness which is ineffable by a series of ejaculations which still use the signs and tools of the failing linguistic system. The idea of the ineffable is expressed in this case by expressions which are modelled on the 'face to face', such as the 'eyes in eyes', the 'kiss to kiss', which translate the desire for a direct contact with the divinity, without having recourse to intermediaries such as images, symbols or tropes:

> I am weary, she says, of these storerooms, empty because of the Bridegroom's absence; I am weary of these daily repeated promises, these obscure secrets, these parables and proverbs, the glass and the riddle. I desire the mystery of the kingdom of God; I entreat that the Father may be spoken to me plainly – face to face, eye to eye, kiss to kiss: 'Let him kiss me with the kiss of his mouth!'[35]

Performing the role of the bride allows William access into the deepest recesses of the human understanding (*conscientia*), and leads him to the realm where words and cognitive signs have no *raison d'être*. The 'face to face' and the 'kiss to kiss' are used to bridge the cataphatic with the apophatic, the figurative with the inexpressible. At this stage of the contemplative experience, when the soul searches to enter the mystery of God, mediators are useless. The revelation implies direct participation, breath to breath, mouth to mouth: 'but what the breath of his mouth and of his kiss inspires, gives savor; and it will give full savor when my joy in him shall be full'.[36] If the soul cannot sustain the brightness of God's charity, she must lower her spiritual demands and, from the kiss and the brightness of the face of God, move to the breasts.[37]

The breast image does not bear the same apophatic qualities as the 'face to face', the 'kiss to kiss' or the 'eyes to eyes' expressions.[38] Its use in late medieval devotional practices attests to its success and demonstrates the need for more homely images answering the needs of practitioners whose devotions still demand pictorial, visual and physical representations of the humanity of Christ.[39]

Although William engages in the Song at a personal level, he makes allowances for the needs of his readers who may want to start the spiritual journey at a lower level than that played out by himself. Spiritual progress is circular and implies a need to go back to the basics in order to reach yet again the pinnacle. William thus sets out the preliminaries and the foundations which will make the 'face to face' likely. The latter appears only again in the antepenultimate strophe of the first song.[40] Mentions are made of the face of the Lord prior to that, in the context of the love relationship between the bride and the bridegroom. The completion of the kiss and the embrace described in the same strophe are in fact evocative of what the 'face to face' will be in the other life. The identification of the bride and the bridegroom will be total: each meritorious soul will not only see the bridegroom as he is, but will become the bridegroom himself. This idea lies at the core of the *unitas spiritus*.[41] The ambitious mystical assumptions of William lack the descriptive terms which could express such unity.[42] The *unitas spiritus* is a 'face to face' between two beings identical in nature, who have reached that stage through an exchange and blending of their being. William recurs to the kiss and the embrace to describe the highest mystical stage: 'The kiss will also know its plenitude when, kiss to kiss and embrace to embrace, full and abiding fruition shall be attained. Then nevermore shall anyone stir up the Bride nor make her to awake, until she please; and never again will she please.'[43] Further in the same strophe, the importance of the virtues, more especially charity, is stressed. The bed of flowers and the beamed-roof house described by William are signs of invitation for God, her confidant, to enter into her heart. For an exchange of such intimate love, there is need for a better and more joyful room, which stands as *caritas,* described as *cor in Deum solitarium*.[44] Depicted as the wine cellar in strophe 10, *caritas* transforms all incoming goods into wine, which symbolizes the Holy Spirit. Indeed, for the lover of God everything is changed into goodness. Once filled with the desire for the love of God, the immature soul is equipped to deal with her memory and intelligence in their ramblings on topics alien to the love of God. An ordered *caritas* is therefore a prerequisite for any mystical experience, as William forcefully points out: 'Thus he whose charity is well-ordered loves the Lord his God, and himself in him, and his neighbor as himself, with a love of the same quality and intensity.'⁴⁵ The love of God is felt according to the levels at which the soul finds itself. William posits three levels for the soul: the animal, the rational and the spiritual levels. The *Expositio* offers access into the performance played out by the bride and bridegroom for each level at which a soul finds itself. To satisfy this new framework, the images and the vocabulary of the Song of Songs are given new meaning, and additional biblical images and quotations are added. Before reappearing in strophe 10, the 'face to face' expression is contextually reassessed as part of the reading process which prepares the audience for a subtle metaphorical understanding of its meaning.⁴⁶ The notion of *caritas*, the images of the kiss and the embrace and the 'face to face' make a semantic field from which more cognitive meaning can be gleaned:

> Therefore whoever is a Bride has but one desire, one aspiration – namely that her face may continually be joined to your Face in the kiss of charity, that is, that she may become one spirit with you through unity of will with you; that the form of her life may be ardently impressed to the form of your love, by the ardor of great love . . .⁴⁷

The discrepancy which exists between the *unitas spiritus* and the beatific vision is made explicit by William in strophe 11: 'This deep calls on another deep; this ecstasy dreams of something far other than what it sees; this secret sighs for another secret; this joy evokes another joy; this sweetness foretells another sweetness.'⁴⁸ How can the yet unknown bliss of the beatific vision be foreseen? William answers by encoding his feelings about the beatific vision with the same terms he used to express the *unitas spiritus*, thus implying that there are no differences of nature between the mystical vision and the beatific vision, but that the quality and abundance of the latter makes them markedly different. The differentiation between the two is stressed by William with a finer qualification about the fullness of the kiss and the embrace, as well as the perfection of the vision:

> For when Face shall be fully revealed to face, and mutual knowledge shall be perfect, and the Bride shall know even as she is known, it will then be the full kiss and the full embrace; for she will not need the left hand to stay her up, but the delights of the Bridegroom's right hand shall completely embrace the Bride even to the end of infinite eternity. Then, I say, it will be the full kiss and the full embrace, the power of which is the wisdom of God . . .⁴⁹

By contextualizing the 'face to face' expression within the semantic field of the courtship between the bride and bridegroom of the Song, William achieves both a textual and mystical feat. His use of metaphorical language goes beyond the expectations of the commentary genre by deciphering the possibilities a soul can have in encountering the essence of God. By doing so, William also equips himself to make serious propositions about the nature of the beatific vision. If his attempt is successful, it is because he has seized the performative qualities of the Song and raised himself to the level of the bride in order to feel what he believes she could feel when playing this game of love with God. One should remember how theologically daring such an enterprise is, since, in the eyes of twelfth-century theologians, William is appropriating God's text and making the voice of the bride his own.

THE COMMENTARY ON THE SONG OF SONGS: BOOK 2

Through the voice of the bride, William manifests his own desire for union with God. The identification of the soul as the bride, a common practice in monastic writings on the Song of Songs, suggests male commentators and their readers felt no anxiety about performing and identifying a role which in the Song is a female one. Whether this appropriation of the female characteristics of the bride is another aspect of 'the rise of affective piety and the feminization of religious imagery' described by Bynum is worth discussing here.[50] Although the bride and the bridegroom of the Song of Songs are respectively female and male, when this relationship is transposed to the level of the soul and God, it is not systematically seen as a female entity seeking union with a male God. On the contrary, this never seems to be the case in the writings of William. In the *Golden Epistle*, he sees the *anima*, the lowest level of the soul, as an impediment in the search for spiritual love. His comments are virulent and aggressive and denounce the effeminate in the *anima*, while praising the virility of the *animus*, which stands for the spiritual part of the soul:

> The animal soul makes bestial those among men who are fond of the objects of the flesh and submit to the bodily senses. When this soul begins to become not only capable, but also endowed with a perfect reason, she immediately rejects away from her the sign of the feminine gender: from

anima she becomes *animus*, reasonable soul, fit to guide the body; spirit that possesses itself. As long as she remains *anima*, she effeminates herself willingly by carrying herself towards the carnal; once *animus* on the other hand, once spirit, she falls only on virile and spiritual objects.[51]

If William attributes great importance to the masculinization of the soul as it matures into an entity capable and willing to set its desire on God, he is very flexible as to the grammatical gender which he attributes to the bridegroom. The bridegroom is also to William *caritas* or *sapientia* which he describes as feminine figures. The interiorized language of love addresses the soul and, in view of the intimacy which William assumes in the *unitas spiritus*, that is, the bond which joins the soul to God in a trinitarian fashion, he speaks of a fusion which is ineffable, therefore beyond considerations of gender relationships.

This feminization of the self occurs at the lower levels of the contemplative life. However, according to William one should be careful to make the discovery and conversion of the *affectiones* binding to the idea of the feminine. When Bernard reshapes the psyche of his novices and young monks by redirecting their amorous desires and carnal *affectiones* to the person of Christ in his humanity and, eventually, to God, he rather choses the Fin' Amor male figure as model for his disciples, and reshapes this model before them to make their conversion to spiritual love possible. William's project provides a field of performance for those who have already achieved such affective conversion, who have already been instilled with the desire for God, when the soul and the reader, with the verse of the Song of Songs, can proclaim: 'curramus in odorem Sponsi'.[52]

The language of love fulfils several functions in twelfth-century spiritual writings. In the first song of William's *Expositio*, the ordering of charity is described in great detail. It presupposes and assumes the completion of the reformation of the *affectiones*. If the metaphorical discourse of love operated only for this reformation, its presence in William's *Expositio* would be superfluous. Richard of St Victor demonstrates in his treatises the uses that twelfth-century authors made of the metaphorical language of the Bible and the Song of Songs in particular. William's use of language conforms to some of the points assessed in the writings of the Victorine author. It is used here in particular not to operate the conversion of the *affectiones*, but rather to maintain them focused on the exclusive desire for the love of

God. Such is the role of the sensuous and the erotic in spiritual discourse: to maintain the former *affectio carnalis* focused on a non-carnal entity. Thirdly, another function of the language of love emerges from the inadequacy of discursive language to express the encounter of the soul with the deity. When the dramatic fiction couched in the Song, until then played outside of himself, becomes *historia veritatis*, an interiorized story, then its mode of perception, stripped of all intellection or ratiocination, becomes intellective love, expressed by William in the famed catchphrase, *Amor ipse intellectus est*:[53] 'Then all will be able to see, in your light, how much the devotion of the simplest lover surpasses, in your judgement, the prudence of the most learned thinker; for where reason draws back, devout love itself will become its own understanding.'[54] The process by which one reaches this state is the subject of the second song of William. After its first *accubitus*, that is, being side by side with God, the soul understands the necessity for further purification, through speculations and mirrors, in preparation for the 'face to face'.[55] The soul can ruminate over the *accubitus* in the privacy of its cell, in a sitting posture, away from the turmoil of public places.[56] The exposition of Song of Songs 2: 8–10 leads William to consider the ways by which the soul may come nearer the 'face to face'. Insinuations and encouragements from the bridegroom by means of images resembling a model or archetype (*figura*) allow the soul to progress further towards its final destination. Its itinerary is activated by a divinely arranged sequence of images which succeed one another in the soul: each new image surpasses the preceding one in its resemblance to the model. As Javelet remarks, the soul of the creature must return to its creator, as it is predestined to divinization, and its existence is oriented from the beginning to this goal. Javelet stresses the multi-layered movement towards the source, at all levels, from the ontologic to the noetic: 'the sign tends towards the signified, the image towards the Archetype'.[57] Stress is put on the transformation of love into charity, and charity into wisdom. Charity is the cause which makes us look like the Creator. Javelet's portrayal of twelfth-century mystical practices omits the role that images borrowed from the world have in shaping the creature in the likeness of its creator. This phenomenon is crucial to the soul's progress: 'The Bridegroom, in his coming, is now drawing nearer to the Bride; even if not yet face to face, he already introduces himself to her under figures more nearly resembling the reality.'[58] The presence of God is manifest within his whole creation. The more the ordered *caritas* fills and governs the soul, the more it is able to perceive and decode the divine message embedded in the creation. To William, the creation is a book which must be read metaphorically: the simplest of its objects is a mirror in which God can be known.[59] Religious texts are part of this cosmological metaphor: sophisticated answers about God are embedded in their (figurative) language. This knowledge of God is defined by William as the *affectus* (affection, disposition) mode.[60] The second mode, the *effectus* (execution, accomplishment), relies on the effects of the facts and the life of the Word made flesh.[61]

The humanity of Jesus is central to William's mystical doctrine. First, it fills scripture with divine light and becomes the matrix by which it can be deciphered. The humanity of Jesus allows man to understand and taste the divine reality. This special mode of apprehension is encapsulated in a formula typical of William: 'Gustare hoc est intelligere'. Secondly, although the discovery of the divine reality is a gift of Spirit, it comes into fruition in Jesus, who acts as mediator between heaven and earth.[62] The decoding of scripture in the light of his passion and resurrection provides answers to its most intricate literal passages. Thus, the discourse of the Song of Songs matures into metaphorical discourse to encode the union of the soul with God because of the mediating influence of the person of Christ. However important this mediating role for making sense of all the biblical books, there is no indication in William that the vocabulary of love specifically addresses the relation between the soul and Jesus in his humanity, as is the case in later devotional texts. The metaphorical sense, or inner sense, is moulded by individual experience balanced with the perusing of scripture through the lens of his humanity.[63] The emergence of such sophisticated and individual responses to the biblical books depends largely on the humanity of Jesus, who himself stands as the living embodiment of God, the Christ-book metaphor.[64]

William uses in paragraph 154 a new expression, *paries hujus mortalitatis* or *velum hujus mortalitatis* (the wall or veil of his mortality), which indicates the limitations forced upon the soul while living in the earthly life: a mortal veil prevents the full acceptance of the kiss and the embrace.[65] Possibly borrowing from Gregory of Nyssa (d. 385/6), William articulates another of his powerful statements: 'To see the Invisible behind the wall, means therefore to see him insofar as is possible in this life.'[66] The recognition of the limitations imposed by the earthly state of the soul does not prevent William from anticipating in a powerful lyrical style the beatific vision. This passage shows best and most beautifully how the 'face to face' expression evolves within the context of the nuptial imagery. William condenses in a short paragraph (given here *in extenso*) the most meaningful images of the Song of Songs:

> For when the day breaks and the shadows retire, Bridegroom and Bride will pass beyond the point of belonging one to the other for mutual accord and be present one to the other for their mutual enjoyment and delight. And the Bridegroom will no longer feed amid the sterile loveliness of the lilies, but amid the full fertility of the fruits of the Spirit. For when by the daybreak of the Holy Spirit our night in this life shall be light as the day, for a moment, for an hour, and the shadows of worldly vanity shall retire, yielding to the light of truth – or rather in the sunset of this life, which is night and not light, and in the morning of the opening of the other life, and above all in the morning of eternity, on the day of the general resurrection, then Bridegroom and Bride will begin no longer to belong one to the other by faith, but to be mutually present by vision, face to face; and the Bridegroom will not feed the Bride as it were among the sterile lilies in the flower of hope, but in the fruit of reality. And then all the shadows of the vanity of this world shall retire; that is, they shall be cast down from the pedestal of their self-esteem.[67]

Insistence is put on the absolute perfection of the vision 'face to face' at the end of all ends. The intelligence will then set its knowledge on the fullness of the *summum bonum*. The *affectus*, not shaped by the will of mortal man, but effected by God, will be completely possessed by him. The subservience of both intelligence and the *affectus* to the will of God is necessary for the glorification of man with God:

> All the moral force, the virtues, wills, intentions and affections of the man glorified with God, which are delivered through the power of the resurrection from the servitude of corruption and subjection to vanity, will be immutably stabilized in full vision of what he had believed in an incomplete manner; in secure possession of what he had hoped for with trepidation; and in entire fruition of what he had loved by faith.[68]

The mystical system of William addresses issues which touch upon the discovery of the self through the perusal and meditation of the Song of Songs. The vocabulary of love of this book has an important part to play in the reformation of the *affectiones* of the contemplative. In the following phase, they help in keeping them focused on a spiritual object, be it Jesus in his humanity or God. The vocabulary of love also expresses the achievements which ensue from such a rigorous discipline: the mystical experiences acquired during contemplation. The same vocabulary serves to describe hypothetically the beatific vision. William uses the terms of love especially for the fourth and fifth phases.

However, the steady progress of the contemplative life is only theoretical. As a passionate lover, the bridegroom plays hide and seek with his beloved.[69] The theme of the game of love is new in this work, and William emphasizes again the necessity to borrow the terms of carnal love to express this new spiritual game: 'And indeed, as we have already said above, by analogy with what takes place in fleshly love, we perceive a certain sense of experience as regards spiritual love and the affection of Bridegroom and Bride.'[70] William addresses an issue which has already been evoked in his writings, namely that the use of the terminology which describes carnal love is ineffective at circumscribing spiritual love if the practices (*usus*) of carnal love are not felt by those who use or read the terms. The metaphorical discourse of love is cognitively meaningful if the primary meaning, carnal love, is kept in the mind to explicate the secondary meaning. There are no dead metaphors of love in the works of William of St Thierry. He can anticipate an audience with a high level of literary competence, for whom description of the spiritual union can be expressed with the most enticing vocabulary:

> Often the Bridegroom seems to play the game of wanton love with the Bride; repeatedly he snatches himself away from her love with violence and then restores himself again to her desires. Sometimes he withdraws and departs as if he would not return, to make her seek him with greater ardor; and sometimes he returns and comes where she is, as if he would remain forever, the more sweetly to invite her to receive his kisses. Sometimes he stands behind the wall and looks through the windows, to arouse his lover's desire by letting himself be seen with his charms, but not wholly . . .[71]

This literary competence is fuelled by the grace which pours into the soul. Without such grace, metaphorical utterances encoding a divine message become indecipherable: 'For when God turns away his face, all is trouble. Words remain nothing but words, and writings nothing but letters.'[72] The end of William's *Expositio* stresses the necessity for the soul to reach beyond the states where reading, meditation, prayer, spiritual and physical exercises lead. This is the realm of the Book of Truth, of the *aeterna sapientia*, of the vision, and of the 'face to face'.[73]

Of all the twelfth-century commentators expounding the Song of Songs as the narration of a love relationship between the soul and God, William best represents how the terms of love define and explicate the itinerary of the soul in its quest for the 'face to face'. William also extends language to the limits of its expressive and cognitive capacities in its apprehension of the ineffability of the mystical experience. The language of love contributes in an important way to the broadening of the semantic field used to define the union of the soul to God, either on its own, or in conjunction with other biblical terms. Three points should be made concerning the use of the Song by William. First, it is essential to point out the extreme significance of the performative nature of this text, and William's full endorsement of this quality. Secondly, his writing of the commentary stands as the result of a performative act. His writing takes place as William lives out the role of the bride of the Song. Thirdly, such performative writing depends on the way the *affectiones* of the writer have been purified in order to sustain such an effort.

My aim is to see whether such conditions are met outside the period which is regarded as an apogee in the tradition of the commentary on the Song of Songs. We shall see how Richard Rolle, a fourteenth-century Yorkshire hermit, modulates those paradigms in expressing his own mystical system.

Part Two

*Self and Tradition: Richard Rolle and the
Commentary Tradition of the Song of Songs*

Prologue

The tradition of the commentaries on the Song of Songs has a long history which is beyond the grasp of a single volume, or indeed of a single author. As we have seen in Part 1, theologians such as Ohly, Matter, Astell and Turner, among others, have offered studies whose aim has been to cover relatively broad periods and consider the most important commentaries.[1] The aim of this volume, as mentioned in the introduction, is both to demonstrate the importance of the genre as literature and to show how a language of interiority and a consciousness of the self are seen to emerge from those writings. Part 1 offers a substantial discussion for the emergence of this language of interiority by discussing the making of metaphorical language in the writings of Richard of St Victor. I have argued that Richard's familiarity and internalization of the tropes of the Song of Songs are a catalyst for the making of his linguistic system. The chapters following, rather than considering texts which offer conceptualizations of notions dealing with language issues and interiority, engage with texts showing narrative involvement and use of those tropes which become instrumental to the discovery of the medieval self. The experiential and performative elements of those texts are essential to the discovery of the self.

The tradition of the commentaries on the Song of Songs is yet to be fully disclosed, as some treatises have not even appeared in Migne's *Patrologia latina*, not to mention modern critical editions. However, the substantial amount of treatises made already available would allow for a coverage which would extend from the twelfth century onwards. Indeed, the commentaries of Thomas Gallus (d. 1246), Thomas Aquinas (1224/5–74), Giles of Rome (1243–1316), Nicholas of Lyra (*c*.1270–1349) and Denys the Carthusian (*c*.1402–71), to name only some of the treatises selected and briefly discussed by Turner, would make apt objects for a general investigation of that tradition.[2] Since this study in its second part is geared towards the production of Latin and vernacular writings on the English soil, a consideration of the commentary by the English Cistercian Gilbert of Hoyland (d. 1172), a sequel to Bernard's enterprise, or some of the commentaries from the masters of theology from the universities of Oxford and Cambridge, sometimes delivered as part of their lecture courses, would also make interesting objects of investigation. Commentaries on the Song of Songs are also attributed to two English Dominicans, Thomas de Jorz (d. 1310) and Thomas Waleys (*c*.1287–1349).[3] Another Dominican friar, Robert Holcot (d. 1349), is credited with a commentary on the Song of Songs. In addition to the authors mentioned above, Stegmüller lists several commentaries written during the fifteenth century, some of them by British authors, like Guillaume Blackeney (d. 1490), William Byntree (d. 1493) and John Russell (d. 1494).[4]

The history of the tradition of the commentaries on the Song of Songs goes well beyond the medieval period, as the fine and extensive study by Max Engammare demonstrates.[5] However, rather than offering a diachronic evolution of the genre in medieval Europe, or even in England, this study in its second part proceeds by emphasizing instead the sustained engagement described by one of the narrative voices with the tropes of the Song.

In Part 1 William of St Thierry is shown to construct a self which works towards union with the divine by having recourse to a process of inner purification supplied by the love language of the Song. Although William works within a tradition marked by the weight of the Bernardine interpretation, he nevertheless offers an individualistic approach which differentiates him from some of his contemporaries. Such idiosyncratic engagement with the Song finds interesting echoes in William's peculiar itinerary within the religious monastic establishments, marked by changes from the Benedictine house of Saint-Thierry to the Cistercian one of Signy, with the late development of a great interest in Carthusian spirituality, attested by William's *Golden Letter* written to the attention of the monks of the Carthusian house of Mont-Dieu, where William spent several weeks there, if not months.[6]

It is more than apt in the prologue to the second part of this volume to mention William's late interest in using the epistolary genre for providing guidance to those interested in the solitary life. Indeed, a parallel can be found with the writing career of Richard

Rolle (*c*.1300-49) whose interest in the solitary life is one of his ongoing concerns. But my main reason for such a juxtaposition is that Rolle participates more than any of his contemporaries in the development of the mystical commentary on the Song of Songs, while at the same time redeploying a concern for the self shaped by the tropes of the Song of Songs and its use in former commentaries. In this second part I argue for the pervasive influence of Rolle's own acquaintance with the Song of Songs on the making of his own self, and the way that self is going to address its audience in the works which follow the writing of Rolle's own commentary on the first verses of the Song.

4
From *Interpres* to *Auctor*: New Contexts for the Vocabulary of Love

The history of the making of Richard Rolle's corpus and literary career has received careful attention. Following the work of the nineteenth-century German scholar Horstmann, Hope Emily Allen identified Rolle's canon by a meticulous study of a large body of manuscripts, with the aim of publishing his biography. No serious study of Rolle can bypass the extensive scholarship in her magisterial and imposing volume on the hermit.[1] More recently, Nicholas Watson, in *Richard Rolle and the Invention of Authority*, pays particular attention to the strategies used by Rolle for his self-fashioning as an *auctor*.[2] My own study of Rolle differentiates itself from Allen and Watson by considering exclusively his mystical writings. More importantly, one of the aims of this book is to demonstrate the process by which Rolle's development of a mystical discourse went hand in hand with the experience itself. As the first three chapters of this book demonstrate, several twelfth-century authors made effective use of the commentary tradition on the Song of Songs to finesse and develop language's metaphorical potential for the expression of their mystical experiences.

This book therefore places Richard Rolle in the same literary context by demonstrating the significance of this tradition for the making of his own mystical discourse. Rolle wrote a commentary on the first verses of the Song of Songs, *Super canticum canticorum*, and dealt further with the Song of Songs material in another treatise, *Melos amoris*, which is defined as being a postil on the Song.[3] This chapter looks at the ways Rolle handles the issues prompted by his reading and performance of this difficult biblical book.

But before moving on to a specific study of those texts, I would like to delineate the writing career of Rolle in three broad categories according to the dominant elements which mark his writing style. The experience of Rolle as biblical commentator is not limited to his treatment of the Song of Songs. The *English* and *Latin Psalters*, *Super threnos*, *Super apocalypsim*, *Six Old Testament Canticles* and the *English Magnificat* follow and rely on an exegetical pattern established by Peter Lombard (*c.*1100–60), among other commentators. In those pieces, Rolle's literary role consists essentially of that of an *interpres*. The next general term which best describes his literary activities is that of *auctor*, and under this label one can see the making of *Super canticum*, *Melos amoris* and *Contra amatores*. Rolle then absorbs exegetical practices for the writing of his Latin and Middle English epistles to become a 'messager', an intermediary between the divine voice and the audience. At this stage, Rolle addresses the specific spiritual needs of his audience by shaping a mystical system and making it available to his following.

Broadly speaking, the literary style of the Vulgate and its commentaries has a bearing on the whole of Rolle's writings.[4] Even the triad of *calor*, *dulcor* and *canor*, considered to be idiosyncratic, and which attests to Rolle's tendency to compress thoughts to verbal formulas, echoes biblical practice.[5] In fact, the structure of the Rollean sentence in many respects imitates favourite medieval biblical texts such as the Psalter and the Song of Songs. Alford argues that some of Rolle's rhetorical devices, such as association, substitution and amplification, owe more to the commentary tradition than to school rhetoric.[6] Rolle's use of some of the stylistic features of the Bible and its commentaries is crucial to our understanding of his style in both his Latin and English works. With regard to the *Melos amoris* for instance, it has been pointed out that the general form of the commentary is hardly disguised, and the structure of this piece has been characterized as 'postil-form'.[7] Yet, in looking at the commentary tradition of the Song and Rolle's own contribution to this literary genre, one has to acknowledge his dependence on this tradition while at the same time recognizing the new forces which are behind the writing of Rolle's commentary. This chapter argues that both *Super canticum* and *Melos amoris* show Rolle to engage more importantly with authorial activity, principally by displacing and assimilating materials which are generally used for biblical hermeneutic investigation in the commentary tradition.[8] As a result of *inventio*, Rolle sets a surrogate to the biblical context which allows for a widespread and strategic deployment of the terms of love. The opposition *amor carnalis–caritas* constitutes the dynamic foundation from which Rolle can impart cognitive meaning to the terms of love.[9]

Such strategy is commonplace among the twelfth-century commentators, but with Rolle one has to contend with three new important elements. First, outside the monastic context, the terms of love can be more loosely interpreted. Secondly, Rolle probably has less control over the inner dispositions of his putative audience. While the primary audience of Bernard or William is an intimate monastic one, Rolle's audience may be made of clerics, priests and perhaps even educated lay people. And, last, Rolle's discussion of women reveals interesting evidence on his psychological make-up and speaks for his own understanding of the concept of the *affectus* and its attendant *affectiones*. Some of his utterances reveal the inner conflict between *amor carnalis* and *amor spiritualis* which is still going on as he engages with the Song of Songs.

WOMEN AND *AFFECTIONES*

The process by which Rolle, interpreter of scripture, becomes translator of his spiritual experience, appropriating the imagery and displacing the textual practices of the commentary and accommodating them to his effusive prose, relies on the ways he manages to sort out psychologically his inclinations for women. The first part of this chapter looks at passages in his corpus revealing this phenomenon.

One passage in *Super canticum* makes use of the traditional representation of the devil disguised as a beautiful woman to demonstrate the power of the invocation to Jesus. Rolle offers this moment as a turning point in his life:

> While I had seized the single intention and, giving up the secular habit, and declined in my serving of God rather than man, it happened to me that on a certain night in the beginning of my conversion in my quiet state there appeared to me a certain maiden, very beautiful; before I had noticed, she was loving me quite a bit with good love. When I had gazed at her and marveled why indeed she had come to me by night in my solitude, suddenly without delay or speech she let herself free next to me. Because, sensing and feeling that she might entice me to evil, I told myself to wish to rise and bless us with the sign of the cross, invoking the holy Trinity. But she so strongly bound me that I felt neither my mouth for speaking nor my hands for moving. Seeing this, I thought that not a woman but a devil in the form of a woman was there tempting me. Therefore I turned to God

and with him in my mind, I said, 'O Jesus, how precious is your blood,' pressing the cross onto my breast with my finger, which now I could move a little, and, behold, suddenly all disappeared and I gave thanks to God, who freed me.[10]

The figure of the woman plays a significant role by emphasizing Rolle's weaker points. There is elsewhere supporting evidence for the way the making of his spirituality is intermingled with tense relationships with women. In the *Incendium amoris*, Rolle is rebuked by four different women for showing an usual interest in their attire, complexion and physicality.[11] Those accounts throw light on an important aspect of Rolle's psychological make-up which partakes in the elaboration of his mysticism and its expression through metaphorical discourse.

The fight against concupiscence is an ongoing and pervasive process in most of Rolle's writings. The fiercest diatribes against women appear in *Melos amoris*, the most ambitious of his mystical treatises.[12] Notwithstanding his brief acknowledgement of the craftsmanship necessary for the making of songs praising the *delectatio carnalis* – indicative of a familiarity with such practice – Rolle concentrates otherwise on the dangers of a carnal passion.[13] The use of biblical authorities, in this instance Ecclesiastes 7: 27, makes his case more authoritative:

> Moreover, to confound our enemies, a word from the wise one comes at the right time: *I find*, he says, *more bitter than death the woman whose heart is a snare and a net*. Yes, he holds woman far more cruel than temporal death, because how many rash persons who seemed to have deserved eternal life didn't she cover with her impure kisses and lead to eternal death! In this passage of Scripture, she is said also to be the net of the hunting demons; by which is meant the world in its almost totality, because, by her, almost the entire world is clasped in the illusory whips and snares of roaring hell.[14]

Such statements make it difficult for anyone not to treat Rolle as a misogynist. According to him, the entire world is trapped by women in the nets of hell. Rolle's diatribes are only a small reflection of the misogyny pervading all aspects of medieval culture. However, the surprise arises from the fact that misogynist statements are used to shape a mystical doctrine. In *Melos,* a text which presents highly sophisticated articulations of the contemplative state, there are also passages expressing views on carnal concupiscence which, in view of their supplicatory tone, read like wishful thinking:

> O dear Spirit, fill me with your breath, as I wish to despise the flesh and to be free from this filthily clothed concupiscence, and I want also, fully invigorated by the love of my Maker, to walk towards the summits in the ardour of this love. The beauty of woman will not move me, because I am henceforth stronger. In its purity and peace, my heart full of tenderness cannot let corruption invade it. Despising impurity, I yearn for the vision of the God of Beauty in his radiance. I strive with my gaze to define his depths, setting my eyes audaciously on the eyes of the Beloved.[15]

Within the same sentence, diatribes against women and concupiscence serve to contextualize the utterances expressing Rolle's higher mystical aspirations. For that reason, those misogynist ejaculations express a fundamental psychological trait of their writer. My contention is that Rolle is not filling in his text with material which would generally appeal to the misogynist audience of the medieval period. On the contrary, there is no rhetorical gesture on his part: those utterances are fundamental to Rolle's psychological make-up, and they make his use of the language of love more difficult than that of Bernard of Clairvaux or William of St Thierry.

By making those morally shocking utterances most relevant to his mysticism, one runs the risk of alienating him from a great majority of his twenty-first-century audience. Worse, such interest in women could be regarded by many as a sign of spiritual immaturity.[16] Be that as it may, it is remarkable to find how daring and frank an approach Rolle takes with regard to this particular issue. Diatribes against feminine beauty are rampant in *Melos*. Most often, a devilish association is set up with the feminine gender. Those who fall prey to the charms of feminine beauty for instance will not be spared from the bite of immortal death (*morsio mortis mortalis*). The invective points to a sense of the pervasive threat posed by alluring young women to the rich and the poor, the young and the old. The pretty seductive woman receives attention as if representative of womankind in general:

> This woman with her beauty has deceived creatures. She slits the throat of the young ones before it is possible to appear at court, and she corrupts the old ones to prevent them from blossoming again in justice. She makes

fall the poor, who seemed to be privileged and who thought were making great progress towards paradise, and the rich are ridiculed after she has wasted their gifts.[17]

The spectre of the sexually attractive woman is overwhelmingly present in the writings of Rolle. She bears great responsibility in bringing chaos and failure in the spiritual enterprises of many. No doubt Rolle is here projecting his own psychological doubts to a more general application. It may very well be that Rolle's sexual drive was the greatest impediment to his spiritual development. The passages exhale great bitterness and frustration which point to this possibility. For Rolle, the spiritual battle and its victorious outcome depend on the ability of the contemplative to operate a psychological self-castration and thus erase from the memory the image of this type of woman. It is impossible not to see the possibility for a former involvement with debauched women in statements as this one:

> No, don't like this beauty which deceives and fades. Don't set your eyes on a virgin, for fear that your beauty becomes an occasion for downfall. The make up of women is like plaster on a wall. Take away from them all those ornaments, they are disgusting to look at. As says the poet, *There is little to a woman which is truly herself*. Her unblushing lovers, by way of aromatic perfumes, will have their heart lifted up by the stench and they will taste the bitterness of absinthe. The jewels of the friend will be changed into misery. The crown of the carnal lovers will fall from their head into the abyss. There, in the middle of terrible terrors, the slaves of the flesh will be gulped down with their desires. Thus avoid debauched women, don't break the sworn faith. Appetites and madness are put to flight by a faithful life; they are poisons, vomited by sensual pleasure.[18]

It is as if Rolle had signed a pact to avoid being yet again lured into sexual debauchery. Although concern with lustful thoughts goes back to the tradition of the desert fathers, such a sustained attitude towards women is found nowhere else in Western mystical writings. And yet it pervades all the mystical writings of Rolle which make his experience the core of their concerns.

Argumentation against a certain type of woman is an important element of Rolle's apologetic and self-canonizing mysticism. It marks, among other works, *Melos*. Evidence in other texts, such as the *Incendium amoris*, tends to show that Rolle did not have clean hands over this matter. However, misogynist and vituperative passages, rather than exonerating him, emphasize his high anxiety. Chapter 43 stands as a response to enemies wanting him to account for his time spent among perverts and debauched girls:

> And that is why they were striving to hamper my journey. They judged me scheming and vicious, and if I was delayed so among the perverts, it was, they thought, because of the girls. The truth was that I did not slip away from any of those who wanted to hear some talk on the love of the maker. I want them to know once and for all that I live in sanctity. They should repent promptly, all those who judged me badly, so that they would not be chastised themselves. Yes, they were wrong when they thought I was evil. Women cannot deceive me, nor am I subservient to girls, nor do I set my happiness in those orgies which spoil the pagans. The soul which his majesty has purified from her faults takes time to modulate her song, and stays in this protected mystery of sweetness.[19]

The tension prompted by the encounter or visualization of enticing women forces Rolle to effect a drastic transfer of the sexual desire, which is then directed to God. Although this notion of transference is found in the writings of Bernard of Clairvaux, especially in the way he reminds his monks of their former carnal practices, Rolle's psychological conversion is tested as he walks in the middle of depraved and debauched women. Once established among the *electi*, Rolle still deems it necessary to demonstrate his ability to touch fire without being burnt, as he exclaims: 'we are indeed able to live among women and feel no delight of women in the soul'.[20] There is a tangible quality to his infatuation with the female gender which raises questions as to the state of his *affectiones*, the nature of his mysticism and the metaphorical meaning of the terms of love so expansively used in several of his Latin and Middle English writings. One has to admit that to use women as a gauge to measure spiritual progress is a remarkable and very idiosyncratic characteristic.

However, such is not the complete picture which Rolle offers with regard to women. An early Latin poem, the *Canticum amoris*, accommodates a wide catalogue of secular love motifs in praise of the queen of heaven.[21] The most typical characteristics from the medieval catalogue of feminine beauty describe the Virgin: golden locks, lovely cheeks, lofty eyebrows, rosy lips, graceful mouth, 'sparkling eyes of love', beautiful white neck, hands, breasts and arms. All the attributes of the idealized secular lady are conferred upon the Virgin:

A. The loveliest of girls bowled over the pleasure seeker./ And the serenest of brows makes him a languisher./ Her locks like gold consume the sad one;/ Her wonderfully lovely cheeks console the sitter.
B. The arching eyebrows of the flower of flowers shine,/ Her lips redden like the roses;/ Her mouth extremely beautiful./ Her eyes are very bright, abounding in passionate longings./ The young ones rejoice in those, from the scourges of sorrow.[22]

Idealized feminine figures do not threaten Rolle's psychological make-up. This description of the Virgin goes back to a tradition in which the twelfth-century Cistercians contributed significantly. Some of the vernacular lyrics which are part of the Wooing Group have accommodated to the Middle English language those attributes which, when applied to the Virgin, appeared first in the Latin language.[23]

The three Middle English epistles written during Rolle's later career each address a female recipient. If they are all devoid of the misogynist passages characteristic of his Latin writings, it is because Rolle is addressing women who belong to a different category from those he uses to measure his spiritual maturity. Moreover, the epistles, as we shall see in Chapter 6, fulfil functions drastically opposite to the Latin writings. It is therefore crucial to notice that Rolle has three categories of women in mind, all of which give rise to a particular response on his part. The Virgin Mary, idealized feminine figure, receives utmost poetic praise in Rolle's early career. Women living or entering the religious life, such as nuns or anchoresses, receive in the epistles written to their attention the advice a spiritual guide would wish to offer. The third category, that of debauched women, is used by Rolle to check his *affectiones* and his spiritual maturity. Whether Rolle went through a change of attitude with regard to the feminine gender later in life is difficult to assess, especially if one does not pay specific attention to those significant categories.[24]

In view of this particular feature of his mysticism, a careful appraisal of the use of the discourse of love in *Super canticum* and *Melos amoris* yields significant evidence about metaphorical meaning, language and the self.

SUPER CANTICUM CANTICORUM

The long but accurate title given to Rolle's commentary on the Song of Songs is that copied by the scribe in Dublin, MS Trinity College 153: *Exposicio super primum versiculum canticum canticorum secundum Ricardum heremitam.*[25] Rolle's commentary deals only with the first two-and-a-half verses of the Song of Songs. The length of the existing commentary indicates that, like many of his predecessors, Rolle never intended to write a commentary on the whole of the Song of Songs. A prologue, which would account for the difficulties of unveiling the mystery hidden in the book and reveal some of the author's strategies, is curiously absent from the commentary.[26] Rolle's commentary on the Song of Songs belongs to the category of the mystical commentaries, which were so fashionable in the twelfth century. In her introduction to her transcription of Dublin, MS Trinity College 153, Elizabeth Murray notes that the commentary written by Rolle follows the form of the Oxford postil, which was much longer and more discursive than the concise Paris postil. She finds that the term postil is the most appropriate term to define what Rolle does in this text.[27] Indeed, it is true that Rolle does not only provide an exegesis on the verses which have been selected for exposition, but he appropriates them to offer his very personal views on the contemplative life. The imagery of the spiritual marriage serves for the development of the most significant aspects of his mysticism. Rolle, who claims to have experienced the spiritual kiss (Sg. 1: 1), will offer substantial evidence for it. The image of the breasts (Sg. 1: 1) serves also to develop the theme of growth in charity, which Rolle believes to be best achieved while living the solitary life. The fragrance of the perfumes (Sg. 1: 2) is considered by Rolle to be the gift of the Holy Spirit, the perfumes themselves being the virtues, with charity as the most prominent one. The oil poured out (Sg. 1: 2) leads Rolle to develop one of the characteristics of his mysticism, the devotion to the Name, inspired by Bernard of Clairvaux and the Bernardine tradition to the Name in general.[28] Then the chosen soul cries to God (Sg. 1: 3) for help, as she needs God's support to find the peace provided by the discovery of charity. The last portion of the commentary dwells on the line *curremus in odore unguentorum tuorum* (Sg 1: 3) which serves to describe the joyous exaltation provided by steadfast love towards God. In disagreement with traditional mysticism, he claims the joyous experience of God to be a lasting one for holy and contemplative men.[29]

However, such a brief and seemingly ordered account does not do justice to what Rolle attempts in this treatise. For that reason, I would like to consider the ways by which he appropriates the Song and the commentary genre for the couching of a very personal account which leads to a radical transformation of the contextual setting of the Song. If Rolle's radicalism is extreme, especially in the way the authorial text is subject to displacement, it nevertheless follows a long tradition which shows how the appropriation of the Song serves for the expression of the mystical experiences of individuals such as, for instance, Bernard of Clairvaux, Richard of St Victor, or William of St Thierry, not to mention the mariological commentaries or the uses of some of its verses in various liturgical offices, which are discussed at length by Matter and Fulton.[30] As Chapter 2 has shown, commentators on this particular book are unable to accept its literal meaning within the biblical context. The overt sensuality of the vocabulary of love challenges any simple view of the divine origins of the Bible. For instance, William of St Thierry believes that God placed it with the other books in a condescending gesture to man's frailty, as a compound of both the material and the spiritual. Pseudo-Richard of St Victor regards the implausible literal sense as a means for the contemplative to look beyond the literal horizon.[31] The necessity for a constant reappraisal of its place within the Bible provides clear evidence of the difficulty of making sense of the vocabulary of love within the biblical context. A literal understanding, that is, is not appropriate within this special context. The task of the commentators is to create a new context for the text which allows for new conditions of reading.[32] As one can gather, the literal and allegorical interpretations occupied the minds of twelfth-century authors, as they did that of Richard Rolle.[33]

The dichotomy *affectio carnalis – affectio spiritualis* becomes the main line on which spiritual progress will be measured. When one has moved to a level regulated by the *affectio spiritualis*, then *caritas* becomes an essential element to facilitate a new reading of the Song.[34] William of St Thierry makes important references to this notion, while Richard of St Victor, in *De IV gradibus violentae charitatis*, offers a detailed and systematic study of this virtue.[35] Some of the major ideas and images of this important work are echoed in *Super canticum* and *Melos*.[36] The metaphor of love as fire, with its strong physical basis, as well as the degrees of love, called *insuperabilis*, *inseparabilis*, *singularis* and *insatiabilis* – with the omission in Rolle of the final degree – are without doubt borrowed from the Victorine treatise.[37] Moreover, as we have seen, Richard of St Victor defines further his four degrees as the love of the heart, the love of the whole heart, the love of the soul and the love of all the virtues. When talking of and describing further those degrees of *caritas*, he uses the model of natural love, so that the first degree is the celebration of the betrothal between the soul and God, the second celebrates their wedding, the third the consummation of their marriage, and the fourth the childbirth.[38]

The presentation of the contemplative life by means of the fusion of the carnal with the spiritual is echoed in the writings of Rolle. In *Super canticum*, the latter offers what can be regarded as an example of the expression of the third degree of violent charity of Richard of St Victor.[39] The *jubilatio* theme, which covers in *Super canticum* the fourth section of the commentary, called the *Encomium nominis Jesu*,[40] the image of the *incendium amoris*, the theme expressed by the *Quia amore langueo* verse, the image of liquefaction, and of course the *caritas* image, all present in *De IV gradibus*, become important elements of Rolle's mysticism and theology.[41]

The conflation of those traditions with Rolle's more idiosyncratic characteristics creates a context suitable for the articulation of more daring utterances. However, because of Rolle's particular stance towards carnal love, the latter is more used to modulate a contrast rather than as a springboard for spiritual love. Hence a particular style in his commentary is marked by the juxtaposition of castigation against carnal love with effusive passages inspired by the Song:

> Henceforth accordingly look up to heaven, o virgins; there seek the bridegroom; don't corrupt yourselves with the lovers of the world. Indeed Christ declares he will not recognize the foolish virgins, whom he then drives away from him because of their worldly vanity. In any case at present those pompous little women with their curled hair, going (about) with elevated horns, strive to be adorned only for carnal love. They hate and abhor this only way which leads to Christ, because they don't worry about casting out the form and substance given by God in deception and worthlessly.[42]

Rolle's commentary on the Song of Songs serves several purposes. It is crucial to strengthening his psychological make-up and making him confident in his spiritual claims. The utterances of love play a crucial role in the formulation of his mysticism. If expressed in the light of *caritas*, they will exonerate him from the constant references by his enemies to his shady past in the company of women. *Super canticum* is offered as a testimony, a piece of evidence to his innocence, in the form of a linguistic demonstration of the metaphorical use of carnal language on his part. The transfer of the terms of love into a new semantic field belongs to a process of spiritual purgation.

The *Osculetur me osculo oris sui* (Sg. 1: 1) is used as a formula to express the soul's desire for four important elements, such as the burning of eternal love, the sweetness of supernal contemplation, the dissolving of carnal corruptibility and the union with the unseen beloved:

> Certainly the burning of the speculation about divine love goes before the sweetness, because unless someone rightly loves Christ, doubtless he will not rejoice in the song of the celestial contemplation. Truly contemplative sweetness precedes the desire for death, because when we contemplate the belovedness that is only in God, singing the delights of eternal love, then we die with joy. For every delight of transitory desire is sent out as long as we truly ignite with the fire of the Holy Spirit and desire incessantly the glory of eternity. *He who, however, adheres to God*, as the Apostle says, *is one spirit* with him. Thus also our joy consists in this: God lives in us, so that we live in him.[43]

Rolle attributes the *Osculetur* verse with the potential of leading the contemplative to the *raptus*, which takes place when he involves Christ as recipient of his loving attention, nurtured by the kisses of God.

Other commentators are startled by this first line of the Song. Bernard of Clairvaux develops from it a theory of contemplative progression. The kissing of Christ's feet, hands and face symbolizes the different stages of the contemplative life, from a love of Christ in his humanity to the love of his Godhead. From a lexical term borrowed from the semantic field of love, Bernard creates a new set of functions for the kiss, unrelated to the originating field. The symbolic potential of the Song is used to inscribe a contemplative system of a sophisticated nature. Carnal imagery's transference from the field of physical love to that of the spiritual is clearly established in Bernard's writings, whereas in the case of Rolle, the double meaning of the terms of love is maintained, so that the gesture of kissing applies to both the semantic field of love and the conceptual domain of God. In the context of medieval courtly culture, the kiss expresses an advanced stage of the love relationship, which is maintained when it is transferred to the content domain of the mystical union, and when expressing the mutual love of soul and God in the contemplative experience. The evaluation of the meaning of this verse by Rolle leads to a contemptuous comment about carnal love, juxtaposed to the beauty of its spiritual meaning:

> Surely the lovers of filth in those words by no means have pleased Christ. On the other hand she is ravished by the sweetness of divine contemplation, truly she feels beforehand the flame of the infinite light, who in those words, 'That he may kiss me with the kiss of his mouth', glorifies God properly.[44]

Rolle is making a link between the moral worth of a putative audience and its ability to read metaphorically his discourse and that of the Song of Songs. Those who perform and enjoy fornication and impurity, the *amatores immundicie*, will not be able to understand and learn from the metaphorical meaning of those terms. The ways in which Rolle ponders on the language of love, projecting thus his anxieties and high aspirations about its use, must be treated as an essential component of his spiritual experience. This aspect, which is part of his psychological make-up and which defines also his linguistic approach, is responsible for the way the encoding of his mystical experience takes place at the metaphorical level. For it would be erroneous to consider the use of metaphorical terms by Rolle as being arbitrary and conventional. On the contrary, they carry the experience itself.[45]

The vehemence with which Rolle opposes two sets of meaning for the whole range of the vocabulary of love indicates how he charges his metaphorical utterances with more than an ornamental or affective value. The metaphorical meaning of Rolle's lexical terms of love conveys the contemplative experience.[46] As a concept taken from the domain of the *affectiones*, love, as *eros* or *caritas*, has a basis in bodily experience.[47] The process of interiorization of the external language of love marks out Rolle's most mystical pages. The interiorized language of love comes out as metaphorical discourse. In the course of the process, Rolle operates the transfer of meaning from the semantic field of carnal love to that of the conceptual domain of God by attempting to assign to the latter a series of defining terms. The terms of love lead to the understanding of some of God's attributes as the eternal light, *caritas*, the celestial melody, *dulcor*, the fire and its heat. The kisses of God are at one point described as the eternal light which embraces the mind. The contrasting of the heart burning with eternal light with the burning of evil desires leads Rolle to compare eternal light with natural light:

> By this, however, we understand that true light is uncircumscribed and eternal; for, when it illuminates our minds, when we are inwardly burned up by its heat, then we are glorified more sweetly in God. It is not, however, of the same material as the sun which blinds itself by considering punishment for a long time. But he who, doubtless, does not look back upon that sun of the celestial homeland with desire and diligence will be blind without end. Certainly we recognize that eternal light because when we live longer in this life, then we more truly sense it.[48]

Rolle opposes the literal meaning to many of his metaphorical utterances. This attitude is set with even more insistence when lexical terms of love are used. In another of his long and acerbic condemnations of carnal lovers, he argues for the incompatibility between joy in the world and happiness with Christ for the future life. In his crude language he asserts: 'A full stomach embraces more easily Venus than Christ', thus borrowing and adapting from Ovid's *Ars amatoria*.[49] The terms of love retain in Rolle's mind their double meaning, the literal and the metaphorical, because he does not stand too far from carnal desires, as he knows he can be easily led into a sexual act with a woman. This psychological background adds metaphorical meaning to the lexical terms of love. On the other hand, because of his propensity, Rolle is somewhat less daring in contextualizing those terms. Even more than other commentators, Rolle builds up a context for the vocabulary of love to limit their literal meaning. Linguistically, he is impressive and extreme in his efforts at opposing the literal sense of the love imagery. As I have noted, some of his utterances reflect his psychological difficulties in using the material taken from the semantic field of love to express his contemplative experience. But metaphorical utterances make sense only if their literal meaning is known. The accounts of Rolle's carnal experiences with women, so dramatically and expansively offered in his mystical writings, contribute to fire with life the metaphorical utterances whose literal meaning Rolle is trying to block. The man and his experiences have the better hand in this contest. If the reader sees Rolle the author deleting the literal meaning of the utterances of love, he keeps in mind the reports of his carnal experiences. The effort at deleting the literal meaning is anyhow counterproductive, since Rolle, by putting so much attention on the negative value of the literal meaning, makes its presence strongly felt by his audience. It is most likely he is not fully aware of the effects his vituperations against carnal love have on his audience. But if first *Super canticum* must be recognized as the site where Rolle makes use of textual commentary practices to fix the metaphorical meaning of the terms of love as translation and gloss of a mystical experience, it also raises important questions about the use of metaphorical discourse for the expression of mystical experiences.

The oddity in delineating the essence of God, and the relationship of the soul to him, is caused by the impossibility for the mystic of expressing it in the discursive mode. For that reason, Rolle resorts to, and counts on, both traditional vehicles and made-up terms as cognitive tools expressing the conceptual reality of the mystical experience, without saturating his commentary with a list of symbols. Instead, Rolle's preference for metaphorical meaning implies the resurgence and the interplay of two distinct components: on the one hand that of the world of love and courtship, and on the other that of the field of contemplation. The notion of transference of meaning from one component to another does not imply the rejection of the meaning given in the first semantic field. Moreover, the cognitive force of metaphorical meaning depends largely on the virtuosity with which the writer organizes his metaphorical utterances according to the relations of affinities and contrasts between the terms.[50] *Super canticum* demonstrates the difficulties with which Rolle, like most commentators, maintains those relations. If the Song provides most of its vocabulary of love to define the contemplative experience, it does not however unfold itself according to the natural progression of a human love relationship. Furthermore, the displacement of the text into commentary format makes it vulnerable to the intentions of its interpreters. As the human *auctor* becomes more inquisitive before the divinely inspired texts, he acquires the techniques to set them in his own chosen context, at his own pace.[51]

Super canticum is structured around a series of discussions of the sinful nature of carnal love, so as to establish a contrast with the most elevating passages using the same vocabulary of love. Apart from the bearing it has on Rolle's self-fashioning, this textual practice warns readers whose assumptions and expectations would not be those of a lover of God. Unlike the monastic and scholastic commentaries which were aimed at a certain milieu, the circulation of Rolle's work was not circumscribed by any social or religious barriers. Rolle makes a reference to the layman eager to hear divine words right after an audacious passage discussing the meaning of the breasts in comparison to the kiss, based on the joining of the verses *Osculetur me osculo oris sui* and *Quia meliora sunt ubera tua vino fragrancia unguentis optimis*:

> Yet and on that account she languishes for the kiss *because your breasts are better than wine*. For if she did not understand that the breasts of Christ were better than wine, certainly she would not dare ask for a kiss. Because if we are not busy to be pleased in divine instructions, without doubt we do not truly long for the pleasantness of the eternal sweetness. This is plain seeing that even the layman, as soon as he has experienced himself touched by divine love, impetuously burns to hear and to talk about God, neglecting secular concerns. Hence much more we who, with the help of God, can understand sacred scriptures, we must gird ourselves to read and hear the word of God and for other things which are to be written and taught.[52]

Being a lover of God implies an understanding and knowledge of the religious background, as well as the ability to trace the different layers of discourse. Rolle assumes that God's lovers will read his text with a set of inbuilt assumptions helping them to understand the terms of love spiritually. However, the spiritual reading has to be hammered into the consciousness of the audience:

> Then the reprobate is excluded from this godly protection, who, unstable in prosperity, falling in mischief, is carried away by the demon. So indeed blessed are the breasts which the saints sucked, but accursed are the breasts which nourished the sinners. But I want you to understand nothing here carnally, but everything spiritually. As the devil is first the inventor and the father of sin, so the evil ones are as if they were born from him when they sin. His breasts nourish them, while rejoicing they rush towards gluttony, lust and other vices.[53]

Rolle, like William of St Thierry, identifies strongly with the bride's point of view, and encourages his audience to do the same. But because of a new contextual setting, miles apart from the twelfth-century monastic revival from which most mystical commentaries emerged, the rendering by Rolle has a completely new flavour. The Song becomes the means by which his effusive voice will find a medium. Such drastic appropriation of the Song defies the rules governing the commentary genre: the narrative voice conveys both the concerns Rolle has for himself and for his audience, while it identifies at the same time with the bride. This double role makes the move from one level of scripture to another much more difficult.

Thus, the new context in which the terms from the semantic field of love are set requires a reinterpretation of their metaphorical meaning. Rolle, and any reader after him, has to solve the incongruities of the metaphorical meaning individually, according to the spiritual level and aspirations of the reader. *Ruminatio* on the Bible and other mystical texts allows readers to measure their spiritual progress by checking the gap which separates the literal meaning of the lexical terms against their understanding of the term's metaphorical meaning.[54] Rolle in fact actualizes this process textually, when he opposes the two senses of the vocabulary of love. Whether this process is didactically motivated is unclear, but it inevitably leads readers to compare their own understanding with that of the narrative voice, which becomes a matrix against which a measurement and a comparison are possible. Seductive as it may be, the process implies an acceptance of a form of contemplative experience which is circumscribed by the assumptions of the narrative voice. Nevertheless, if the opposition of the different meanings of the vocabulary of love throws light on the different layers of interpretation of the lexical terms, it does not explicate the nature of the higher meaning. Metaphors force the audience to rethink accepted concepts, to extend them or to invent new conceptualizations. They may bring the reader closer to an understanding of the higher meaning, even though the latter remains ineffable.

The ways by which the narrative voice moves from the effusive tone inspired by the anagogic sense to an interpretation of carnal love support the argument for a metaphorical interpretation of the conventional terms of love. Conceptually, the domain of God has no set pattern, is discursively non-expressible, visually non-describable. It therefore needs metaphorical utterances to have existence and meaning. Thus the function of metaphorical language is far from being only ornamental. Metaphors are essential components of the expressive capacity of language, which is not devoid of cognitive import. Rolle has no interest in constructing a mystical theology. Unlike Bernard, who systematizes through the use of symbols, Rolle sticks closely to the metaphorical interpretation. The ways in which both treat the kiss in the contemplative life are significant. Bernard elaborates an entire system around this term, whereas Rolle uses the terms *osculum* and *osculare* in their different forms thirty-nine times in *Super canticum*. He combines the kiss metaphor with other terms to enhance its expressive capacity, or alters its meaning by setting it in new contexts. Thus, Rolle's concern with the vocabulary of love is poetical, expressive and cognitive, as he tries to improve its strategic force within the contemplative field by widening the meaning of its metaphorical sense. The *Osculetur me* exclamation becomes a favourite utterance for the articulation of God's presence in the soul. The more often it is combined with words from other semantic fields, the greater the informational content conveyed by the metaphorical utterance will become. After his prophetic description of the Apocalypse, Rolle reverts to the *Osculum* formula. Combined with the wound and the lance motifs, it becomes one of the most dynamic and poetic metaphorical uses in this text:[55]

Let him kiss me. As the blessed soul repeats those sweet words so many times, what else does she insinuate except that she strives to expose herself. Every chosen soul truly indeed is wounded by divine love. However, the injured seeks a medicine, and the soul touched by charity is inflamed in the creator. It is surely apparent that such wound is not made of malice but of love, not of suffering but of sweetness. She never ceases to ask for the kiss, because she is not sluggish in desiring the joy of eternity. And when she ardently begs for the kiss, God pours himself totally into the soul and rejoices her marvellously, that then she is made drunk by eternal love and, wounded by the salutary arrow, she is raised above all terrestrial desires.[56]

In his quest for a linguistic system that serves for communication and fusion between the soul and God, Rolle posits his high style, rich in metaphors and metonymies, as a potential solution. His incessant warnings against a carnal understanding of the terms of love may be accounted not only as the result of a personal sexual inhibition, but also as a fear of seeing truthful meaning misinterpreted.[57] The reconciling of the erotic and the spiritual are a major concern of his. The two voices are brought together in *Super canticum* by a broadening of the metaphorical meaning of the terms of love. For instance, the association of the kiss with the eternal light plays a significant function in his mysticism:

> Truly I know that she feels great joy in God who asks a kiss from him. Therefore I should not dare to ask this, unless I know that he wished this of me. For from the great delight of love the spirit is snatched away to supernal things and, abounding in the secrets of God, is deeply examined by the splendor of eternal light . . . Thus truly, as long as she unceasingly collects all of herself in one blaze of eternal love, continually holding herself inwardly, now she never tends to desirable exterior attractions. And because she is consumed by the delectableness of internal delights, she rejoices to be dissolved, panting in the desire of the Creator. Therefore it is no marvel that the soul that melts so much with the eternal fire of sweetness also says, sighing, *Let him kiss me.*[58]

The joy, the sweet kiss, the madness, the inebriation, the panting, the sighs and the melting belong to the semantic field of love. They bear an important cognitive value in the Rollean context by being instrumental to the affective voice of the author who claims direct participation in the experience described. Rolle does not provide a definition of *caritas*, but makes extensive use of the term and associates it with one aspect of the content domain he tries to define with the vocabulary of love. Song of Songs 8: 1, which refers to the spouses as brothers sucking the same breasts, gains meaning in a passage where Rolle associates it with the notion of *caritas*.[59] Such association may very well be influenced by representations of the *caritas* personification as a lady with her two children sucking her breasts.[60] But Rolle adds to this association. To him, the *fragrancia unguentis optimis* refers to the breasts providing celestial knowledge for the lovers of God. With that as a starting-point, Rolle adds Luke 11: 27, *Beatus venter qui te portavit et ubera quae suxisti*, to make up one of his most interesting analogies. Allegorically speaking, he uses the formula to characterize the relationship between the saints and Christ. He portrays a detailed allegorical figure of Christ as mother, patiently waiting for her children to undergo baptism and penitence. After that, they will be fed from the milk flowing from her breasts.[61] The analogy contributes to the making of a forceful relationship between the contemplative and the person of Christ:

> Whence also, speaking allegorically, it can be said to any saint that which the woman spoke in the Gospel to Christ: *Blessed the womb which bore you*

and the breast which you sucked. For just as before we are born corporally in the world we are carried in the mother's womb, and before we are able to walk strongly or run or take any food, it is necessary that we take milk from the breasts of a mother; thus spiritually, before baptism or before penance, we are carried about in Christ's womb, that is, in his patience, lest we suffocate as aborted fetuses or be damned by diverse pollutions. When truly through baptism or through penance we had been extracted by God from the prison of infidelity or the labor pains of iniquity, we have the job of hanging from the breasts sucking the milk by which we are nourished.[62]

The wound motif which is often used to express the desire of the soul to enter into the body of Christ reflects the primal position of the soul in the womb of Christ, our spiritual mother. The technique Rolle uses here in the writing of his commentary is based on elaboration of biblical images which recur in his mind while he is writing. The transfer of the maternal imagery of the Virgin Mary to Christ is affectively very powerful. Luke 11: 27–8, traditionally used in the gospel of vigil to commemorate the Assumption of the Blessed Virgin, assists the creation of this new image.[63] It is followed by Psalms 70: 6. Nevertheless, the biblical connection which allows for the making of the metaphorical meaning is derived from Ps. 70: 5: *quoniam tu es patientia mea, Domine. Domine, spes mea a iuventute mea.* The ways by which Rolle links biblical passages mirrors the mental itinerary which shapes his mysticism: it is marked by a multiplicity of images, formulas and symbols which are used as cornerstones within the affective edifice. From each of them Rolle ceaselessly shapes affective utterances, either to stress a moral point or to move the soul to the love of God. Yet Rolle sometimes has to lower his language from what he calls the spiritual sense to the literal sense. From a mystical exploration of the meaning of the breasts of Song of Songs 1: 1, we have moved to the wound and the womb motifs, to return ultimately to a vituperative outburst against the breasts of evil.

The conclusion of the exposition on the first verse of the Song of Songs emphasizes the importance of the virtues, more especially *caritas*. The passage is central to our understanding of Rolle's mysticism. Its style, elaborate in poetical devices, makes effective use of the language of love to describe the role played by this virtue:

Thus love is the most perfect of virtues, the noblest and sweetest, which that saint deserved to possess who, passing from virtue to virtue, arrived at the summit. We know this virtue joins lover and beloved, that is, Christ eternally joining with the elect soul. Love moreover forms anew in us the image of the highest Trinity and makes the created similar to the Creator.[64]

Rolle uses explicit sexual terms to describe the ultimate effects of *caritas* on the relationship between the soul and God. Both terms convey either a sexual or spiritual meaning, as *coniungere* means to unite (sexually or spiritually) and *copulare* to couple.[65] Rolle expounds further on the relationship in an expressive and incantatory style:[66]

> O gift of love, how you prevail over all things because you recommend for yourself only the highest grade with the angels, for the more someone receives things from you in the way, the more will he be sublime and glorious in his homeland. O singular joy of love, that you bind your own with chains by which you snatch them above earthly to heavenly things! He who does not have you in the earth loses whatever he has; he who however strives to be able to rejoice in you through all things quickly is raised above earthly matters. O lovely love, how good you are, because you do not arrange to appear alone before the Creator! You boldly enter into the cell of the eternal king; you alone are not afraid to seize Christ. Christ is yours; hold him. He cannot refuse to receive you, whom alone you desire to obey. Without you absolutely no works are pleasing to Christ. Therefore your seat is heavenly; your society is angelic; your holiness is marvellous; your vision of God is glorious; yours is life abiding without end. All who do not trust in your salvation will be damned. O love to be desired, you raise up fame and extinguish it immediately; you make the cold warm! You are the vestments by which we will stand motionlessly by, clothed to the measure of Christ. What should I say about your praise? Whatever I shall have said, I admit I am not adequate. O how great you are, who make even the miserable great! O how glorious, who make mortals incapable of suffering! Rightly therefore it is said: that strong is the *love* which *conquers all things*.[67]

Rolle's impassioned lyric style characterizes this passage. According to Copeland, this style is always used as 'a suggestive transcription of ecstatic spirituality, and of the compulsion of a love which is violent and overpowering'.[68] Some of Rolle's most characteristic rhetorical devices are used in this passage.[69] Praise of *caritas* concludes and summarizes the commentary on the first verse. In order to impart cognitive meaning to the conceptual domain of God, Rolle applies terms of carnal love drawn from the Song of Songs and reinforces them with terms from secular love poetry.[70]

THE POWER OF METAPHORS

One of the strengths of Rolle's discourse is the ability of its author to expand the cognitive meaning of the metaphorical utterances of love. Despite Rolle's uneasiness with sexual topics, he exploits the field of courtship and carnal love to articulate the target field of mystical love. Without the literary theories and textual practices which emerged from the commentaries of the Song of Songs and preceded his own work, Rolle would be at a loss expressing his affective spirituality. His discourse rests on a tissue of biblical analogies which were already woven in the early days of this specific commentary tradition. The vocabulary of love translates the mystical phenomena best, and the relations the terms of love bear to one another in the originating field, serve to guide the relations which they continue to share with one another in the new field. The contemplative experience can thus be scanned in an epistemic way by defining the relations each term bears to the other. The high-powered emotional potential of the terms of love can affect the audience when they are used in a strategically effective way. The sequence in which each term of love is placed *vis-à-vis* other terms in this new context is essential to the development of the new affective strategies of the text.[71] Terms like *osculum* and *amplexio* each convey a certain aspect of physical love which, transposed to a mystical context, expresses also a notion of the contemplative experience. Rolle uses the terms together three times, first at the beginning of his exposition: 'He therefore embraces his brides, who are all one bride, and sweetly with the kiss of love he satisfies each and all and comforts with eternal embraces'.[72] The two terms are linked again towards the middle of the exposition, in a passage dealing with the maidens and their love for Jesus.

> And accordingly it is true love, chaste, sacred, loving freely the beloved for himself, not for his goods, setting itself completely in the beloved, seeking nothing outside of him, contented about himself, blazing, being inflamed, taking fire from the lover, ardent, binding itself to him, impetuous in a marvelous way, exceeding all measure, stretching out to the only beloved, despising and also forgetting all other things, singing in the beloved,

thinking him, remembering him constantly, increasing in desire, proceeding in the beloved, rushing towards embraces, absorbed in kisses, melting completely in the fire of ardent love, so that to you, O good Jesus, it is said justly: *The Young maidens loved you exceedingly*.[73]

A juncture between the two terms appears again in the last fourth of *Super canticum*: 'And when she melts because of the prior chilliness and the hurtful cold, neither dragged along nor called, she runs to the beloved sometimes to embrace and kiss.'[74] In the three examples offered here, the tension created between vehicle and topic serves to define the topic of God and its relationship to the contemplative soul. Such a domain of experience needs the tangible love imagery to take a visual form.[75] Applied to an essentially abstract entity, the use of the vocabulary of love fulfils altogether different functions than those when defining Jesus in his humanity. As the latter can be articulated outside the sphere of metaphorical expressions, the conceptual domain evades a clear delineation by means of those expressions. Without an appropriate and moderate application of the terms of love, the depiction of the relationship of the soul with Jesus in his humanity echoes with powerful and explicit sexual allusions.[76]

However, Rolle provides an artful demonstration of the use of the language of love to define the humanity of Jesus. The exposition on the *Oleum effusum nomen tuum* focuses on the repetition of the name of Jesus as a devotional exercise.[77] If the Virgin Mary in *Canticum amoris* was represented as an object of praise and envy, towering solitarily in her excellence, here she is subtly appraised within the general scheme of the humanity of Jesus. The reciprocity of their relationship, expressed in a tender and homely vocabulary, contributes to a powerful depiction. In this context, the kiss, the embrace and the breasts carry a strong literal meaning:

> For you truly, O Lady, it is fitting to ask and receive a kiss from the eternal king, for indeed you have merited to suck his mouth and deservedly, *because better are your breasts than wine*. O blessed breasts, which the eternal creator did not refuse to suck, and from them, according to the custom of infants, absorb milk. O Mother, elect and truly glorious, with so great delights you have flowed when that mouth, the mouth of the eternal Father, joined to yours and touched with tender fingers your breasts. Weeping with consolation, you expect jesting.[78]

The conflation of images pertaining to two respective domains, that of the maternal relationship and that of the lover relationship, creates an interesting tension. Rolle appropriates images of the nativity which evoke the physical tenderness of the maternal relationship. While the babe sucks the breasts and touches them with his delicate fingers, the Virgin Mary asks for the spiritual kiss from the mouth which her breasts fed. There is a parallel between the new-born infant's desire for physical comfort and that of the Virgin Mary for spiritual experience. With delicate artistry and by the use of the literal and metaphorical meanings of the terms *ubera* and *osculum*, Rolle successfully describes the mystical field with a new range of images drawn from popular iconography and literature.

After having created a particular emotional landscape for the expression of the mother and son relationship, Rolle reverts to the *oleum effusum* verse to create an emotionally strong bond between the soul and Jesus: 'O pious Jesus, pour in our wombs this oil; write on our hearts your name. Since poured out oil is called your name for us, give us that oil to taste, to love, to embrace.'[79] The narrative voice appropriates the imagery of motherhood and pregnancy to express the desire to be filled by the oil, which stands for the Name. Pregnant with such a powerful linguistic sign, one which deserves to be loved, tasted, and embraced, the narrator continues with multi-layered metaphorical passages which abound with an affective charge: 'This oil refreshes us; this oil perfects us; this oil smears us; this oil delights.'[80] Making use of a cadenced prose, the narrator continues his praise of the oil, insisting on how it clothes the soul with the virtues necessary to gain insight into the spiritual worlds. Following a passage insisting especially on the healing power of the oil, an association is made between *oleum* and *caritatis* in the significant expression *oleum caritatis*. Deconstructing such a passage reveals how linguistic competence informs the meditative process by which one may have access to the spiritual sphere. Being infused by the oil, which stands for the Name of Jesus, leads to a higher state of awareness, a certain degree of love which Rolle defines as the third degree of love, called *singularis*. Such a degree of love is concomitant with *caritas*.[81] At a later stage in the commentary, *caritas* is defined as God, according to the First Epistle of St John: *Deus caritas est qui manet in caritate, in deo manet et deus in eo* (1, John 4: 16).[82] The principle of reciprocity already expressed in the maternal love of Mary for her son recurs in this passage where the association *deus–caritas* is made.

> To be sure this is manifest when, indeed in holy men, God pours himself out according to their capacity. Since therefore God grows not in himself but in us, we are able to make the clear connection that he shows himself most grand in those souls in whom he pours himself more fully and perfectly through his grace. Wherefore, since Holy Mother Church agrees about all its sons that no one has God abiding in himself except he who has love, since he who does not love God mistakenly says he has God, it follows certainly that he who loves God less indeed senses God less and he who burns more greatly in love has God more perfectly and abundantly.[83]

Although the mystical *unio* and the so-called *excessus mentis* could logically be part of the description following, there is instead a concerted effort on the part of the narrative voice to put attention on the *caritas* theme and its attendant vocabulary of love.[84] The addition *radix cordis nostri sit caritatis* to Song of Songs 1: 3 allows for an ongoing development of the theme in the remaining part of the commentary. The description of this virtue as a wedding dress, for instance, underscores the extent of the transfer of the nuptial vocabulary to describe the domain of God:

> Many are called to faith; few are chosen for salvation, because unless someone is clothed in love, without doubt he will rather be expelled from the nuptials. This virtue which is love is great and very great, since others do not find it unless they are dear friends of God. Let him not, moreover, fear to stand before the tribunal of God who will be able to carry love with him. Many judge many things; others make great things; others endure hardships; but he alone is saved who is about to have love. None love mistakenly although many act mistakenly. Moreover, this love, if it will be true, is acquired by the greatest labor, but it is truly possessed, held by unthinkable sweetness.[85]

Caritas, gained through prayers and meditations on the Name of Jesus, creates new conditions for the decoding of the terms of love. To Rolle, who is the narrator of the commentary, God is light, celestial melody, sweetness, heat and charity. The expression of those inner visions and sensations into an affective and metaphorical language supports the hypothesis of the authenticity of his experiences which cannot be explained discursively, since the *ratio* is not equipped to express the joy and the love which it contains: 'And love is not drawn but spontaneous, moving itself freely for the beloved, indeed running with delight to the beloved.'[86] If the affective response prevails in the eyes of Rolle, it is because it alone produces an idea of what the mystical experience can be. As Rolle states, 'No one therefore is drawn to God, unless he who indeed is drawn by all his feelings strives to love.'[87]

Both the method of the mystical life and its written account rely on, and emphasize, the importance of the affective side of the soul, described as the *affectus* by medieval theologians. As this close analysis of *Super canticum* demonstrates, the kind of literary production which Rolle offers here serves more to embed glimpses of his own spiritual experience than to make sense of the biblical text. However, most commentators of the Song before Rolle invest the Song with a strong personal involvement as well, even if they pretend to show a greater concern for the naked truth of the text. In both cases, the kind of introspection which this kind of literary activity allows does not pass unnoticed by the commentators. The construction of their subjectivity goes hand in hand with the writing of their text.

MELOS AMORIS

The writing career of Rolle as mystic depends greatly on his interaction and work with the commentary tradition. The earlier chapters of this book demonstrate how commentaries on the Song of Songs help to shape a mystical language in the Western tradition. Bernard of Clairvaux, William of St Thierry, Richard of St Victor and Pseudo-Richard all participate in the making of a powerful mystical discourse shaped by the images of the Song and translated into metaphorical utterances. Richard Rolle's own contribution to the making of this language, as shown above, appears forcibly in his own commentary on the Song. My contention is that, however momentous the writing of this piece in his writing career as a mystic, it stands as a turning point rather than an ultimate achievement, as is the case with many of the twelfth-century authors. *Super canticum* is the first step by Rolle in his appropriation of a tradition for the making of his own peculiar language and mysticism. Once this appropriation is solidly established, he proceeds to translate it into the other genres which are going to be used to disseminate his mystical message. This move away from the commentary genre, noticeable in the commentary as such in the first instance, never attempts to sever itself completely from that tradition. On the contrary, each text following this turning point in his writing career resonates with elements of the commentary tradition on the Song. Indeed, in his later writings in Latin and the vernacular, the imagery, the performance-based passages, the intimate and seductive tone, all attest to the overall significance of that tradition. *Melos amoris*, a text which, according to Watson's chronology, was written shortly after *Super canticum*, demonstrates both its author's dependence on the Song and its tradition while providing signs of an even greater independence of composition.

Rolle calls *Melos amoris* a postil and, indeed, this work bears these characteristics more than *Super canticum*. Indeed, this treatise makes a looser use of the verses of the Song of Songs and does not attempt to offer a verse-by-verse hermeneutics on the Song. However, the postil form provides evidence for its strong dependence on the commentary genre, not only in terms of its forms, but also with regard to the reading process which the writing of mystical commentaries implies. The monastic practice of *lectio, ruminatio* and *oratio* accounts for the kind of material embedded in the commentaries of Rolle and his monastic predecessors. Similarly, *Melos* projects a voice much preoccupied with the construction of its own self through love. This fashioning of the self through the process of writing about love takes a new impetus in a treatise much more loosely framed than the commentary which precedes it.

Melos amoris is divided into fifty-eight chapters. The first fifty-five chapters describe spiritual progress and make part 1. Part 2 is made of three chapters only. They consider the rewards of the *electi* and the punishments of the *reprobi* after Judgement Day. Vandenbroucke describes nine units in part 1, interspersed by personal accounts. Each unit offers a theme particular to Richard Rolle, and introduced by a biblical quotation. The call to the mystical life is introduced by Song of Songs 1: 1, *Osculetur me osculo oris sui*. It discusses the call to the mystical life and the role played by spiritual song in this process. The excellence of the mystical life makes the second unit, introduced by Song of Songs 1: 3. Stress is put on the value of spiritual goods; it therefore praises those with few material possessions and discusses the path of the *electi*. The third unit is entirely devoted to the contemplative soul's process of purification, introduced with Song of Songs 1: 5: *Pugnaverunt contra me*. A verse from a psalm (Ps. 21: 15) serves for the discussion of the divine action in the purified soul which makes the fourth unit. The following unit opposes the love of Christ to carnal love. It is followed by an account by Rolle about his own conversion, and how it may serve as a model for those who want to enter the spiritual life. Unit seven is devoted to a discussion of the paradoxes of the mystical life, which is introduced by Song of Songs 1: 5: *Nolite considerare me quod fusca sim, quia decoloravit me sol*. The penultimate unit is about *melos* itself, the most divine of songs. Following another personal account of the greatness of the solitary life, the last unit discusses the theme of perfect love, based on Song of Songs 2: 4, *Ordinavit in me charitatem*. A short epilogue also based on Song of Songs 2: 4 (*Fulcite me floribus, stipate me malis, quia amore langueo*) discusses the languishing of the lover. The second part of the treatise is divided into three units which discuss, in the following order, the gathering of the *electi*, final judgement and the chastizement of hell.[88] As Vandenbroucke admits, the division of *Melos amoris* into several units demonstrates a certain amount of coherence, which scholars have usually been at pains to attribute to the treatise. However, the internal structure of each unit leaves much to be desired. It is as if the scriptural quotation was used as trigger for the development of a discourse largely dependent upon biblical association. In that respect, the postil form of *Melos* allows for a much looser development of ideas than the commentary structure of *Super canticum*.

Such contextual frame allows for a more adventurous use of metaphorical discourse. As Rolle has graduated here from the more restricted form of the commentary genre, his personal insights are deployed more frequently in the text.[89] Arnould notes in his introduction to *Melos* that some sentences from *Super canticum* are repeated word for word in *Melos*. Watson carries this investigation even further by providing evidence of appropriation from *Super canticum* into *Melos* in eight different extracts.[90] One can argue along the same lines as Arnould by saying that they are indeed explained more fully and given 'a more mature and forceful expression' in the latter text.[91] I would like to show that this is true as well of the large body of metaphorical utterances found in this difficult treatise. This fourth section therefore considers how, despite the use of a traditional imagery, the conceptual domain of God is substantially enlarged in this new context.

Melos is didactic in its own peculiar way. For instance, the *proemium* emphasizes the importance of love as the *causa scribendi*. It continues with a definition of the *forma materialis*:

Therefore, this violence of love presses me so much, that I dare open the conversation in order to instruct others and show them the greatness of those who love ardently, the justice of those who rejoice in Jesus, the love of those who sing in harmony with the heaven, and finally the clarity of those who can capture in their consciousness the uncreated ardour and the unwaning pleasure.[92]

Eloquium, translated as conversation here, is the term used to define the medium which will serve to express the various feelings of those who have an experience with the divine. The narrator, surely including himself among those who have a claim to the spiritual life, devotes little attention to his audience, while laying emphasis on the particularities of those who deserve mention as spiritual beings.

If *Melos* marks an important step in Rolle's programme of self-aggrandisement as an *auctor*, I rather doubt that this next episode in his writing career was as carefully planned as Watson argues.[93] When looking back at the commentary tradition, and Rolle's own role within it, *Melos amoris* stands as a logical, natural continuation. The commentary tradition has provided him with a range of linguistic tools which express best his intimate self. The treatise, following his own commentary, is a tribute to the Song of Songs itself, an acknowledgement of its decisive role in the construction of Rolle's mystical language and persona. *Canor*, which is at the heart of *Melos amoris*, translates idiosyncratically the inner state which resulted from an intimate and sustained meditation on the biblical book. If Rolle experienced *canor* early in his career, as the chapel episode in *Incendium amoris* attests, it required a long religious and literary engagement with the Song of Songs before it found its means of expression.[94] *Melos* is the most daring and fanciful attempt at encoding the ineffable in the affective vocabulary borrowed from carnal love. Moreover, the textual transcription of *canor*, a difficult act of translation as such, calls for a vast array of rhetorical techniques, such as the use of alliteration, balance, and anaphora.[95] My interest with this work lies in the way the vocabulary of love serves in setting a spiritual context for *canor*.

The significance of spiritual song in *Melos* is as important as its musical vocabulary is varied and numerous.[96] In the context of this text, song receives the same attributes as *caritas* in *Super canticum*. Song is the eternal beatitude, the peak of mystical life, God himself. When described as a mystical state, it is compared to a large number of musicians playing a symphony in beautiful style.[97] The celestial court, the home of the purified souls, resounds with sweet melodies. Access into the court is sealed by the kiss given to the chosen soul by the creator:

> Going about her own inner occupations, the soul, liberated from human consolations, purifies herself from the stain of the world. She strives to reach the celestial court. Loved by God, she expresses her desire to receive the kiss of the creator of the universe. And soon she receives this token of bounty which is the kiss of the lips, by the meeting of the spirits. Because, I insist, the union about which I am about to reveal the sweetness to God's beloved, is invisible and spiritual, and it is by the tip of the spirit, and without return shock, that we look forward to be ravished in this light of perfect joy.[98]

Rolle further describes the joy of the *justi* with a great number of musical terms:

> They gorge themselves on the consolations of the celestial symphony, and stand among the verdant and spring riches of virtues. They sing in chorus, with the inhabitants of heaven, the songs of love. The honey of his majesty softens them marvellously. Without respite, the uncreated fire consumes the rust of all their sins.[99]

Synaesthesia, which is defined as 'the production, from a sense impression of one kind, of an associated mental image of a sense-impression of another kind' (*OED*), and which is generously used by Rolle – as the first sentence just quoted demonstrates – may serve several functions. First, it participates in conveying the notion that the spiritual world belongs to a dimension which cannot find expression via the use of mental images produced by one sense impression only. Synaesthesia therefore expresses difference and ineffability. Second, it may be representative of a mnemonic intention on the part of Rolle. Sounds, for instance, are rendered into visual images, which may facilitate memorization. Hence, Rolle may be following medieval memory advice when using synaesthesia.[100] In the context of the role of the language of love in defining the relationship of the self with the divine, synaesthesia partakes also in giving new meaning to imagery borrowed from the Song of Songs.

The spiritual kiss for instance is regarded as offering joy by the fact that it allows the music of invisible life to be tasted. Synaesthesia therefore participates importantly in providing textual accesss into the highest degree of the mystical experience:

> They live in glory and taste the music of invisible life. What a kiss, sweet, delicious and desirable, which gives rise to such joy. It gives birth to devotion, nourishes fervour and makes piety. Because as we let sing within us the delights of eternal love, we are carried away above ourselves, we exult in an astonishing joy of love according to the measure that the divine will allows us to relish. Such are the song of songs and the joy of joys.[101]

The conceptual domain which expresses the relationship of the soul with God is discursively inexplicable. Copeland has emphasized how Rolle's metaphorical language, from its sensual base, brings the reader towards an understanding of the spiritual experience and how the linguistic signs (or lexical terms) constitute the experience itself when placed in a transcendent sphere.[102] The cognitive value of the metaphors of love, which are associated here with music and song, carries a real significance within the affective system. Each utterance touches upon a reality which exists beyond language. As a figure of speech, it provides insufficient evidence to investigate fully the inner world of the mystic. Yet, as metaphorical discourse, it provides a means of describing the mystical world and also of decoding the network made up of the connections which link the terms from two semantic fields. The conceptual domain for the mystical experience varies from one mystic to another, in accordance with the links and bridges which the mind has been able to make between the different terms. Rolle looks for a multiplicity of meaning from the biblical text. During *ruminatio*, the text takes on meaning according to the contemplative's state of consciousness.[103] The insights into the spiritual reality, which may be developed from the text, are uncircumscribable, infinite, while at the same time very personal. Rolle's awareness of this linguistic diversity for the translation of a personal mystical experience appears in the way he expresses his fascination for the spiritual potential of the *Osculetur* verse: 'The prophetic oracle declares in his exordium concerning those who love: *Let him kiss me with the kiss of his mouth*. Those words breathe a vital force and a jubilant joy. One finds in them marvellous mystical senses.'[104] His definition of the kiss stresses the affective response which the term should bring about in the mind: 'The divine kiss is to feel the comfort of eternal love.'[105] Engrossed in such a mode of thinking, Rolle continues with a description of the joy of contemplation based on a biblical reference: 'She it was I loved and searched for from my youth; I resolved to have her as my bride; I fell in love with her beauty.'[106] The infectious spiralling effect of such affective writing produces a highly metaphoric discourse whose meaning depends on the connection each utterance bears with the other.

One wonders whether Rolle does not have in mind the contemplative system offered by Richard of St Victor in *The Twelve Patriarchs* when he associates clothing imagery to the image of the kiss borrowed from the Song of Songs. For, indeed, *tunicam talarem*, found at least twice in *Melos*, and which should be translated as a gown or long cloak, is a borrowing from Genesis 37: 23, which is part of the episode describing the attempt by the brothers of Joseph to kill him. Joseph stands for full self-knowledge in *The Twelve Patriarchs*.[107] By dressing the holy hermit – which probably stands as representation of his own self – with the long tunic which was snatched from Joseph by his brothers, Rolle makes a claim for the heavenly reward which will be offered to those who, like him, have engaged in the work of contemplation:

> The holy hermit who, for his Savior, has accepted to dwell in a sitting posture as a solitary, will receive in heaven a magnificent golden seat among the angelic choirs. Instead of the coarse clothing that he has worn for the love of the Creator, he will wear the *long cloak* of eternity, weaved in the divine light. Among the celestial powers, he will wear forever a superb mantle adorned with precious jewels.[108]

Earlier in the text, the gift of the cloak stands for the practice of all the virtues. Further demonstration is made about the way the biblical context serves in the making of Rolle's discourse:

> We will receive the immaculate cloak and our soul will be clothed with it. Wrapped up in a flawless happiness, she will be enlightened by the flash of the glittering vision. Soon established in heaven, she will reach in an ascending march to the glorious heavenly body and will seek the shadow of the beloved's kisses, author of the infinite precious gift.[109]

The association of the term *osculum* with *obumbratio*, which results from the conflation of Song of Songs 1: 1 and 2: 3, appears for the first time in this text, but is used on several occasions in the second half of the work.[110] In the following passage, elaboration on this association produces a new set of images highlighting the meaning of the shadow of the kiss:

> *And where from* does this happiness come to the elected soul? She is placed in the helpful shadow of the creator, she is equally sitting in the shelter of the storeroom of a haven. A magnificent wall protects her from evil. A refreshing dew restores her radically. And really, it would be impossible for her to be removed from the goad of sin and, insensitive to the burning of tribulation, to believe herself to be in peace until the trial of the fight, if she had not tasted by pure grace the joy in those words: 'And her fruit is sweet to my palate.' Undoubtedly she possesses love and knows the burning embraces. The kiss that she desired, she has received it under the tree. This tree of joy has placed her in the shadow of his mystery, shielded from sin and guilty deviations. His fruit, bursting out of a fertile flower, has put to flight all imagination, all disastrous passion. The beloved of God, the elected which He consecrated to Himself, gorges on it with delight.[111]

If, as I have noted, the ferment of this association is biblical, the first part of Song of Songs 2: 3, *Sub umbra illius quem desideraveram,* is omitted, so that the association becomes much less apparent.[112] In fact, a significant web of biblical images participates in the making of this contextual frame, as the cellar image is inspired by Song of Songs 2: 4: 'Introduxit me in cellam vinariam, ordinavit in me caritatem.' Such careful and inspired use of biblical imagery to describe the mystical experience relies on a process borrowed from the monastic reading and study of the Bible. *Obumbratio osculi,* for instance, is the work of an inspired and meditative mind. The reference to the tree designates both Christ as *arbor vitae* and the cross itself.[113] The combination of traditional lexical terms to give multiple meaning to the expression assumes a readership familiar with the biblical tissue which stands behind the making of those complex metaphoric utterances. In order for the utterance to convey its two senses at the same time, the literal meaning has to be coherent: without the clarity of the literal sense the figurative sense itself fails to be construed. In the case of the example above, the metaphorical meaning can be decoded only once Rolle has brought further clarification on the literal sense.

If the carnal imagery of the Song of Songs provides most of the material for the making of Rolle's mystical discourse, elements of other traditions contribute importantly as well. Secular love poetry was not unfamiliar to Rolle, and the use of the arrow motif in *Melos* attests to it.[114] Transposed into this context, it is the binding effect of the wound of love caused by the arrow which attracts attention here:

> The divine sweetness moves him away from all evil. He practices in the spiritual art and pronounces in the vigour of his virtue those words of truth: *The arrows of the all-powerful are driven in me, their bite consumes my life*. By the spirit of penitence indeed the bottom of his heart is stabbed and the intimate part of his being purified. He acquires the strength to suffer.
>
> Souls wounded in this manner know very well that it is from above that the arrows departed. On this point their belief is unshakeable: yes, saved from the wreck, they are really tied up with the nobles, and their birth is for them a title to remain with the saints.[115]

In the initial stages of the contemplative life, the wound of divine love secures the contemplative against the seven vices.[116] Further on, and particularly in the epistles, the wound of divine love is going to drive the contemplative to a state of languishing which Rolle is going to express via the *Amore langueo* verse of the Song. Here, however, the celestial arrows, the *incendium amoris*, the *jubilatio*, the devotion to the name of Jesus, the kiss and the shadow of sweetness contribute to making the heart burn with charity and becoming *canor*.[117] The comparison of the wounds of the arrows to the kiss is interesting, as Rolle himself suggests a similarity of functions for those terms as metaphorical expressions. The slow death which is induced by the wounds is attributed to the kiss. In order to make sense of this semantic transfer, the reader is first forced to invest separately the literal sense of each term used to build up the association. Secondly, the cohesion of the association is referred for accuracy at the literal level before it can yield metaphorical meaning. Such metaphorical associations in *Melos* demonstrate the ways by which dead metaphors are rejuvenated. By bringing the literal sense to the foreground and decoding its simple meaning, new light is thrown on the metaphorical association.

If the nuptial relationship of the soul and God leaves important marks throughout the entire treatise, nowhere is it more pervasive than in chapter 27. The different stages of the relationship are described one after the other, from the desire to meet the master until the soul is allowed to sit next to the Creator and be crowned queen of heaven. The terms of love used to express *caritas* belong to the common stock. During the course of the soul's purification, God enters into contact with her and the soul's readiness to encounter her lover is attested by her wounded heart and the exchange of kisses.[118] The epithalamium continues by describing the beauty of Christ and mentioning his predilection for chaste souls. The description of the future crowning of the bride is most apt in this context, making use again of the clothing imagery mentioned earlier in this chapter:

> That is why if the king has a very beautiful and completely pure friend, all the honour comes to Him. Dressed with precious gifts, charming with grace, terror of the demons, she puts an end to their sinister empire. Her head will receive the crown of glory; triumphant, she will carry the diadem of honour. She will be bathed in the pure joy of light, she who today languishes with love, melts completely in praise and plays easily in its torrent. She will return to the quiet. Proclaimed queen, carried by her impetus, full of respect in the arms of the bridegroom, she will sit in the company of angels on the celestial throne where, very near the beloved, she will burn with a love as perfect as that of a seraphim. There, clothed in a glittering dress, her beauty will blossom under the precious stones. Would it be just an ephemeral ornament, as plaster against a wall? Not at all! Because this costume will be eternal. In this radiant beauty, souls will shine forever in the gorging vision of the very glorious creator.[119]

In this particular understanding of the beatific vision, clothing imagery, with the numerous details underlining the texture of the material and its precious stones, contrasts forcefully with the everlasting and evanescent qualities usually attributed to the experience. Such discrepancy between the abstract nature of the spiritual worlds, often defined as *canor* by Rolle, and the detailed visual representation of a royal wedding, surprises if one does not consider the binding force of *caritas* within the system.[120]

Caritas gives meaning and direction to Rolle's expression. The postil on Song of Songs 4: 9, *Vulnerasti cor meum in uno occulorum tuorum et in uno crine colli tui*, which makes up most of chapter 28, uses a sensuous vocabulary suited to the theme. The key to understanding the hidden meaning of this biblical passage is also the mother of all the virtues: 'The hairs of the neck stand for the thoughts of the heart, glued together by charity in a song without dissonance.'[119] *Caritas* embellishes the bride with its colour in order to appear beautiful to the master. The latter inspires her to introduce him to the secrets of her intimacy and to make her sweet heart a nuptial chamber.[122] Rolle compares himself to the nightingale when he expresses the primitive force of harmonious and repeated ejaculations:[123]

> Here is what happens to my loving soul: it is in the light that I run towards the canticle of the elects and I press on with fervour in future trustworthiness. I am carried away spontaneously towards the one who gives joy and to whom my desire is curbed. I rejoice in my creator and I am so deeply touched that I become similar to the nightingale whose song lasts till death. It expresses so wonderfully its love that it ends up dying of it, enraptured by its song, and he fails because of its love, we hear, under the pressure of the desire of what it loves. So the souls which walk in the path of love languish. The charity of the creator consumes their heart. The song as sweet as honey softens their soul. The ears resound inwardly with the instruments of divine praise.[124]

The special resourcefulness of the language of love in conveying metaphorical meaning to express different aspects of the contemplative life is due to the essential similarities of the two fields. Indeed, the notions of desire and love expressed by the terms of love also define the contemplative experience. Those notions constitute the common boundary of the two fields, which is exploited by the mystics and other religious writers to persuade the audience to accept a metaphorical transposition of relations. Rolle works with the Latin language to carry out the encoding of his mystical experience.

CONCLUSION

Super canticum and *Melos amoris* present compelling evidence for the conflation of textual commentary practice and imagery for the making of a mystical discourse. The discourse of *Super canticum* and *Melos amoris* account for a self constructing its specific identity with reference to a language community using the Latin idiom, and a tradition based upon the commentaries of the Song of Songs. Rolle's self-fashioning depends on a community of selves familiar with those practices. I want to argue therefore that, at this stage of his career as a mystic, Rolle engages by proxy with the selves who have left traces of their own encounter with the Song of Songs. This textual community of writers constitutes the context in which Rolle's own self situates itself among other selves. Whatever the significance of this desire to speak with the dead in his maturation as a mystical writer, Rolle needs to turn his gaze away to engage with a more dynamic community. It is this process of distancing from an original community, and the creation of a new dynamic pattern involving the community of the living, which shapes *Contra amatores mundi*, discussed in Chapter 5.

5
Love of God and Lovers of the World: Self and Audience in *Contra amatores mundi*

The encoding of the ineffable experience is at the heart of both *Super canticum* and *Melos amoris*. This chapter looks at a mature work which encapsulates this process as well, although its deliberations on the mystical life make room for an imaginary audience whose presence is partly acknowledged in the full title of the work, *Liber de amore Dei contra amatores mundi*.[1] As the title suggests, this particular segment of the imaginary audience will serve to highlight two contrasting forms of love, spiritual love and love of the world.

Contra is neither a commentary nor a postil like *Melos*, nor is it as conventional in structure as the later epistles or the strongly autobiographical *Incendium amoris*. Theiner, the editor and translator of this treatise, recognizes a division into seven chapters. Unlike *Melos* which describes progress in the spiritual journey, *Contra* instead seems to develop cyclically an ongoing theme, the one which makes the title of the treatise, that is the consideration of the love of God against the lovers of the world. Each chapter comes back to this topic, bringing always a slightly new angle to the topic, and adding new material to move Rolle's potential audience to the love of God. Theiner nevertheless considers two distinct parts to the main topic. In the first Rolle is careful to describe the ascetic practices and labours necessary to reach the state of contemplation itself, the latter being the second part.[2] What is particularly striking in this treatise, unlike those considered so far, is that Rolle here invents a new pose in which he no longer impersonates the voice of the beloved experiencing ecstasy, but he rather aims to demonstrate what it means to be a lover of God. Such attitude is audience-orientated, in a way which was not tried in the other treatises.

But before engaging with a work which constitutes a turning point in the career of Rolle, a few words are needed on its place in the chronology of Rolle's writings. Although the argument of this book makes use of the new chronology of Richard Rolle's writings argued by Watson, it nevertheless challenges some aspects of it. Indeed, Watson himself acknowledges that his new chronology is, in some places, still tentative. My main contention about this chronology has to do with the order in which *Melos* and *Contra* have been written. Here in brief are the reasons why *Contra* is more likely to have been written after *Melos*. As this chapter will demonstrate, *Contra* plays with the idea of an audience in a way which prepares Rolle to engage with particular recipients, as he will do when addressing specific individuals in his epistles. Moreover, *Contra* serves to attenuate the mystical claims so forcefully defended in the preceding treatises, thus marking a new beginning in the description of the mystical experience. Such process of moderation and contextualization for the spiritual experience is endorsed even more fully in the epistles. Unlike *Super canticum* and *Melos*, Rolle's spiritual exploits receive moderate attention and the narrative figure which emerges from the reading of this treatise is devoid of the arrogant and boasting features found in earlier works. Such low-key presentation is found in the epistles as well, with a narrator much less concerned about the display of his own spiritual exploits. One last feature which supports a chronology where *Contra* finds a place between *Melos* and the epistles is the fact that the terms for two of the degrees of love, so central to the epistles, are mentioned in *Contra*. It would seem therefore anachronistic to place *Contra* before *Melos*, as Watson does, for the former marks new beginnings in the politics of accessibility which becomes so prominent in Rolle's middle and late periods.[3]

Incendium amoris, *Super canticum* and *Melos* are essentially engaged with the making and justification of Rolle's spiritual horizon.[4] This takes place with the encoding of his spiritual experience into the metaphorical utterances of love. Although equally obsessed with the power of that kind of language, *Contra amatores mundi* expresses caution about elevated spiritual experiences and their textual articulation. The beatific vision, whose characteristic image is the 'face to face', so prominent in the writings of William of St Thierry, becomes the focus for that discussion in Rolle's *Contra* and is perceived through the eyes of a potential audience. The extent to which Rolle addresses a fictitious or a real audience is difficult to assess. However that may be, that audience's role bears essential consequences in the development of the mystic. It allows for the emergence of a self which delineates its claims and the contextual domain of expression not only on the basis of its experiences with the divine, as has been the case so far, but with the awareness of a communal self which is perceived in different guises: lover of the world, member of the secular clergy or amateur mystic. However, and as the title of the book attests, this representation of the self outside the usual mystical context relies most heavily on the opposition between the spiritual lovers and the carnal lovers. The main discussion in *Contra* will therefore consist in pointing to the qualitative differences between those two loves. Set against carnal love, the metaphorical utterances of love used for the description of spiritual love create a tension which makes their meaning less self-revelatory.[5] As narrator of his own spiritual exploits, Rolle also becomes aware of the difficulties of couching the ineffable in written language. As a preamble to the more moderate posture of the epistles, he takes here a much more self-effacing attitude as spiritual writer and adviser.

Although one undoubtedly perceives Rolle shaping his own self and making use of it to lay important claims about the mystical life in his other treatises, here the constructed self serves more to be used as a vehicle for the expression of a mysticism which extends beyond the persona of Rolle to incorporate less personal, more sophisticated accounts.[6] The textual consequence of such a psychological shift is greater attention being given to the decoding than to the encoding process. While Rolle was initially preoccupied with the construction of a self within an idiosyncratic system which aligned it alongside great spiritual giants, here he suggests deconstruction of that system so as to allow a community of selves to identify with it. In order to do that, the narrator of that treatise must open his self-referential system by comparing it to more traditional beliefs on the mystical life, thus making the use of the concepts conveyed by the system accessible to a larger audience. Still using his own person as model, Rolle reveals the psychological and physical realities of the mystical life to an audience which does not necessarily have first-hand experience of it.[7]

Contra marks a decisive shift in his spiritual career. The unusually long prologue which occupies the first two chapters of the treatise may attest to this shift of literary intention.[8] However, the method used to achieve the so carefully laid out aim is essentially that used in his previous works: the textual strategy of *Contra* relies significantly on the use of the metaphorical utterances of love to make distinctions between carnal and spiritual lovers. The paranomasia on *amore/amatores* indicates how the paradox between carnal and spiritual love can be used didactically.⁹ It reinforces the gap which characterizes the worlds of the *electi* and the *reprobi*.¹⁰

After describing the notion of audience for this text, the chapter considers how the decoding process for metaphorical utterances is linked to which mode of life (active or contemplative) that potential audience is engaged in. Despite this new tendency for accessibility, the eremitic life towers as the best state for that process, and thus demonstrates that Rolle's penchant for self-referentiality still plays importantly in the strategies of the treatise. A discussion on the characteristics of the eremitic life, with special reference to the contemplative life and *canor* follows. The chapter then looks at the only discursive exposition on the contemplative life by Rolle and assesses his new position with regard to his spiritual exploits and the limitations imposed by the linguistic system in making them discursively explicit. In order to highlight the new direction set out by Rolle in his inclusion of an audience as part of his textual strategy, references will be made to William of St Thierry who, in contrast, seems to be completely oblivious of an audience once he embarks in his discussion of the Song of Songs.

AUDIENCE AND SOLITARY LIFE

Although anyone committed to a study of Rolle is indebted to the prodigious work of Allen, one should be careful with her tendency to historicize events and details found in the writings of Rolle. For instance, Allen argues that the acerbic criticism of carnal lovers, their attire and their intellectual preoccupations points necessarily to a secular audience. It is her contention that the hermit of Hampole had difficulties with laymen at that time, which included his former patron and his entourage, and that such experience bolstered the writing of *Contra amatores mundi*.¹¹ The audience of *Contra* is addressed as *pudice virgines* and *muliercule* in chapter 7 of that work. It seems that the text addresses a large audience, male or female, secular or religious. The role of that audience serves as a hermeneutical tool for the decoding of Rolle's mysticism. Here, like in his previous works, the admonitions to young men against the deflowering of virgins echoes preoccupations with women which are a hallmark of his mysticism.¹² However, the pervasive presence of a constructed audience as part of the textual strategies of *Contra* reflects the affective aspirations of a solitary hermit who, as the following passage attests, is now willing to share his experiential approach to the mystical life: 'Ah, wretched me! solitary such as I am, that things are so in my day that not one person can I find who wishes to go along with me, and in repose and silence to long for the delights of eternal love.'[13] Despite such lamentation, Rolle fails to set up guidelines for whoever would want to consider the contemplative life. When he admonishes virgins, male lovers, whores, intellectuals and clergymen, it is not at this point to offer advice with respect to the social standing of each category. Instead, Rolle admonishes to better highlight the sanctity of his own life. Such a strategy is fraught with weaknesses as it fails to complement its initial seductive moment with a method allowing access to the experiences described. Moreover, the partial failure of the exercise follows from Rolle's general address which fails to set a more precise programme for the readership of the book. Even though the readership theme is more a rhetorical exercise in this treatise, it shows him becoming conscious of the future needs of a real audience, and hence the profuse gloss over *dulcor, calor* and *canor*, to prevent unorthodox spiritual experiences and claims on the part of potential readers.

In the particular context of this treatise, Rolle devises two strategies. First, he offers a consistent attack against carnal lovers throughout the treatise. The first sentence of the treatise shrewdly denounces their practices and insists on the corruption the mind undergoes when contemplating the pursuit of physical goods. The invitation to such a composite audience forces Rolle to delineate a suitable context for the reception of his work. Such process depends on his ability to break the antagonism of the lovers of the world against the contemplative life by attracting the *decepti iuvenes* to spiritual love, while discouraging their carnal practices.[14] In order for the language of love to establish itself as an appropriate medium in that context, Rolle associates it with the privileged status of the solitary. This is the second aspect of his strategy: the spiritual life is so intimately connected to the eremitic status that no other state seems adequate for serious spiritual progress.[15] If Rolle in this treatise neglects his own persona as model for the mystical life, he adopts instead a broader model, that of the wandering hermit with no ecclesiastical backing, to warrant the sanity of his mysticism. The representation of a self voicing personal experience gathered from a contemplative practice based on the perusal of the Song of Songs seems less importantly marked in this text. This slight move away from personal representation is indicative of the new direction which the career of Rolle is about to take. But the aggressive tone of the treatise is a reflection of the ways in which Rolle, as a young rebel, embraced the eremitic life.[16] The aim of the treatise is to offer a model which provides the readership with the tools to trigger conversion. Despite a tendency to make his system more accessible, the prevailing role given to that model sets limitations to the strategy of the treatise. In short, if the persona of Rolle stands less importantly in this treatise, the model of the solitary eremitic life nevertheless overshadows the monastic, regular and secular lives. We shall see that, despite moderation in the presentation of his own persona, Rolle will often set his experience as example when praising the state of the solitary life.

For instance, chapter 1 offers a comment on the *electus* which is clearly drawn from personal experience. It emphasizes the difference between the *electus* and the rest of the community, with the provision of practical details for a justification of the behaviour of the former:

> Because he has forgotten other things and does not stop singing the love of God, either in church or in town, or because, intent only upon this love, he does not, in some other place, cease to meditate, some who see him think that he is mad, and say that he offers irreverence to God and does not observe the laws of the Church.[17]

Equipped with the gift of grace, the *electus* reaches a mode of perception alien to the ordinary *homo catholicus*. The latter cannot make meaning out of the unusual behaviour of the *electus* because he lacks the grace which would allow him to decode such behaviour. The *electus* is therefore as difficult to read as The Book: he needs to be glossed, he becomes unreadable if the reader does not keep his face turned to God for inspiration. The awkward behaviour of the *electus* hides a deeper meaning. The application of the commentary practice to the *electus* makes him a book as well, a mouthpiece through which the audacious and daring reader may discover the mysteries of the spiritual experience.[18]

The *electus* leads the eremitic life, a state capable of granting the gifts of *dulcor*, *calor* and *canor*. The last is Rolle's most sophisticated way of translating the ineffable.[19] Such translation depends on conditions which only the eremitic life can provide: silence is necessary both for hearing and singing *canor*. The special status attributed to *canor* is attested by its important presence in all the Latin writings, with the exception of *Emendatio vitae*. Although *Melos amoris* translates and glosses *canor*, *Contra amatores mundi* provides information about the necessary conditions for the experience to take place.[20] Emphasis is put on two prerequisites for the *canor* experience to take place. Spiritually, the mind must be put on fire by *caritas*, whose heat and light set it in a state of inebriation. Absorbed in that state, the mind becomes totally oblivious of mortal life. However, for that to happen, the tumult of worldly activities has to be avoided, so as not to disrupt the conditions necessary for *canor*. Solitude and peace must be sought to allow the divine melody to be heard and sung.[21] If *canor* does not receive similar attention in the vernacular writings, it is perhaps because, as we shall see in Chapter 6, the performance of *canor* is not deemed possible for the recipients of the epistles. *Canor* becomes song; *canor* translates a spiritual experience which Rolle has shaped when dealing with the Song of Songs. It substantiates the need for the eremitic life, and Rolle has a good case in point for constructing an argument on the superiority of the eremitic life, especially since its material conditions, unlike fourteenth-century monastic life, allow for the experience to emerge in the self. *Incendium amoris* indicates as well that the absence of external sound, even the recitation of the liturgy, is necessary in order to hear *canor*.[22] Rolle insists that the solitary has a much greater chance of becoming one of the *perfecti*:

> Because I am called 'hermit' and do not intentionally live as an unworthy man, I do indeed praise the goodness of my God, who transported me from this world and in His kindness lifted me up to the praiseworthy delights of eternal love. Now one should call him a true hermit who, because of the greatness of the divine, spiritual love and because of song filled with sweetness, has fled to a *heremus*; that is, a place of solitude.[23]

Contra offers a view where the status of the solitary becomes a necessary element for the decoding of his text. The transference of the commentary technique, applied to the *electus*, demonstrates a move away from the authority of scripture, already noticeable in the hybrid text which is *Super canticum*. The experience of the contemplative becomes authoritative: 'but now in truth I know through my own experience that true love is with God'.[24]

DESCRIBING THE JOURNEY OF THE SOUL

The description of the inebriated mind, from the piercing of the thick cloud, the starry skies, the choirs of angels, the celestial court and, finally, the splendour of the deified Christ, borrows some of its imagery from the Pseudo-Dionysian tradition.[25] However succinct, it is the only systematic description of the journey of the soul in the corpus of Rolle.[26] His disgust at carnal love has an interesting effect on the ways its terminology defines the progress of the soul towards God, and the spiritual union. The love imagery and its polysemous meaning accord well with the various psychological traits of Rolle, who often portrays himself in conflicting situations generated by sexual impulses. The imbalance created by Rolle's avowed imperfection and his audacious spiritual claims challenges the latter, as well as the medium in which they are couched. Indeed, in contradistinction to twelfth-century practices, which have been exposed in preceding chapters, he denigrates carnal love, thus not allowing the topic to be used as springboard for the spiritual experience: 'Consequently I am constrained to treat of eternal love to the confusion and contempt of temporal love, and this in every way delights me.'[27] The import of such statements on the textual strategy is momentous. The personal pleasure which the narrator finds at rebuking carnal love has a liberating effect which he wishes to share with his audience: 'For this frees my conscience entirely from the bite of the immortal serpent and pleasantly covers my will with heavenly sweetness.'[28] Rather than being used as a springboard to a higher form of love, carnal love is here stressed as an opposing force with which one has to contend.

The metaphorical discourse of love in *Contra amatores mundi* takes cognitive meaning according to the special context in which it is set. Rolle builds an imposing contrast between secular and spiritual love in the third chapter of his treatise. The argument evolves around a well-known set of oppositions: the glory and pleasure of this world lead to hell, whereas the sufferings endured for the love of Christ lead to the eternal exultation. The use made by Rolle of terms distinguishing the outer and the inner man emphasizes his growing awareness of the psychological make-up of man:

> For they all give themselves vainly to the joys of the world; and the mind of the inner man, with its mental sharpness impaired by the sickness of

visible form, does not yield to the celestial embrace. And finally, because they never attempted in any way to rise to this embrace while they were able, at last, when they are fixed in their evil ways, they see not God.[29]

The object of the celestial embrace is the *sapiencia increata*, familiarly called *dilecta mea* by Rolle. The soul described by Rolle changes gender depending on the grammatical gender of the divine attributes with which it is associated, be they God, *sapiencia increata* or *caritas*. The switch from one gender to another prevents the audience from qualifying the soul with a specific gender and allows for a mixed audience of male and female participants to project themselves into the described drama.[30]

Chapter 3 addresses young men who have been deceived by carnal love. The strategy used to convince them to forsake the world for the love of God sets imitation as the most effective method. Rolle offers himself as the model lover never disappointed with the object of his love. The narrative voice invites the young men to partake in an embrace with the *sapiencia increata*:

> Come with me; hear of delight; desire to love; but taste of eternal love, which gives life, and not of temporal love, which kills. For so far I, too, am a young lover, but still a wonderful one, because I think continually of my beloved, and I do not withdraw from her embrace. This beloved of mine is Uncreated Wisdom, truly worthy of love and most gratifying in love.[31]

The recourse to *sapiencia increata* qualified by the love vocabulary allows for a flexible transfer of the carnal *affectiones*. It allows the addressees to operate smoothly a transfer from a gender-based love to a genderless one. To contrast the baseness of carnal of love with the purity of spiritual love, Rolle creates a divide between the visible and the invisible, the immaterial and the created, the descent and the ascent, the abyss and the heaven. His aspirations and those he expects of his audience are high on the ladder of the contemplative life, far beyond devotional practices. Rolle invites entry into the apophatic realm: 'cast away the burden of the flesh; despise the love of the world and of visible things; fly away with me to the love of the invisible Creator!'[32]

Issues dealing with the notions of ineffability, imagination and language take important place when Rolle demonstrates his awareness of the paradoxical nature of the language of love. Chapter 4 emphasizes how the *oculus mentali* perceives the heavenly worlds, beyond clouds and stars. The terms of love express a reality which stands beyond those different layers. The song of rejoicing is beyond the visible, part and parcel of the inexpressible realm. The use of superlatives leads to the negative approach: the soul experiences the inexpressible delight, is bathed in the ardour of the immaterial light and is absorbed by the sweetness of the incomprehensible love.[33] Rolle claims to describe here the highest spiritual experience any mortal can achieve while in the body: 'absorbed with the delightfulness of incomprehensible love and inspired with eternal grace, it enjoys the happiness of heaven as thoroughly as mortals ever can; and, transcending all visible things, it is raised to the sweetness of the song of rejoicing'.[34] Song features prominently in the ecstatic language of Rolle.[35] The invention of the concept of *canor* gives Rolle the means to transfer and condense written discourse into musical language. The Song of Songs contributes to ascertaining the mystical dimension of *canor* and the authority of its recipient, who asks: 'Truly, with the hand of God guiding him, how could he stray?'[36] Rolle demonstrates the reciprocity of the *canor* experience by showing how the heavenly sounds descend into the mind, to be then voiced through the mouth and be heard as physical sound.[37] To explain the ineffability of the experience and the impossibility of making it cognitively valid, the hermit of Hampole indulges in a discussion by quoting Song of Songs 1: 4 and 5. Rolle, like Richard of St Victor and other writers preoccupied with the textual strategies of the Song of Songs, builds up a system which explicates his literary performance.[38]

This textual strategy leads to a consideration of the inexpressibility topos. Rolle begins with the following question: why should one write so many little books (*opusculi*) on a topic which can hardly be written down, which can only be experienced? 'For truly no man knows this gift, unless he has received it', Rolle asserts.[39] Yet, despite this comment, explanations are provided to establish the authoritative claims made by the narrator. First, he accounts for the fact that some mystics have kept silent about their experiences by reason of their inexpressibility. Most people would not understand their meaning. Secondly, he argues that only a small number of people have been given the grace of those special gifts. The experience of St Paul mentioned in the treatise demonstrates that only the experience of a few saints is necessary to strengthen the authority of the Church against the attacks of heretics.

The implications of this discussion are momentous. Rolle records St Paul's words in the following way: 'whence the apostle says that "caught up into the third heaven", he heard the secrets of God, which it is not granted to men to utter' (cf. 2 Cor. 12: 2–4).[40] In opposition to St Paul, Rolle indulges in spreading his own private experience for a general audience. At the same time however, writing about the experience has the potential to bring back the experience to the mind of the contemplative. The hermit of Hampole claims this ability of calling the experience back at his own will. However, translating the ineffable and allowing it a new lease of life in the self pose serious difficulties. The process of encoding such an experience into a system of linguistic signs refers to sensory perceptions. Hence, the very act of encoding is by the nature of the experience an anticipated failure from which the contemplative must distance himself. The written text stands only as the deficient translation of a mystical experience:

> In truth I confess that my powers fail me when I try to speak of eternal love, because I cannot express in words in what abundance I conceive the sweetness of divine love in my own mind. My tongue fails me; my mind is not up to the task, for this is beyond all human intellect.[41]

The loss of perceptual consciousness during the ecstatic experience prevents the use of the rational tools for the proper delineation of the events experienced at that particular moment. While Rolle provides a sort of apology for the failure of his writings to account for the experience, he also echoes the statements recorded by St Paul and attempts thus to establish himself among the great authorities on the contemplative life:

> I opened my mouth to my God, and such great sweetness was poured into me that I was oblivious to myself; thinking only of God, I knew not where I was; either I was carried up to heaven, or the song of heaven descended upon me.[42]

It is particularly significant to note that Rolle's perception of the kind of authority to which he wants to make reference forces him to reconsider his achievements as a writer. Nowhere else in his writings does such subtle awareness on the complexity of the relationship between language and the mystical experience appear more forcefully. It is marked by the antinomy which makes it impossible to reconcile the act of writing with the loss of consciousness the experience implies. The annihilation of the senses and the intellect during ecstasy, the inebriation due to the infusion of the *melos celicum* make Rolle indifferent to the spatio-temporal environment in which it took place.[43] Such dislocation between the experience and the material context necessary for its expression implies a distinct gap between the experience itself and its textual translation. It is to this aspect that the remaining part of this chapter devotes its attention. In order to highlight the considerations found in *Contra*, parallels and comparisons are made with some of the writings of William of St Thierry.

LANGUAGE OF LOVE AND THE INEFFABLE

The long and detailed discussion on the differences between speculative visions and the vision 'face to face' has an important bearing on the functions of the metaphors of love within Rolle's system.[44] Now that language has been denied a role as an adequate means of translating the mystical experience, the apophatic aspirations assigned to the *canor* experience suffer in credibility. Although Rolle is far from offering a retraction of the claims described in *Melos amoris*, passages of *Contra* set important limitations to their potential achievements: 'Still this mental vision of mine is not bright and clear, but dark and speculative; for when we operate through faith, "we see now through a glass in a dark manner"' (1 Cor. 13: 12).[45] If Rolle previously used St Paul as a counter-example to his own gullibility, here the same authority serves to moderate his claims in relation to the experience which one will be given to witness after one leaves the physical body. In his case however, the *enigmata et speculativa visio* applies to a limited range of experiences: according to Rolle, the objects of the world should be despised. They cannot therefore reflect the beauty of the divine in the same way the Neo-Platonic twelfth-century mystical writers perceived them: 'For if one were to hold a dark and heavy cloth between himself and the sun, he would not see the sun at all on account of the obstacle which blocks his vision, although he may perhaps be able to feel something from the sky.'[46] The revelations come to us impaired and incomplete. Their perception via the sensory faculties, more especially through vision, is therefore disappointing. On the other hand, the feeling reveals better the nature of the experience. The marked reservation on the visionary quality of the experience leads Rolle to emphasize the importance of *sensatio* over *visio*.

This is an important characteristic of his mysticism, which stands out when compared with the attitude of William of St Thierry. The latter acknowledges as well that a wall, which he calls *paries*, impedes the proper vision. However, the wall is pierced with a multitude of barred windows which give access into the divine realm and allow for the mutual glance.[47] Such a positive outlook on the mystical vision is lost in Rolle. A substantial list of biblical passages serves to confirm that the vision, according to Rolle, is dark and shadowy,[48] and that *sensatio* takes precedence: 'because though what is felt is very delightful; still what is seen is dark and cloudy'.[49] In his challenge against the *moderni* on this issue, Rolle, keeping the account of the biblical character St Paul as his source, attests to the truthfulness of his approach by demonstrating that the saint was not granted the face-to-face vision:

> Even Paul, who was caught up to the third heaven, did not say that he saw God or those in heaven face to face, but that he heard the secret words of God. And afterwards he said, 'We see now through a glass in a dark manner: but then face to face.'[50]

Further evidence given by Rolle argues that Paul would not have been proud and not been tempted to sin had he seen God face to face. Moreover, he points out the use by Paul of the word *revelacio* rather than *visio*, the former not being necessarily linked to a visual referent. Rolle can thus safely conclude on this issue: 'Wherefore I make bold to say that a perfect vision of eternal things is granted to none of the saints in this life, unless it be out of some spiritual need, so that someone may be converted.'[51] It is clear from this discussion that *sensatio* fulfils an important function in his mysticism. Since the flesh does not let the soul have a glimpse of the eternal light, it has to feel (*palpitare*) its way towards it. In view of the bold assertions made in the preceding pieces, one is struck by the comparative humility of *Contra* where Rolle recognizes his weaknesses against the learning and *caritas* of the Holy Fathers, when he ultimately pronounces in the most humble fashion: 'I, in truth, am a small figure, and a lesser one in comparison with them.'[52] The evidence presented so far points to a drastic turning point in the career of Richard Rolle. One notable change is the new humility which will be necessary for sharing the important tenets of his system with a specific audience. Such a change indicates a growing awareness of the perceptions of a potential audience towards his writings and corroborates the argument for a chronology which places the writing of *Contra* between *Melos* and the epistles.

Visual elements are not part of the trinitarian concept of belief, hope and desire which is at the heart of the contemplative experience in this life, but which becomes knowledge, vision and possession in the other life:

> And what I believe now, I shall know then; and what I hope for now, I shall see then; and what I desire now, I shall have then. But the one I love now, I shall love forever: for love does not fall away, but remains for all eternity.[53]

Here as well, *caritas* stands out as the element whose immanence crosses the divide between the earthly and the divine. The mystical claims are unpretentious, devoid of the power of prophecy, of the knowledge of the mysteries, not making miraculous claims, and lacking the description of the attributes proffered by Paul in 1 Corinthians 12: 7–11. *Caritas* is at the heart of *Contra*. As in *Super canticum* and *Melos amoris*, the metaphorical discourse of love defines this divine conceptual domain, which Rolle places as his main referent: 'It is this which I undertake to talk about, to which and for which I ascribe all things.'[54] When reminiscing about Rolle's earlier treatises, one is struck here by the absence of comments making reference to the many para-mystical phenomena which pervaded his earlier writings. Here, Rolle, neglecting the sensational and the idiosyncratic, emphasizes that the essence of his mysticism is based on the quest for *caritas* in this earthly life:

> In truth, whoever does not have it, nothing is useful to him, whatever he possesses; and whoever possesses it completely, however much he does not have prophecy, nor has been acquainted with the divine mysteries or seen wonders performed, truly I daresay that he is the most holy, the most blessed and the most excellent, and he will be closer, nearer and more similar to God forever.[55]

The end of chapter 5 uses most profusely the metaphorical discourse of love in this treatise. One of the textual strategies which makes possible the description of two opposed worlds, the carnal and the spiritual, with a similar terminology, is the recurring use of *caritas* as signpost for the use of the metaphorical discourse of love. Conditions for the reception of *caritas* are closely modelled on those of the solitary:

> Seek out this love, my brothers, and keep it firmly in your minds. This virtue, dearly beloved, has ever been at its fullest, not in those who work hard, not in those who are always on their feet, not in those who dash and scurry about, nor in those who speak much; but rather in those who are at rest, and in those who sit in silence.[56]

The inner itinerary of the contemplative depends on the individual history, the social and historical conditions and the nature of the mystical claims. *Contra* reveals openly the importance of those factors for the setting of the textual strategy. Furthermore, the particular stress paid to conditions experienced in the solitary life portends significant repercussions for the process of decoding the metaphorical discourse of love. This perception accounts for the carefully prepared use of the metaphorical discourse of love to define *caritas*. Before chapter 5, metaphors of love appear only as a contrast to the long diatribes against carnal love and worldly goods. Yet once his mysticism is clearly defined and its attributes explained, it acquires poignant qualities in such a context. It serves to define the unique lasting attribute of his mysticism.

The way by which Rolle is led to use his metaphorical discourse of love is revealing of the associations which build up within his mind: *caritas* is found in a life of silence, and silence is found only by those who are at rest and sit. The bed image of the Song of Songs demonstrates the use of the associative power of metaphors in this treatise:[57] 'That is why the woman, desiring the embrace and kisses of her lover, says "Our bed is flourishing" (Cant. 1: 15). One who goes to bed seeks rest, but if his bed is hard, he very quickly gets up and goes away, even though his beloved is beautiful.'[58] Song of Songs 1: 15 is used by other mystics as a means of association between the bed image and the *quies mentis*.[59] William of St Thierry describes in the following terms: 'The little flowery bed is a conscience full of charm, and the joy of the Holy Spirit in it; it is the constant fruition of truth in its very fountainhead.'[60] Further, he calls the *lectulus floridus* the abode of the *unitas spiritus* which is, he writes, the Holy Ghost, God, and Charity.

Rolle's definition of the *lectulus floridus* partakes of his view of contemplation as being a state where silence is paramount. Thus the quality of the bed, its hardness or softness, stands as the metaphor for the quality of silence the contemplative is able to maintain:

> Therefore the devoted and holy soul, longing for continual sweetness in Christ, gets into a bed fragrant with flowers and made pleasing to her Beloved with delightful softness; so that when Christ comes – whom she loves, whom she desires, in longing for whom alone she sighs – He will never leave her bed, but will make her happy by their continual union, since she rejoices in remaining forever in His embrace.[61]

Rolle invites carnal lovers to shift their desire from deceptive sexual unions to the eternal union with God. To demonstrate the advantage of the offer, the description of the joy which the desire for spiritual love provides must be affectively convincing. Yet, as Rolle denies the possibility of a glimpse of the beatific vision, the vocabulary of love serves instead to describe the enduring quality of the feeling which the desire induces. It is therefore important to stress that the metaphorical discourse of love where *sensatio* is the mode of cognition loses some of its potential cognitive power. In the visual world of William's commentary on the Song, the accretion of the 'face to face' to the terms of love allows for a momentary exploration of the perfect vision of God. Rolle instead is content with the delight which the desire for the glory of God produces in the contemplative. Thus the core of his spiritual experience in *Contra* consists in the way the desire for the union with the Beloved pervades his state of consciousness.[62] However, the narrator does not refrain from describing the future beatific vision to come, face to face, which will supplant the tasting and feeling of God: 'Still, I sigh with desire, and I languish with love, because I do not see the face of my God; nevertheless I look forward to such a joy in heaven, because while still in the flesh I taste and feel it.'[63]

There seems to be a paradox in using so extensively a language of union to define a state of consciousness which does not allow union to happen. Again, when looking at the use made by William of the language of love, one notices that the delight experienced by the soul is to William the result of an exchange between the soul and God. In an original way, William makes this intimate partnership between the soul and God possible because of his depiction of a malleable God who can humble himself to the level of the soul without, however, losing his perfect and pure nature. As the result of God calling the soul beautiful and ascribing to it qualities, the latter realizes that all those qualities come from the one who is the good of all goods, the beauty of all beauties. She strives therefore to conform to the shape of the Creator, and the result of this modelling depends on the strength of her faith, the light of her intelligence and the capacity of her love. William continues by explaining how the experiential loving knowledge of God surpasses in realism the knowledge dependent upon the senses or the reason.[64] In order to demonstrate how the experiential loving knowledge is activated in the soul, William draws an analogy with the ways the bodily senses are activated. The act of sensation consists in the realisation – through the intermediary of a mental image which bears a certain resemblance with the object felt to conform to the nature of the receptive sense – that the visible element of an object is drawn in the shape of a resembling image which transforms the feeling subject into the felt object.[65] Such explanation accounts for the ambitious claims made by twelfth-century mystics, for the vision of God implies the same process, at a much higher level, love being the only 'sense' at work.

It is while dealing with the metaphorical discourse of love of the Song of Songs that William reaches to those elevating and creative thoughts. It is important to see that William does not conceive the terms of the biblical book as images. The *lectulus floridus* for instance will not lead to the contemplative experience if it is stored in the mind as an image resembling the object. The feeling subject would not otherwise be able to make spiritual meaning out of this image, and of all the others which are present in the Song. In fact, the metaphorical discourse of love is the link between the perceptual knowledge and the experiential loving knowledge which surpasses everything. If the metaphorical discourse of love still uses images, it is however not to make them the essential means of the loving knowledge. The analogy drawn between carnal love and spiritual love is an essential element of the metaphorical discourse of love. It is responsible for activating in the mind of the reader a discriminating process which forces him both to deny and to accept the analogy. Among the mystical affective writers, William is possibly the craftsman best at elucidating the possibilities which can be conveyed through the language of love. He is able to seize the essential aspect conveyed by the metaphorical discourse of love in his description of the vision of God, where only love operates:

But in the vision of God, where love alone is operative without the cooperation of any other sense, in a manner incomparably nobler and more refined than any imagination due to the senses, purity of love and the divine attraction play this same role; they arouse more sweetly him who perceives, they attract him more strongly and master him more gently; they transform the faithful lover wholly, mind and activity, into God, not only strengthening him, but conforming him and vivifying him that he may have fruition. Therefore the Bride immediately goes on to speak of fruition and says: 'Our little bed is flowery.'[66]

The interplay of cataphatic and apophatic characteristics in the use by William of the metaphorical discourse of love makes it extremely efficient in affecting the soul towards union with God. There is as little contextual limitation as possible, in order to allow the metaphorical discourse of love to lead to the peaks of the contemplative experience. When making use of the 'face to face' William makes possible the most elevated spiritual experience. Indeed, the *Expositio* of William recounts the attempts of an individual who, by interiorizing the love relationship described in the Song of Songs within himself, experiences and speaks of a *fruitio* which in nature is equivalent to the beatific vision. Initially, faith is responsible for the birth of the desire for spiritual love. Moreover, the more the interiorization is being processed, the more faith grows, as the felt and visual experience of spiritual love demonstrates its validity. The re-enacting in the mind of the love relationship encoded in the Song demands from the reader the capacity to accept the carnal imagery as a gift from God to facilitate the awakening of the desire for spiritual love. Because William perceives images as mediators between the contemplative and the spiritual world, the carnal images of love play the most important role in making the experience of the beatific vision possible in this life. The carnal images are useful for the description of the transfusion of the loving soul into God. William's success with the love imagery of the Song of Songs resides in the faith he has shown in the commentary genre, as well as the strict self-referential focus which allows for the exploration of new intimate landscapes, without implying an audience as part of the textual strategy.[67]

Because Rolle wants his audience to use the tools for the exploration of those landscapes, he has to set less ambitious functions for the metaphorical discourse of love in *Contra amatores mundi*. The images of love express the experience of *caritas*, and convey the desire for the beatific vision in the afterlife. The metaphorical discourse of love complies with the limitations which have been set in the treatise, and which could reflect contemporary preoccupations with the beatific vision.[68] Their function consists in keeping the feeling of God present within, while expecting the 'face to face', the perfect vision, in the afterlife:

> I do not wish that another glory be given me, but that this be given in a different way; namely that I may see my God in all His beauty, brightly and clearly. I wish that the joy of love, which is beginning in me in this life, be truly brought to perfection in the kingdom of my God.[69]

Chapter 5 is demonstrably the most explicit passage by Rolle on the aims of his mysticism. It uses both discursive and affective discourses to define and describe his idiosyncratic mysticism. Rolle, conscious of the ineffability of his topic, answers this difficulty by giving a brief and yet unsystematic account of the degrees of love:

> O vehement, flaming, strong, ravishing love! who call all that we are into your service, and do not permit anything beyond yourself to be pondered, claiming for yourself our whole lives – everything that we know and everything that we are ...
> O love inseparable and invulnerable, insuperable, violent, and impetuous![70]

CONCLUSION

Some of the terms which are going to characterize the degrees of love are used here by Rolle in one of his affective outbursts celebrating *caritas*. However, *Contra amatores mundi* provides evidence that the form of writing which Rolle has used in the three treatises studied so far is unsatisfactory for a conscious and audience-orientated textual strategy. Rolle's self-referential statements, however successful for the couching of his experiences, lose their force in *Contra*. The importance of the solitary life as an essential condition for the decoding of the metaphorical meaning of the language of love reveals the deficiencies of that strategy. The self-referential metaphorical discourse of love needs substantial modifications for a general audience, which Rolle has failed to implement in this treatise. It is the epistolary genre which will allow Rolle to make those changes.

6
Hermeneutics and Degrees of Love in the Epistles

The postulate that I have developed from *Contra amatores mundi* argues for Rolle's construction of a referential frame for his mystical language. The latter, in the earlier Latin treatises, expresses states known only to him. Greatly indebted to the Song of Songs and its commentaries, the language of *Super canticum* and *Melos amoris* departs from its biblical referents without supplying a new set of textual modalities. Before *Contra amatores mundi*, in all of his texts, Rolle's persona stands as unique referent against which his language can be measured. The metaphoric meaning of that language, rather than enticing the audience into personal practice, rebounds to its originator. Perhaps overtaken, even surprised, by his own performance, Rolle in those treatises plays innocently, and perhaps dangerously, with self-referential, hermetic, literary practices.

Tentative and rough a sketch as it is, *Contra amatores mundi* does ground some of its elements in important Christian references, such as, for instance, the words of St Paul.[1] Hesitant about its claims and the audience it seeks to address, *Contra* nevertheless offers interpretive clues by which those claims can be assessed. Associated with this broader contextualization, Rolle also depicts himself in a less extravagant and offputting manner. In structure and substance, with a passing mention of the terms which will define the degrees of love, *Contra amatores mundi* stands as a pivotal piece for the understanding of the momentous changes – psychological, mystical and literary – whose effects are fully manifested in the epistles and lyrics.[2]

The translation and accommodation of passages borrowed from his Latin treatises in the Middle English works are part of the process (however extreme with Rolle) which Rita Copeland calls 'secondary translation'.[3] My contention is that those Middle English pieces, although remote from the Song of Songs in form, structure and substance, are produced in part through the appropriation of its hermeneutical practices. Furthermore, this practice plays its part in shaping the theory of the degrees of love, which reads as a transposition of an exegetical system with the *affectiones* as object of inquiry. This system presents a framework for moral and religious conduct in which *inventio* is transferred to the reader. As Copeland demonstrates, the ambiguities in holy writ are presented in the *signa* which the reader must interpret. In such a creative setting as Rolle's, the empowered reader discovers and makes his or her own meaning of the *signa*.[4]

The integration of lyrics within some of the epistles is testimony to this transfer of creative function. The four epistles participate in this ambitious project, with variations in emphasis and development to accommodate the recipients they seek to address.[5] The reader, invested with the degrees of love and the faculty of *inventio*, may perform the lyrics as an actualization of their spiritual tenets. That kind of performance requires complete empathy with the level of consciousness which defines the lyric. Each one of them presents the reader with a programme of *signa* to be performed and decoded through performance. *Inventio* is especially important to the decoding of metaphorical discourse, whose cognitive value bears an essential function within religious language.[6] The degree of inventive reading depends on the way the imagination works in subservience to the state of consciousness of the performer. The higher that consciousness, the more the imagination works creatively. The lyrics do not effect a change: they reinforce the state which is assumed of the performer.

Before his presentation of the theory of the degrees of love, Rolle has very little to say about reading. Although replete with metaphorical discourse, the high-flyers *Super canticum*, *Melos* and *Contra amatores mundi* do not encourage *inventio* on the part of the reader. The new intentions which appear in the later pieces, devoid of demonstrative posturing, are geared towards the accessibility of spiritual experience. Although vernacularity and the fragmentation of the Latin culture are pivotal phenomena to this new politics of accessibility, they do not fully account for it. Exegetical practice, traditionally charged with the task of extracting meaning from *sacra scriptura*, provides here both a rhetorical system and the tools for the making of hermeneutic poetry, and also contributes devices which allow recitation and reading to become creative individual performance.[7] In the *Breviloquium*, Bonaventure (*c*.1217–74) not only claims depth for holy scripture, but puts attention on the reader and his ability in hermeneutic practice:

> This manifold meaning of Scripture is appropriate to the hearer. For no one is a fitting hearer of Scripture unless he is humble, pure, faithful, and attentive. So, under the shell of the obvious literal meaning are hidden mystical and profound understandings, to humble pride, so that the profound truths hidden within the humble letter of the text may abash the arrogant, keep out the unclean, drive away the deceitful, and arouse the idle to an understanding of the mysteries. And, because the recipients of this teaching do not belong to any one class (*genus*) of people, but come from all classes – for all who are to be saved must know something of this teaching – Scripture has a manifold meaning so that it may win over every mind, reach the level of every mind, rise above every mind, and illuminate and fire with its many rays of light every mind which diligently searches for it.[8]

Rolle makes use of the method of Bonaventure and other theologians associated with the University of Paris in the thirteenth century, but he displaces the Bible as object of investigation in order to make room for his own writings. In that respect, he participates also in what Minnis, Scott and Wallace call the 'transformation of critical tradition', with Dante as a precursor, followed by Petrarch, Boccaccio and Gower, among others.[9] The Middle English writings (with the English Psalter as a notable exception) and *Emendatio vitae* stand as extreme forms of 'secondary translation': the displacement of the Word and its Latin commentaries (some of the latter written by Rolle) is essential to the making of Rolle's own *sacra scriptura*. The decoding of that kind of *scriptura*, as part of the inner performance it proposes, relies on the same sequence *lectio–oratio–meditatio* which was traditionally used for the decoding of the messages encrypted in the Bible.[10] To achieve this shift of textual focus, Rolle has to appropriate some of the authorial attributes of the commentary genre. It is the history of this complex and gradual process which this chapter traces.

The internal logic of this process, manifest in the works discussed in this book, suggests a new chronology for the treatises discussed. The sequence of composition offered here departs only slightly from Watson's own suggestions: it places *Contra amatores mundi* after *Super canticum* and *Melos amoris*, with *Ego dormio* in their immediate vicinity. In *Contra*, the terms for the degrees of love are first used to define the quality of spiritual love. They then appear, qualifying specific degrees of love, in *Emendatio vitae*, *The Commandment* and *The Form of Living*.[11] Thus the sequence is *Super canticum*, *Melos amoris*, *Contra amatores mundi* and *Ego dormio*, the latter two written close to one another, but not necessarily in this order, and followed by *Emendatio vitae*, *The Commandment* and *The Form of Living*. Such a chronology manifests, as this chapter will argue for the epistles, an evolving interest in materials related to the Song of Songs.

Ego dormio is a critical vehicle for the transfer of that material in the epistles, and in the vernacular. *Emendatio vitae*, on the other hand, warns the reader against an over-forceful appraisal of vernacularity as part of this process. *The Commandment* and especially *The Form of Living* are further evidence of the tension between Rolle's new politics of accessibility and his ingrained élitist assumptions.

Of the twenty works credited to Rolle, eleven are commentaries, and one is a postil.[12] Rolle had written at least nine commentaries before engaging in *Ego dormio*, the first of the epistles, which was written for the spiritual direction of a Cistercian nun of Yedingham.[13] This relatively short epistle (313 lines), written for a nun with some experience of the contemplative life, offers an interesting prologue where Rolle's persona plays a significant affective role in addressing the issue of the relationship the female reader should build with Christ.[14] Several elements in the epistle concur to convey the sense of spiritual progression, as Rolle provides a careful account of the hierarchical organization of the heavens, which is followed by a definition of the degrees of love in ascending order. The feeling of progression from the first to the third degree is not only passed on by a precise description of the ever-growing spiritual states associated with each degree, but also by the use of a more and more sophisticated rhetoric. The performative quality of *Ego dormio*, another characteristic deserving sustained attention, is well attested by two lyrical passages accompanied by short advisory precepts for their proper performance. The first lyrical passage, a meditation on the passion, placed between the second and the third degree, allows the performer to move from one level of consciousness to another, corresponding to the third degree of love. The second lyrical passage, called a song of love, serves to mark the state of consciousness of the performer who already is solidly grounded in the third degree. Imagery borrowed from the Song of Songs and focused attention on the name Jesus are the hallmarks of this poetic passage.

However, it is not just the Bible and its imagery which will receive direct attention here, but the techniques associated with the commentary as a genre, which have a lasting influence on this work and the other epistles.[15] The first fifteen lines of *Ego dormio*, an epistolary prologue, set out the main paradigms by which the appropriation of exegetical strategies takes place in the vernacular:

> Ego Dormio 'et' cor meum vigilat. Þe þat lust loue, hold þyn ere and hyre of loue. In þe songe of loue I fynd hit written þat I haue set at þe begennynge of my writynge: 'I slepe and my hert waketh.' Mich loue he sheweth þat neuer is wery to loue, bot euer, standynge, sittynge, goynge, or any oþer dede doynge, is euer his loue þynkynge, and oft sithe þerof dremynge. Forþi þat I loue þe, I wowe þe, þat I myght haue þe as I wold, nat to me, bot to my Lord. I wil becum a messager to brynge þe to his bed þat hath mad þe and boght þe, Crist, þe kynges son of heuyn, for he wil wed þe if þou wil loue hym. He asketh þe no more bot þi love, and my wil þou dost, if þou loue hym. Crist couaiteth þy fayrnesse in soule, þat þou gif holy þi herte, and I prech noght elles bot þat þou his wille, and afforce þe day and nyght to leue al fleisshely loue, and al lykynge þat letteth the to loue Ihesu Crist verraily. For whils þi hert is holdynge to loue of any bodily thynge, þou may nat perfitly be cowpled with God. (26.1–15)

The biblical quotation of Song of Songs 5: 2 as the beginning of the epistle, followed one and a half sentences later by its Middle English translation, imitates basic exegetical practices. Displacement of the biblical source is, however, forcefully marked by the immediate presence of the narrative voice addressing the recipient. While the reference to the source ('þe songe of love'), unusual with Rolle, denotes a certain reverence before this particular book, the structural emphasis of the sentence gestures towards the new contextualization he offers. This moment attests to a particularly bold appropriation of biblical authority. Although somewhat personal, the following sentence comprises the commentary proper, explicating aptly the traditional spiritual meaning commonly given to this verse. So, despite the Latin verse, its vernacular translation and a short gloss, the stability of the exegetical practice has been fragmented by the immediate address to the recipient as well as by the overwhelming presence of the narrative voice. Although hermeneutic practices are foregrounded at the very outset of the epistle, they point away from scripture to the narrative voice and its message, conveyed to the recipient. The web of pronouns, without referents in this introduction, facilitates the encoding of essential information. The commentary proper describes in the third person the performance which the verse may induce. Such a strategy avoids both the boasting tone which a first-person pronoun would arouse, and the hasty appropriation by the recipient of the quality depicted, which the use of a second-person pronoun could have prompted. This play with pronouns contributes to the making of *auctoritas* for the epistle. Through prosopopeia, text and author seem to speak with the same 'I' voice, so that the courting passage may also refer to the epistle. The overwhelming presence of this voice partakes in this process of displacement of the original source, and posits the epistle as its valuable extension. We are witness to the making of a peculiar *sacra scriptura*; Rolle suggests that his sophisticated hermeneutics empowers him with authority equal to that of the writers of the Bible.

As I have noted in the preceding chapters, Rolle uses Latin exegetical culture for the textual translation of his own mystical exploits. Here, with this first (major) Middle English work, the ideas of vernacularity and translation play an essential part in the definitions of spiritual adviser, mediator, translator, interpreter that Rolle seems to claim in this epistle.[16] By its association with exegetical practice, translation, as interlingual exegesis, has an important part to play in the making of those roles.[17] The collocations of meaning for the word 'messager' unveils a polysemous web of signifieds, both secular and religious, by which Rolle defines himself. In the eleventh century, the Old French 'messagier', from which the Middle English 'messager' is derived, defines the object sent; it is only from the twelfth century onwards that it is applied to the person who is in charge of passing the object from sender to recipient.[18] In Middle English, the latter meaning overtook the former; instances which show the term to be used with the original Old French meaning are late fourteenth or early fifteenth century.[19]

Rolle's definition in *Ego dormio*, possibly anticipating the latter usage, but used jointly with the standard one, contributes to represent the 'I' voice for both author and epistle (the latter an instance of prosopopeia). Authorial presence is thus intricately suffused into the texture of the epistle. Translation as interlingual hermeneutics yields power and credibility to that authorial presence. The 'messager', as the *interpres*, is the one between, the one who carries over. The definition of *interpres* in the *Catholicon* (1286) of

Joannes Balbus (John of Genoa), derived from Isidore of Seville's *Etymologiae*, best describes this twofold notion of mediation:

> And one who knows diverse kinds of languages is called an interpreter. This is evident because he expounds one language through another or translates one language by means of another . . . For an interpreter is in the middle of two languages when he translates or expounds one language through another. But he who mediates between God and men, to whom he reveals the divine mysteries, is also called an interpreter.[20]

With Rolle, the act of translation from one language to another is preceded by a more difficult transference, that of contemplative experience into a system of signifieds. Rolle's exegesis of the Song of Songs, in commentary and postil forms and in the Latin language, manifests this other aspect of translation.[21] Rolle feeds on this tradition to expound his experiential knowledge of the deity. One important function of *Ego dormio* consists in making the vernacular itself the recipient of that authority. The 'Ego dormio' verse and its translation enclose the making of Rolle's authorial intentions within exegetical praxis.[22] From this literary context, the use of the love imagery, expressed in an intimate tone, partakes of and yet escapes the commentary tradition from which it originated.[23]

As a version of the most extreme form of 'secondary translation', the presence of the Song of Songs and its translation in the epistle is indeed only residual. Yet the appropriation of its imagery is part of the strategy which attempts translation at another level: *Ego dormio* is a hermeneutic text, an expanded gloss in the margins of the ineffable contemplative experience which it tries to explicate. The degrees of love are an important element in this process.

What are, then, the changes which this system brings to his mystical claims? In *Contra amatores mundi*, writing follows a logic based on the supposed reactions of a fictive audience which is part of the overall textual strategy of the treatise. The real audience of *Contra*, as in most of Rolle's other Latin pieces, resists identification. Unlike those pieces, articulated around the narrative voice as a beacon of a certain type of contemplative experience, *Ego dormio* makes the actual recipient of the epistle an equally important voice in the textual strategy. In fact, anticipating the needs of its recipient, Rolle manifests an unprecedented eagerness for structure and the rearrangement of the material. The role of the recipient and her relationship with him are apparent in the tone and mode of address of the work. As result of his personal tie with the nun of Yedingham, instances of direct address permeate the text:

> To þe I writ þis speciali, for I hope in þe more goodnes þan in anoþer, þat þou wil gif þi þoght to fulfil in dede þat þou seest is profitable for þi soule, and þat lif gif þe to in þe whoch þou may holyest offre þi [hert] to Ihesu Criste, and lest be in besynesse of þis world. (26. 33–27. 36)[24]

Rolle has a clear didactic intention in mind, sustained throughout the letter. Acting as an intimate spiritual adviser, his tone in the epistle is amiable. Because of his knowledge of the recipient's spiritual potential, Rolle manifests an eagerness to provide access to spiritual realities for which, in most of his other treatises, he claimed exclusivity.[25] In order to move the recipient towards these spiritual realities, their description needs to be structured, so as to be visually memorizable. As in *Contra amatores mundi*, the teachings of St Paul and Pseudo-Dionysius contribute a basic system:

> In heuyn ben ix ordres of angels, þat ben contened in þre gerarchies. Þe lowest gerarchi conteneth angels, archangels, virtus. The mydel gerarchi, potestates, principatis, dominaciones. Þe heghest gerarchi, þat next is to God, conteneth thronus, cherubin and seraphyn. The lowest ordre is angels, the heghest seraphyn; and þat ordre þat lest is bright is sevyn so bryȝt as þe son. (26. 16–21)

Tempting as it is to try to affix to each order one of the degrees of love, there is no evidence to support such a rigorous arrangement. But the theory of the degrees of love which appears here for the first time in Rolle's writings participates in the process of explication and the attempt to provide access to contemplative experience.

The theory of the degrees of love forms an essential exegetical tool for the discovery by the beginner contemplative of those spiritual realities. The depiction of Rolle's own experiences in the epistles is subservient to this new strategy: no longer cherished and displayed in a hermetic textual environment, they become one of the means by which the beginner contemplative may gain access to those ineffable realities. The epistolary genre acquires most of its characteristics, such as intimate tone and dialogic form, in relation to this external element recuperated by the narrative voice as part of the textual materials. The muted presence of this external element within the text implies modifications in the way the materials are organized. The epistles are witness to an important shift of intention for the writing activity. In those pieces, writing no longer acts as agent in the quest for spiritual truth. His personal search completed, Rolle devises a compendium of high-flying passages borrowed from his own Latin treatises and organizes them with devotional principles in a programmatic sequence which prompts the reader to invest the text with meaning. *Inventio* is there for the reader, to be grasped, as part of the decoding process, through perceptive reading of the metaphorical language in which he has chosen to articulate his contemplative experiences.[26] The degrees of love describe a growth in love. Reading mediates the way love will be envisioned in the mind and my emphasis on Rolle's theory of the three degrees of love shows how the individual spiritual progression goes hand in hand with the development of sophisticated ways of reading. To grasp the meaning of the lyrics which accompany the description of the second and third degrees of love, performative reading is essential. This is made clear at the outset. Rolle has no qualms about requiring sustained reading attention from his recipient. It promises considerable spiritual reward:

> Gif al þyn entent to vndrestond þis writynge; and if þou haue set þi desyre to loue God, h[i]re [þese] þre degrees of loue, so þat þou may ry[s]e fro on to anoþer til þat þou be at þe heghest. For I ne wil nat helle fro þe þat I hop may turne þe to holynesse. (27. 65-8)

In *Ego dormio*, the first degree of love requires a literal understanding of how one is being asked to behave, in accordance with the ten commandments and in rejection of the seven deadly sins. The second degree corresponds to a certain degree of self-awareness which allows the reader to understand what is necessary to maintain the desire for the love of God. Meditation on the passion of Jesus is an essential element of this degree. Then follows advice for the practice of meditation on the Name of Jesus, where the Name itself becomes a signifier for both Jesus in his humanity and Jesus in majesty.[27] This stage is important to the process of internalization and abstraction: 'And I pray þe, as þou couaitist be Goddis louer, þat þou loue þis name Ihesu, and þynke hit in þi hert so þat þou foryet neuer hit, whar-so þou be' (29. 139-41). Moving from the passion to the Name of Jesus implies a proficiency on the part of the contemplative at grasping the hidden meaning of this *signum* by means of her creative intelligence. As a signifier, the Name embodies and refers to the entire Christian understanding of the deity. Meditation on the Name of Jesus is recommended to all Christians; St Bernard, one of the instigators of this meditative practice in the West, posits it as a necessary intermediary in the soul's transition from carnal to spiritual love.[28] The first meditation in *Ego dormio* moves from signified (factual description of the passion incidents), to signifier (the Name of Jesus), inviting (and challenging) the contemplative to perceive and decode the meaning of these spiritually charged words.[29] It is from the tradition of biblical commentary, more especially the exegesis of the *Oleum effusum nomen tuum* verse, that the devotion to the Name of Jesus, pervasive in Rolle's Middle English writings, developed in the West.

The third degree of love requires solitude and the absence of all kinds of noisy activities. The pouring out of grace which may ensue from this practice lifts the thoughts to God and sets the soul in charity. In the state described by the third degree, the contemplative needs to have a sophisticated degree of literary expertise to discover the spiritual meaning of the text. The metaphorical sense of the sentences is read in the light of the overwhelming desire for the love of God. The two lyrical meditations in *Ego dormio* demonstrate how, for each degree of love, a certain level of creative interpretive competence is expected on the part of the reader. In Copeland's terms, the intentionality for the meaning of those parts of the text is located in the reader; this process allows him or her to enter in a partnership with God.[30]

Ego dormio, the first of Rolle's works to include the reader in its textual strategy, presents a subtle and careful exegesis of the third degree of love, which encompasses the state of consciousness which has been the concern of Rolle's mystical Latin treatises.[31] Although the inner realization which this degree implies (with its almost surreal linguistic changes) may be too advanced for the nun of Yedingham, it still receives, of all the degrees of love, the most careful attention. The third degree best defines Rolle's postulation about his own inner realization, which he has formulated while perusing the Song of Songs and writing *Super canticum* and *Melos amoris*. Composed shortly before *Ego dormio*, these two texts influence its tenor and emphasis. It should be no surprise to find the third degree of love articulating the qualities of the eremitic life so dear to Rolle:

This degre of loue is cald contemplatif lif, þat loueth to be [onely] withouten ryngen or dyn and syngynge and criynge. At þe begynnynge, when þou comest thereto, þi goostly egh is taken vp in to þe light of heuyn, and þare enlumyned in grace and kyndlet of þe fyre of Cristes loue, so þat þou shal feel verraily þe brennnynge of loue in þi herte, euermore lyftynge þi thoght to God, and fillynge þe ful of ioy and swetnesse, so myche þat no s[eke]nesse ne shame ne anguys ne penaunce may gref þe, bot al þi lif shal turne in to ioy. And þan for heynesse of þi hert, þi praiers turneth in to ioyful songe and þi þoghtes to melodi. Þan Ihesu is al þi desire, al þi delit, al þi ioy, al þi solace, al þi comfort, so þat on hym wil euer be þi songe, and [in] hym al þi rest. Þan may þou say 'I slepe and my hert waketh. Who shal to my leman say, for his loue me longeth ay?' (31. 224–32. 236)

The 'Ego dormio' verse, followed here by a paraphrase of Song of Songs 5: 8, is an important marker for the state of the third degree. A long tradition associates this verse with the notion of continuous prayer. Rolle, as practitioner of one form of continuous prayer (the prayer to the Name of Jesus) and also as one who claims to hear divine song at all times, has chosen an apt biblical verse to define his third degree of love.

So, although the recipient becomes an important element of the general textual strategy of the epistle, the textual strategies of the Latin treatises in which Rolle is impersonated as an *auctor* still remain visible. Underneath the epistolary style, with its specific attributes, Rolle gives his text a particular focus on the state of the third degree, the one which he claims to be his own and which was fed by his active involvement with Song of Songs material. In some passages, *Ego dormio* reads as a commentary on that degree, accompanied by the 'Ego dormio' verse as important marker for that state.

EMENDATIO VITAE AND *THE COMMANDMENT*

With the popular Latin *Emendatio vitae*, written for a certain 'William', surviving in 110 manuscripts, and translated into Middle English into seven different versions, we touch upon a new phase in the development of the politics of accessibility characteristic of Rolle's later period.[32] The provision of a twelve-chapter frame encapsulating the whole spectrum of the religious life, from conversion to contemplation, signals a new didactic method on his part. Here, Rolle broadens his depiction of the spiritual life, either to satisfy his known recipient, or allow access to other readers placed at various levels of the spiritual life. In this context, it is significant that Rolle resorts to Latin which, in view of the large number of extant manuscripts of this piece, still invites a broad readership.[33] The tension which makes *Ego dormio* so interesting, that of self-referentiality fed by the Song of Songs and its traditional translation into a coherent and decodable system, is diminished in *Emendatio vitae* by the provision of six chapters introducing the early phase of the spiritual life. On the other hand, unlike *Melos amoris* which progresses cyclically, with the repetition of the most important tenets of Rolle's mysticism, the chapter division of *Emendatio vitae* seems to work on the same structuring principle which prevails in *Ego dormio*, with a progression from the lowest aspects of the spiritual life to the rapturous states of the highest degrees. The reader is offered therefore a most systematic account of the spiritual journey offered by Rolle so far, with discussions based on conversion, contempt of the world, poverty, the setting of one's life, tribulation and patience in the first six chapters, followed by more high-flyer topics in the following six: prayer, meditation and reading are the topics of chapters 7–9, while purification of the soul, divine love and contemplation complete this Latin epistle.

The first chapter of *Emendatio*, 'De Conversione', familiarizes the reader with figurative language by educating him or her to read the expression 'turning to God' metaphorically. Turning to God implies a gathering of oneself inwardly and a lifting up in Christ. Basically, it is a change of consciousness, where the values of this world are replaced by the unchanging attributes of the eternal life. The interrogative mode invites serious cogitation on the spiritual meaning of this expression:

> What is conversion to God if not a turning away from sin, the world, the devil and the flesh? What is indeed turning away from God if not turning to changeable goods, to the pleasing beauty of creatures, to the works of the devil, to the lust of the flesh and the world! We are not converted to God with a movement of our feet, but with a change in our desires and manners.[34]

At these early stages of the spiritual progress, Rolle advocates the total rejection of the sensual faculties. This point is reiterated in chapters 2 and 5. So, like his recommendations for the recitation and singing of psalms, hymns and responses from the secular psalter, such advice reveals a significant reliance on traditional medieval practice for the lower levels of spiritual life.[35] *Emendatio vitae* contributes to our understanding of the way traditional material shaped the more idiosyncratic aspects of Rolle's mysticism in the higher levels. Treatments of prayer, meditation and reading, each discussed in a separate chapter, are particularly revealing of Rolle's spiritual hermeneutics:[36]

> Truly then we pray when we think of nothing else, but our whole attention is directed towards the peak and our soul is kindled with the fire through the holy spirit. Thus indeed a great abundance of divine good is found in us, for the love of God grows from the innermost centre of our heart. And then our whole prayer with desire and effect shall be, so that we will not pass over the words quickly, but will rather offer completely to our God all the syllables with a powerful shout of joy and an intense desire. Our heart indeed kindled and made fertile by love, and the prayer itself kindled, it is then offered in worship from our mouth to the gaze of God in the scent of sweetness, so that it is a great joy to pray, for while an ineffable sweetness is given to the one praying, the prayer itself is changed into jubilation.[37]

Rolle's ideas about prayer become a poetic definition of *canor*, the continuous spiritual song which he claims to have been able to hear – a claim of spiritual superiority impossible to prove or disprove but which enhances his own authority.[38] Rolle presents a broad spectrum of religious practices – for example, there is his inclusion of meditation on the Passion and his acceptance of other forms of meditation (119. 17–120. 2). About the latter, he asserts indeed that: 'All however, since they come from one source, to one end they go, and to one virtue they reach or lead, although by diverse paths, through the same charity which is more important in one than in another.'[39] Unlike in his major Latin treatises, Rolle's self-effacement as a source of authority contrasts with his warnings against proud despising of the teaching of the doctors (120. 32–9). Equally striking is the fact that Rolle confesses his own wretchedness, as his flesh is often assailed and tempted (122. 24–8).

The mood and tone clearly do not allow the expression of the lasting spiritual characteristics of *calor*, *dulcor* and *canor*, so pervasive in his other works. After the euphoria of *Incendium amoris*, *Super canticum* and *Melos*, and his first major attempt in the vernacular with *Ego dormio*, Rolle enters a stage where, in the Latin language, he fashions a coherent and successful spiritual treatise with the material provided from these works. For the recipients and readers of those later pieces, Rolle perceives the liturgy as an important tool, both for their understanding and for their use of his mysticism. Some of his minor Middle English writings are paraliturgical pieces and thus evidence of the importance of the liturgy in the early stages of the spiritual life. One other instance of traditional meditative practice using the Latin and English languages is his English Psalter, written at a late stage of his writing career. The Psalter, used in the liturgy as well as for private devotions, appears here in a bilingual edition, provided with an English commentary. The role of the translation is to invite the reader back to the Latin original.[40]

Liturgical practice in those pieces also proposes a system of reading.[41] In this context, does exegetical practice, informed by Rolle's perusal of the Song of Songs, still play a role in those works? The penultimate chapter of *Emendatio*, 'De amore Dei', is a good case in point. The first twenty-eight lines, in the form of an ode, endow the narrative voice with various manifestations representing an aspect of the ineffable God (*conditor incircumscriptis*). The emphasis is on the inner self: there is within the physical body of the narrator an inward face, with white spiritual eyes which nourish, and depend on, spiritual love. Without the infusion of spiritual light, attention cannot remain on the inner self, the locus where Jesus enters into the soul and where the soul sits and rests in him. This subtle and psychologically complex metaphor of interpenetration between the soul and God denotes a sophisticated appropriation of the imagery of love of the Song of Songs:

> O good Jesus, who shall grant me to feel you who now cannot be felt or seen? Pour yourself into the entrails of my soul. Come into my heart and fill it with your clearest sweetness. Inebriate my soul with the spicy wine of your mellifluous love so that, forgetting all the evils and all the illusory images circumscribed by visions, and embracing you only, I may exalt and rejoice in my God Jesus.[42]

The passage recalls the images of the coming into the garden, and the wine drinking and inebriation, which characterize Song of Songs 5: 1. The commentary tradition of this biblical text attributes the *hortus conclusus* imagery to the soul. Similarly, the spicy wine, which is often associated and compared with the breasts of the bride, becomes an attribute of sweet love. Unlike Chaucer's own sexual parody of this versicle in the 'Merchant's Tale', the moistening of the mind described in *Emendatio* obliterates distracting images, visions or thoughts of a non-spiritual nature.[43] The expectations created by such spiritual desire allow for a daring and detailed description of the anticipated ravishment, which surpasses many of its secular love counterparts:

> Burn with your fire my kidneys and my heart, which will be sacrificed endlessly in your altar. O sweet and true glory, I pray you, come! Come, most desired sweetness! Come, my love, who is my whole consolation! Penetrate with your sweet heat a soul languishing for you and to you. Kindle with your heat the recess of my heart and also with your shining light my inner chamber; feed upon myself with the mellifluous song of love by seizing soul and body.[44]

As in *Super canticum*, *Melos* and *Contra amatores mundi*, focus on the desire for spiritual love is one of the most prominent characteristics of the mysticism presented in this work. Instigated by the narrative voice, the reader is invited to prepare the inner chamber for the time when, as a result of complete surrender to Jesus, he will appear in Zyon, the heavenly Jerusalem. Much of the teaching proceeds by means of participation in the meditations which are presented for the recipient. The narrative voice, at times non-dogmatic, encourages empathy with the experience described; at other times, it is clearly dogmatic and preserves a clear-cut demarcation between itself and the reader. Rolle seems to be fully conscious of the effects of such a subtle alternation of voices. It is likely that active participation on his part in the various offices of the liturgy provided him with an understanding of the ways an amalgam of voices had a stronger and deeper effect on his recipients than a single voice.

As in *Super canticum* and *Melos*, charity is the key word for the deployment of the vocabulary of love. The context which the word charity alludes to allows for a use of terms of love in which the metaphorical sense prevails in an unambiguous way. Rolle may therefore claim that:

> Charity is however the noblest, most excellent and sweetest of virtues, which we know to join lover with lover and to couple Christ with the

elected soul for ever. It reforms in us the image of the high trinity and makes the creature most similar to the creator.[45]

The literal meanings given to the word *copulare* in the *OLD* are 'to join physically, connect, couple'.[46] The amorous context between the spiritual lovers calls for those sensuous meanings. Indeed, *copulare* means also 'to unite in marriage' or 'to have sexual intercourse'. Both senses feature in this passage of the *Emendatio*, the literal sense supporting the metaphorical one. The play on the terms of love can be acute when transferred from the semantic field of love to that of charity. Rolle emphasizes the point, and builds up his self-confidence in literary practice, when he says of charity: 'You enter boldly the bedchamber of the everlasting king, you alone are not ashamed to seize Christ.'[47] The way Rolle clarifies the nature of spiritual love is reminiscent of the distinctions he made between carnal love and spiritual love in *Contra amatores mundi*: here, charity is defined as chaste, sweet, holy, wilful, self-sufficient and centred unconditionally on the lover. The kiss, used so profusely in conjunction with the embrace in Rolle's own recollections of his spiritual experiences, is used at a key moment in the treatise: 'rejoicing in the lover, thinking about him, remembering him constantly, growing in desire, falling in love, going in embraces, overcome in kisses, dissolved completely in the fire of love'.[48]

The antecedent chapters of *Emendatio vitae* form a whole reading programme set up to educate or train the reader in preparation for the affective and metaphoric style of the higher reaches. Rolle holds that the meditation and the affective style are essential to lead one to the peak of the contemplative life: 'In this and other such meditations may you be glad, so that you may also ascend to the peak of love.'[49] The grand style which displays a variety of metaphorical utterances is rather scarce in this epistle. This is either because Rolle adjusts his style and the content of his writing according to the gender, education and spiritual needs of particular recipients, in this case William; or, and this is more likely, because *Emendatio vitae* uses the epistolary genre as cover for the presentation of a more general spiritual programme for the attention of a broader audience. Sometimes, however, Rolle plainly speaks his own mind and resorts to the affective mode and the moderate or grand style, as when he defines contemplation.[50]

> It seems to me that contemplation is a song of divine love sustained in the mind, with angelic sweetness of praise. This is jubilation, which is the goal

of perfect prayer and the apex of devotion in this life. This is exultation of the mind obtained before the eternal lover, bursting forth with a melodious voice.[51]

When the language of love is used, the 'I' voice represents Rolle as the model for such an elevated state, and most of the passages which feature it are borrowings from Rolle's earlier Latin writings. They are, in their turn, portioned and remoulded with a stronger emphasis on the needs of specific recipients in *The Commandment* and *The Form of Living*.[52]

Despite a tendency to generalize, *Emendatio vitae* still uses some of the techniques which Rolle had rehearsed in *Ego dormio*. The use of the second pronoun singular, for example, leaves the reader with the impression that a recipient known to Rolle is addressed. Possibly influenced by the relative success of his first epistle, and conscious of the basic needs of practitioners, Rolle sets up in *Emendatio vitae* a spiritual programme accessible to all Christians. It is only through recognition of the needs of others that he becomes able to distance himself from his own achievements. Rolle has thus to retrieve his own persona from the text which serves the politics of accessibility; his treatise has all the elements necessary to make it popular, notably clarity and a high degree of self-confidence. Alongside the paraliturgical chapters which stand as preparation for the higher reaches of spiritual aspiration, hermeneutic practice participates in the making of a rhetoric expressive of the ineffable. The contextualization of this rhetoric within a broad spiritual programme stands as a significant achievement by Rolle. His literary and spiritual horizons have been broadened and finessed by contributing a piece in the vernacular for a beginner in the contemplative life. The dialogue in which Rolle engages with his recipients witnesses the conception of a new outlook on his self, which he maintains in the background to let the recipients develop their own sense of self by exploring the semantic possibilities of the metaphorical discourse of love.

A similar attitude characterizes *The Commandment*, written for another nun recipient whom Rolle knew personally.[53] *The Commandment* is a short epistle (224 lines). Unlike *Emendatio vitae*, it does not claim to offer a systematic account of the spiritual life. Instead, it addresses a specific recipient in need of more basic guidance. Rolle again offers the three degrees of love, asking the recipient to move up from one degree to the next, which assumes a recipient who still needs to enter into the first degree, to move then to the second and the third. In addition to this point, the comments which address the recipient in a more personal way indicate that the nun (perhaps from Hampole), to whom the text is addressed in certain manuscripts, may be fairly new to the spiritual life or needs to be admonished about taking it more seriously.[54] It is interesting to note also that the degrees of love, which are mentioned in *Ego dormio*, are given the names which appear also in *Emendatio* and *The Form of Living*.[55]

Spiritually less high-powered than *Ego dormio*, *The Commandment* concentrates on the fundamental principles of the spiritual life, the commandment to love the Lord in heart, soul and mind. There is little use of extensive metaphorical utterances of love: Rolle refrains from using a grand style which would not be efficient in affecting the recipient at this low level of spiritual awareness. However, where inner conversion is concerned, traces of a hermeneutics based on the positive amorous language of love of the Song of Songs are visible. For example, no source has been found for this passage:

> Wherfor, þat þou may loue hym trewly, vndrestond þat his loue is proued in þre þynges: in thynkynge, in spekynge, and worchynge. Chaunge thy thoght fro þe world and cast hit holy on hym, and he shal nurisshe þe. Chaunge þi mouth fro [vnnayte] and wordys speche and spek of hym, and he shal confort the. Chaunge þi hand fro workes of vanytees and lift ham in his name, and wirche only for his loue, and he shal receyue þe. Do þus, and so þou louest trewly, and þou gost in þe way of perfitnes. Delit þe so in hym þat þi hert receyue noþer worldis ioy ne worldes sorowe, and dred nat anguys or noy þat may bifal bodily on þe or on any of þi frendes, bot bitake al in to Goddis wille, and thanke hym euer of al his sondes, so þat þou may haue reste and sauour in his loue . . . If þou haue delite in þe name of religioun, loke þat þou haue more delite in þe dede þat falleth to religioun. Þi habit seith þat þou hast forsaken þe world, þat þou art gyffen to Goddis seruyce, þat þou delite þe nat in erthly thynge . . . Dight þi soule faire; make þerin a toure of loue to Goddis sun, and mak þi wil be couaitous to receyue hym as gladly as þou wold be at þe comynge of a thynge þat þou loued most of al thynge . . . Also festyn in þi hert þe mynd of his passioun and of his woundes; gret delite and swetnesse shal þou fele if þou hold þi þoght in mynd if þe pyne þat Crist suffred for þe. (37. 137–77)[56]

This passage, with the verb 'delite' and its substantive, and also with 'sauour', points to a positive and pleasurable attitude in the earlier stages of conversion. The early phase of conversion, the shift of focus from the exterior life to the inner self mediated by the humanity of Jesus and depicted in such an endearing tone, invites active participation in the religious life. The confidence with which Rolle posits the greater pleasure of the spiritual against that of the secular relies on his metaphoric understanding of the Song of Songs and the hermeneutics he derived from it to shape his positive mysticism. That he was able to extract the essence of this hermeneutics for this didactic piece is a measure of his own maturity: the nun may not be accomplished enough to decode spiritually the metaphors of love, yet she understands, almost in mercantile terms, how to gauge the affective losses and gains associated with her inner conversion.

By comparison with *Ego dormio*, however, *The Commandment* is more distantly dependent on hermeneutic practices. This is consistent with its aim to provide access to the lower reaches of the spiritual life where those notions have a negligible role to play. The pleasure it describes is imaginatively woven into the devotional and para-liturgical material. Among those devotional manifestations in the later writings, the devotion to the Name of Jesus which concludes this work (39. 214–24) is the most important in all of Rolle's Middle English epistles.[57]

In *The Form of Living*, this devotion has an important role to play within the scheme of the degrees of love. With the *English Psalter*, Rolle's most popular work in Middle English, *The Form of Living* develops further the hermeneutic principles explored in *Ego dormio*. From *Emendatio vitae*, it borrows its pragmatic simplicity and clear organization, while the transfer of hermeneutic practices characteristic of *Ego dormio* makes it a key work in Rolle's corpus for our understanding of the literary strategies of his later works. By finessing the process of appropriation and by blending it with a devotional and para-liturgical material, Rolle makes his later works accessible to a larger audience. The interdependence between Latin culture (in this case *Emendatio vitae* and its sources) and the vernacular here attests to the subtle transfer of the values of Latinate literary culture into the vernacular.[58] In *Ego dormio*, mediation as translation (from the Latin into the vernacular) is a significant element in the making of Rolle's authority in relation to the recipient. For the first time Rolle experiments with the expression of his spiritual beliefs in the vernacular. If this epistle brilliantly expounds the realms of the third degree of love, it is less successful when describing the first and second degrees, which are less familiar to Rolle. This aspect of mediation is present in

The Form, but spiritual mediation plays an equal role in shaping its tone. In my analysis of this epistle, I will show how those two aspects of mediation work side by side to determine the appropriate use of the metaphoric language of love within the most ambitious hermeneutics yet devised by Rolle.

THE FORM OF LIVING

The Form of Living was written for a disciple of Rolle, the recluse Margaret Kirkby, ten months before Rolle's death in September 1349.[59] Although it lacks formal divisions, the epistle falls thematically into two equal parts. In the first (ll. 1–488), the narrative voice provides advice to beginners in the spiritual life. The material is somewhat similar in nature to religious manuals of instruction written for lay people. The second part (ll. 489–897), which begins with the 'Amore langueo' verse, is mainly about contemplation and love. If in its general outline *The Form of Living* follows *Emendatio vitae*, it goes further in presenting a model for performative reading based on hermeneutic practice. *The Form* is a good example of the interdependence between reading and spiritual awareness as necessary preconditions for gaining access to the higher realities described by the second, and more especially by the third, degree of love. Metaphorical utterances saturate the discourse which attempts description of those realms. Rolle provides a key for the decoding of that system (a process which calls for an active and imaginative participation on the part of the reader). This literary process has to be sifted over the spiritual material with which it is intricately linked.

The discourse which articulates the values of spiritual love uses the same terms which constitute the discourse of secular love. Spiritual sophistication grows within this semantic field in a move from a literal to a figurative understanding of the signs it contains. Language use, therefore, reflects and attests to the spiritual proficiency of practitioners. This is, according to Rolle, a more valuable token of religiosity than the external emblems which they wear or carry:

> For euer þe bettre þat þou art, and þe lasse speche þou [hast] of men, þe mor is þi ioy afor God. A, whate 'hit' is mych to ben worþi preisynge and be nat preiset, and whate wrechednesse hit is for to haue þe name and þe

habite of holynesse and be nat so, bot couer pride, wreth or envy vndre þe clothes of Cristes childhode. (5. 87–91)

The lower the desire for human conversation, the greater the spiritual advancement. Yet the terms of that discourse are appropriated for the making of his spiritual language. Transposed metaphorically, the terms of love serve to awaken the recipient to her inner self. Clothing imagery, a recurring motif in Rolle's corpus, becomes an important catalyst in suggesting the inner self as a starting-point from which one may evaluate one's standing in relation to God. In the case above, Rolle looks at the religious habit as a sign defining a certain spiritual state. The meaning of the sign varies. Without the moral and spiritual qualities which the sign generally authorizes, the religious person bearing it stands as an empty construct.

Although those comments are voiced with no particular recipient in mind, they obliterate the spiritual claims which Margaret Kirkby could have made as a former nun from Hampole. Indeed, no reference is made to her expertise as a nun: we must conclude that Rolle still gives no credit to the monastic life. In the context of this epistle, written by a solitary for a solitary, such a reference would only devalue the claims made by a spiritual author anxious about his unofficial position within the Church. The solitary life stands as a model of perfection, with far-reaching implications, touching upon social, spiritual and linguistic dimensions, and shaping the relationship between Rolle and his recipient. Several passages indicate the importance of the solitary life in relation to the spiritual information which Rolle provides in *The Form*. The following long extract is a case in point:

> For þat þou hast forsaken þe solace and þe ioy of þis world, and take þe to solitarie life for Goddis loue, to suffre tribulaciouns and anguysshes here, and aftre to cum to reste and ioye in heuyn, I trow stidfastly þat þe confort of Ihesu Criste and swetnesse of his loue, with þe fyre of þe Holy Goste þat purgeth al syn, shal be in þe and with þe, ledynge and lernynge þe how þou shalt þynke, how þou shalt prey, what þou shalt worche, so þat in a few yers þou shalt haue more delite to be by þyn on and spek to þi loue [and] þi spouse Ihesu, þan if þou were lady of a thousand worldes. Men weneth þat we haue peyn and penaunce, bot we haue more ioy and verrey delite in oon day þan þei haue in þe world al har lyfe. Thei seen our body, bot þei seth nat oure herte wher our solace is. If þei saw þat, many of ham wold forsake al þat þei haue for to folow vs. Forþi be comforted and stalwarth,

and dreed no noy ne anguysshe, bot fast al þyn entent þat þi lif be God to
queme, and þat þer be no thynge in þe þat shold be mispaynge to hym þat
þou ne sone amend hit. (6. 122–37)

The use of the first-person plural binds the narrative voice and the
recipient: 'we' becomes the signifier for the solitary life which they
both lead.[60] The following paragraph begins by making an important
link between the solitary life and spiritual benefits: 'The state þat þou
art in, þat is solitude, þat is most able of al othre to reuelaciouns of þe
Holy Goste' (6. 138–9).

There is, however, another side to this coin, over which Rolle
perorates at great length. The subject of temptation is given particular attention in the first part of *The Form*. Rolle makes it an element
of the eremitic culture (with an appropriate borrowing from
Cassian), which he so stringently constructs in the early pages of this
work. The temptation scene which follows may have been inspired by
Rolle's own temptation, reported in *Super canticum*, which involved
the devil disguised in the form of a beautiful woman.[61] Such visions
here function as a means of self-empowerment in the spiritual role
which the epistle sets for Rolle in relation to Margaret:

Also þe fend oþerwhile tempteth men or wommen þat ben solitarie, bi
ham on, in a quaynt manere and sutile. He transfigure[th] hym in an angel
of light, and appereth to ham and seith þat he is oon of Goddis angels
comen to confort ham, and so he desceyueth foles. Bot ham þat ben wise,
and wol nat anoon trow to al spirites, bot asketh consaille of conynge
men, he may nat begile ham. As I fynd of a recluse written, that was a
good womman, to þe whiche þe yuel angel oft tymes appered in þe fourme
of a good angel, and seid þat he was comen to brynge hir to heuyn.
Wherfor sho was right glaad and ioyful, bot neuerþelatre sho told hit to
hir shrift-fadyre, and he, as a wise man and quaynt, yave hir þis consail:
'Whan he cometh, bid hym þat he shewe þe oure lady Seynt Marie. Whan
he hath don so, sey "Aue Marie".' Sho did so, and þe fend syd 'þou hast
no need to se hir; my presens suffiseth to þe', and sho seid jn al maneres
sho wold se hir. He saw þat hym behoued oþer do hyr wille, or sho wold
dispise hym. Anoon he broght forth þe fairest body of womman þat
myght be, and shewed hit to hir, and 'anon she' set hir on hir knees and
said 'Ave Maria', and al vansshed awey, and for shame sethen he came
neuer aye to hyre. This I sei, nat for I hoop þat he shal haue leue to tempt
þe in þis maner, bot I wol þat þou be warre, if any such temptacioun
befalle [þe], slepynge or wakynge, that þou trow nat ouer sone til þou
knowe þe soth. (7. 161–81)[62]

Both in the general advice and the *exemplum* which follows, male figures – often spiritual advisers or confessors – stand as mediators between individual visions and universal truth. They hold the key to authorize the revelations as part of the divine message. In relation to the female visionary who experiences her transcendental state, they become authorial translators of the received images.

The passage just quoted is reminiscent of the equally deceitful vision Rolle experienced in his youth, which may account for his strong suspicion against visions in *The Form* (8. 203–10). Yet visions were part of the eremitic culture. Their opacity required skilled and trained religious practitioners for the decoding of the messages they might contain. Rolle presents himself as one such practitioner and indirectly suggests himself as the (possible) interpreter of Margaret's visions. In this spiritual relationship between two solitaries, the role of mediation described in *Ego dormio* takes on a new dimension. From the position of authority which Rolle claimed as 'messager', the mediation which he proposes here is couched rather in the terms of a partnership between individuals engaged on a similar religious path. The politics of accessibility, so conspicuous in *Emendatio vitae* and *The Commandment*, is still pursued, as is evidenced by the borrowings of motifs and whole passages from the earlier epistles. Some of the themes (awareness of the brevity of life, uncertainty about its end, final judgement, eternal joy and so on) which in *The Form* are specific to solitaries have been used elsewhere in a more general context. The topic of the brevity of life, for instance, is a translation of *Emendatio vitae*: 'On is þe mesure of þi lif here, þat so short is þat vnnethe is oght; for we lyve bot in apoynt, þat is þe lest þynge þat may be, and sothly oure lif is lasse þan a poynt if we likene hit to þe lif þat lesteth euer' (10. 280–3). The specific recipients of each epistle, and the tone which Rolle uses to address them, demonstrate Rolle's new intentions with regard to the accessibility of his system. They were written in the first instance for individual, known recipients, although Rolle clearly anticipates another readership; the basic religious instruction of part 1 (11. 329–15. 484) in *The Form* seems to be more relevant to beginners than to Margaret. Moreover, the epistle is replete with comments about men or women.[63] They imply a secondary audience, for which Margaret, herself a product of Rolle's scheme, becomes the model. She is the recipient of the epistle, but also a living example (*exemplum*) of the instruction it contains. She is part of the textual strategy, a persona behind which Rolle's own shadow lingers, a textual facade against which his claims can be artfully displayed.

Rolle's focus on the solitary life makes the audience aware of realities foreign to everyday living. It reveals his ambitious project in a crystal-clear light and makes spiritual conversion the logical outcome if those values are to be assimilated. Rolle turns to Margaret to stress his point, which is to infuse meaning into the construct which a person clothed in symbolic religious garments represents. In this way, for the sign which the human construct represents, an excess of meaning is available (9. 261–77). Conversion, expressed metaphorically as 'turning to Christ', is the first stage in the exploration of spiritual realities. Progression through the degrees of love coincides with a greater literary competence at interpreting the signs used to describe the realm of each degree. The meaning of each sign relies on the semantic foundation which has been laid for each term in the preceding degree. Each one of them, with the signs that describe it, have to be investigated and eventually assimilated.

For Rolle, the kiss and the embrace, outside the context which the third degree of love describes, have a negative carnal meaning. They cannot be used to define the first degree, at a point when the individual contemplative is first invited to perceive herself in the light of a new context, devoid of sensual connotations. In the second degree, with prayers and meditations as its most important tools, carnal imagery moves from the literal sense to describe the state which conversion has allowed: an emotional bond with Jesus in his humanity. The carnal imagery processes, as metaphorical utterances, the inner feeling of love for Jesus. The third degree presents the same terms of love in the context of the union of the soul with the Godhead. In this progressive perception of the ineffable, their primary signification supports the metaphorical meaning which they bear in the context of the second and third degrees. The decoding of the metaphorical discourse of love consists of recognizing (and enjoying) the traces, links and connections which each term of love carries when moved from one context into another. This 'hermeneutics of the ineffable' works only if each degree is creatively assimilated in a progressive and controlled quest.[64]

Rolle calls fools those who start at the highest degree: their failure is caused in part by their incompetence at decoding the messages of love couched in such subtle language (10. 310–12). This new hermeneutics is fashioned with the traditional material of the commentary tradition, with love replacing the Bible as object of investigation. The four senses attributed to the Bible provide Rolle with a model for the making of this new hermeneutics. Whereas exegesis, with the Bible at its centre, plays with language in a generative process of meaning, the new hermeneutics, with its focus on love, displaces the Book and seeks the seat of love within the individual. The affective dispositions of the recipient decide the degree of access into the hidden meaning of the contemplative text. The text becomes a field where the transaction of spiritual and literary competence takes place. Within it, affections develop and grow strong enough in love to sustain exchange with the deity in the inner chamber. It is fitting here to give in full Rolle's definition of love, indirectly borrowed from Pomerius' *De vita contemplativa*, in order to determine the role of the degrees of love within this interpretative scheme:

> The firste askynge is: what is loue? And I answare: loue is a brennynge desire in God, with a wonderful delite and sikernesse. God is light and brennynge. Light clarifieth oure skyl; brendynge kyndyls oure couaitise, þat we desire nat bot hym. Loue is a lif coupelynge togiddre þe louynge to þe loued, for mekenes maketh vs s[wete] to god, purtee ioyneth vs to God, loue maketh vs on with God. Loue is fairhede of al vertuz. Loue is a thynge þrogh which God loueth vs, and we loueth God, and euery of vs other. Loue is desire of þe herte euer thynkynge to þat þat hit loueth, [and whan hit hath þat hit loueth], than hit ioyeth, and no thynge may make hit sory. Loue is a desire betwix two, with lestyngnesse of thoghtes. Loue is a stirrynge of þe soule for to loue God for hym self, and al other thynge for God; the whiche loue, when hit is ordeyned in God, hit doth away al vnordeynt loue in any [þynge] þat is noght good. Bot al dedly is vnordynat loue in a thynge þat is nat good; þan loue putteth out al dedly syn. Loue is a vertue þat is þe reghtest affeccioun of mannes soule. Trouth may be withouten loue, bot hit may nat helpe withouten hit. Loue is perfeccioun of lettres, vertu of prophecie, froyt of trouth, heel of sacramentz, stabilynge of witte and conynge, riches of pouer men, lyf of deiynge men. (19. 633–51)

The statement 'Loue is perfeccioun of lettres', an addition by Rolle to Pomerius, demonstrates the working of the association between love and literacy. Words and texts, within the sphere of religious activity, are about love, so that an equivalence and interdependence seem to emerge between the two. This signals the aim of the religious text: its discourse is about love, which surpasses the object through which it is most often mediated. 'Love is perfeccioun of lettres' attributes a portentous role to religious discourse in the quest for spiritual love. That quest is at best only glimpsed behind the semantic web which makes discourse; it leads, via the text, within.

The second part of *The Form* qualifies this discussion of love by advocating the idea of the 'dyuersite of loue' from which the degrees emerge. For the making of this system, Rolle resorts to the Song of Songs and the strategy of *Ego dormio* which, as I have emphasized, uses hermeneutic techniques. The introduction to the second part is an imitation of the prologue of *Ego dormio*:

> Amore langueo. These two wordes ben written in þe boke of loue þat is called þe songe of loue, or þe songe of songes. For he þat mych loueth, hym lust oft to synge of his loue, for ioy þat he or sho hath when þay þynke on þat þat þay loue, namely if har louer be trewe and louynge. And is to þe Englisshe of þese two wordes 'I languysshe for loue.' Dyuers men in erth haue dyuers yiftes and graces of God, bot þe special yift of þo þat ledeth solitary lif is for loue of Ihesu Criste. Thou saist to me 'Al men loueth hym þat holdeth his commaundementz.' Soth hit is, bot al men þat kepeth his biddynge kepeth nat also his consail, and al þat doth his consail is nat as fulfilled of þe swetnesse of his loue, ne feleth nat þe fyre of loue brennynge his herte. Forþi the dyuersite of loue maketh þe dyuersite of holynesse and of mede. In heuyn þe angels þat ben most brennynge in loue ben next God. Also men and wommen þat most hath of Goddis loue, wheþer þei don penaunce or none, þei shal be in þe heghest degre in heuyn; þei þat loue hym lasse, in þe lower ordre. If þou loue hym myche, miche ioy and swetnesse and brennynge thou felest in his loue, þat is þi confort and streynth nyght and day. (15. 489–506)

This diversity of affective engagement is the foundation of the theory of the degrees of love, which, as this passage indicates, are defined *vis-à-vis* the particularities of the solitary life. The viewpoint from which the system is designed belongs to the sphere of the third degree of love. From *Ego dormio* to *The Form*, most of the new material is specific to the first and second degrees, and thus attests to Rolle's exploration of horizons below his own. One notable addition, however, the 'Amore langueo' verse, demonstrates the continuity of approach via hermeneutics which pervades the whole of Rolle's corpus.

The degrees of love are presented in their most complete form in *The Form of Living*. A degree of love defines a state of spiritual consciousness. This religious consciousness is an inner state and Rolle is defiant about those who only wear the external signs of the religious life. Each degree receives a term borrowed from Richard of St Victor's own classification: the first degree is called insuperable, the second inseparable, and the third singular.[65] Each degree defines the intensity of the love one has for God, with an increase of emphasis by Rolle on the pleasure which each degree imparts. Similarly, the states of the first and second degrees are shown to be highly dependent on the faculties of the mind: thoughts and will are the tools to use in order to remain in the first degree, while the second degree also includes the heart. The third degree concentrates exclusively on the heart, the affective part of the soul. Spiritual pleasure grows as the relationship between the recipient and God increases in affective terms. Without the fire of love, the 'delite' is almost nil: 'If þi loue be nat brennynge in hym, litel is þi delite, for hym may no [man] fele in ioy and in swetnesse bot if þai be clene and fild with his loue' (15. 506–8). On the other hand, the person in the third degree feels the intensity of this fire in the soul as if: 'þou may fele þi fynger bren if þou put hit in þe fyre' (17. 554–5). Interesting though the comparison may be, it hardly provides an acceptable means of affective measurement. Recourse is made for that to the two prologue verses used in the second part of *The Form* for the first, and *Ego dormio* for the second:

> þan þou may hardily say 'I langu[y]sshe for loue'; þan may þou say 'I sleep and my hert waketh.'
> In þe first degre men may say 'I langwisshe for loue', or 'Me langeth in loue', and in þe toþer degre also, for languysshynge is whan men failleth for sekenesse. And þat ben in þese two degrees faillen fro al þe couaitise of þis world, and fro lust and lykynge of synful lif, and setteth har entent and har hert to loue of God; forþi þei may say 'I languysshe for loue', and myche more þat ben in þe secunde degree þan in þe first. (17. 563–71)

The *Amore langueo* verse emphatically expresses how the recipient in the first and second degree has to work on the thoughts and the will, and how the state of that desire is still fragile and imperfect. The *Ego dormio* verse on the other hand vividly represents the state of the third degree, where all the faculties of the rational soul are kept dormant, so that slipping into rational scepticism or attraction to sensual objects is no longer possible. The heart is awake and active while all the other faculties remain passive, silent, and useless before the power of love.

In addition to providing most of the imagery of love from which Rolle's metaphors originate, the Song of Songs and its interpretive tradition have a fundamental influence on the shaping of this hermeneutics of love. Rolle's transference of this biblical hermeneutics to the subject of love can be illustrated by contrast with Bernard's reverence before the divine title of the Song of Songs:

> For it is not a melody that resounds abroad but the very music of the heart, not a trilling on the lips but an inward pulsing of delight, a harmony not of voices but of wills. It is a tune you will not hear in the streets; these notes do not sound where crowds assemble; only the singer hears it and the one to whom he sings – the lover and the beloved. It is preeminently a marriage song telling of chaste souls in loving embrace, of their wills in secret concord, of the mutual exchange of the heart's affections.[66]

Bernard's poetic language, replete with musical references of great beauty, always remains subservient to the text it explicates. His commentary emphasizes the divine qualities of the biblical source.

This is not the function of Rolle's new hermeneutics. The assimilation of the language of love and the appropriation of some of the verses of the Song of Songs have a different role here. Early in his career, Rolle writes with the confidence that he has all the attributes necessary for composing another song of love. *Melos amoris,* the *Canticus amoris* of *Ego dormio,* and the early *Canticum amoris* are all medieval remakes of the Song of Songs. It is no fortuitous coincidence that they all translate as the 'songe of loue', the title given by Rolle to the Song of Songs in *Ego dormio* and *The Form*. Proficiency in decoding some of the highly spiritual passages of his writings leads to new performative capabilities for the reader. When the soul operates according to its affective faculties, leaving all the others behind, the recitation of psalms becomes a rhapsodic hymn: 'Than þe songe of preisynge and of loue is comen. Þan þi thoght turneth in to songe and in to melody. Þan þe behoveth synge þe psalmes þat þou before said; than þou mow be longe about fewe psalmes' (17. 559–62).[67]

Recitation becomes effusive singing, guided by love for God, with the stress on the use and articulation of words surrendered by the 'I' voice. Thoughts turned into song and melody, recitation of psalms turned into song, lengthy meditation focused on a few psalms: these are evidence of the translation of common religious practice into spiritual experience.

This translation operates within the consciousness of the individual. Once grasped affectively, the experience of the ineffable does not translate into textual material. Rolle calls some of his texts 'songs' to mark them out from this limited textuality. Like the Song of Songs, they transgress the limitations of textual discourse and demand to be performed, to be sung from the heart.[68] As in *Melos amoris*, Rolle compares this performance to that of the ever-singing nightingale: 'Bot þe soul þat is in þe þrid degre is as a brennynge fyre, and as þe nyghtgalle, þat loueth songe and melody, and failleth for mykel loue; so þat soul is only conforted in praisynge and louynge of God, and til þe deth cum is syngynge gostly to Ihesu and in Ihesu' (17. 571–4).[69] Rolle provides lyrics to be performed when the fire of love has kindled the soul for such spiritual heights. One other item of material used for such performance is the Name of Jesus, the continuous prayer of which has obvious associations with the endless nightingale song (18. 610–25).[70]

CONCLUSION

'The dar nat gretly couait many bokes; hold loue in hert and in werke, and þou hast al done þat we may say or write', says Rolle in *The Form*. From hermeneutics on the Book, Rolle has by stages constructed a system of interpretation of love, a system by which each individual may measure his or her own degree of consciousness by referring to the degrees of love. Although at first hand Rolle's statement may seem odd, coming from the pen of an exceptionally prolific writer, it is evidence of a spiritual evolution deeply intertwined with textual discourse and its founding text, the Bible.[71] It is only such familiarity with the Word and its commentaries which allows the discovery and making of Rolle's hermeneutics of the ineffable.

Afterword

Among the possible influences on the way twelfth-century Europeans came to demonstrate a greater concern for self-awareness and consciousness of others, Benton offers a tentative explanation which makes significant room for the emergence of a richer and more precise vocabulary affecting the way in which individuals perceived themselves.[1] Benton's sweeping study nevertheless neglects the genre of the biblical commentary as a possible site for evidence of the emergence of this new self-awareness. The aim of this book has been to consider the discourses used by some twelfth- and fourteenth-century commentators of the Song of Songs as material in which one witnesses a significant contribution to the more acute understanding of self-awareness and consciousness. If my starting-point, a study of language theory devised at the abbey of St Victor in Paris, does not respect chronological order, it nevertheless reflects an acute awareness on the part of twelfth-century scholars of the complex demands on language in order to lead the self on its journey towards the deity. The account by Richard of St Victor of language and the mind, devised in the rich cultural context of the Victorine tradition which produced Hugh of St Victor's masterpiece, the *Didascalicon*, is echoed in the writings of other twelfth-century writers who make ample use of the Song of Songs for the elaboration of their reflexive meditations. In the case of a theoretician like Richard of St Victor (calling him the medieval precursor of cognitive linguistics is not a usurpation) the discourse of the Song of Songs is repository of a demonstration as to how the mind, divinely inspired, functions for the creation of metaphorical discourse. Richard of St Victor accounts for the making of meaning which has its roots in the divine and which has been generously couched in the sensuous vocabulary of the Song by the Creator. The Victorine author does not so much claim to invent a linguistic system but rather to account for a thought process which made possible the writing of the Song. The theoretical framework devised by Richard of St Victor in *The Twelve Patriarchs* and *The Mystical Ark* never loses sight of the divine element which permeates the Book and the *liber naturae*. The human author who would create by imitation a discourse making similar use of metaphorical utterances as those instilled by God in the Song of Songs aims by this very act to reach towards the divine, to become a mirror of that divine, however imperfect.

The commentaries on the Song of Songs attest to this ambitious claim. Most writers warn their patrons of moral and linguistic incompetence for the task which they have been required to complete. Offering a commentary on this difficult biblical book is regarded as an impossible task by most twelfth-century writers: most authors set limitations to the nature of their offer, stating more often than not in their prologues or the accompanying epistles that their contribution will only consider the allegorical meaning instilled in the book, the mode of reading which relates the Song of Songs to Christ and the Church. All, without exception, and in conformity with the humility topos, describe the task as a most formidable one. Matter has shown the developing complexity of the genre of the commentary on the Song of Songs in the twelfth century, with the elaboration of several sub-genres. The concern of this book has been to consider medieval interpretations which belong to the mystical stream which describes the love between God and the individual soul. While Matter devotes only a short chapter to this sub-genre, with a specific focus on the *Sermones super cantica canticorum* of Bernard of Clairvaux, this book claims that the contribution by William of St Thierry offers a more sustained attempt at exploring the self-reflexivity which is characteristic of this sub-genre.[2] Awareness of the self is at the heart of William's entire corpus: the terminology used is itself revealing of this quest for interiority. Although the contribution by Bernard is the necessary cornerstone for the development of the commentary of the Song of Songs as a specific genre, the psychological dimension whose development the genre makes possible is better exploited by William. This is not to say that Bernard of Clairvaux's contribution lacks psychological depth. Rather, Bernard is less immediately concerned with the notion of subjectivity, as he aims his masterpiece to invite a specific but wide readership to deal with universal aspects of the Catholic doctrine, from the lower to the higher levels which a life devoted to Christ may reach. Hence the narrative voice of the

Sermones super cantica canticorum avoids dialogic exchange with the characters of the Song, but chooses instead the magisterial standpoint from which several modes of reading can be offered to the potential readership. The one-pointed reading of William of St Thierry constitutes in my view a unique contribution to twelfth-century consciousness of the self. I would like to argue that no author in the West since Augustine offers such a complex introspective vision of the self.

In his influential essay, Benton argues for a continuing increase in self-examination and concern with the inner life from the twelfth century up to the present.[3] The second part of this book contributes to a partial assessment of this hypothesis within the confines set up by the Song of Songs commentary as genre. Some pieces which belong to the corpus of Richard Rolle show an individual equally concerned with the notion of interiority. I hope this study has clearly shown the difficulties which mark Rolle's personal journey towards interiority, a journey marked by a conflictual attitude towards women as objects of desire. If Rolle's output does not match the literary and psychological subtleties of William of St Thierry for instance, it is striking nevertheless for its frank depiction of a self which is revealed with all its imperfections, a self which is shown striving to align itself with God in order to achieve the *unitas spiritus*. Acknowledgement of the difficulty of the experience, together with the bold assertions about Rolle's mystical feats, make his itinerary the more appealing because of its fragility. The self which emerges as a result of the dialogic exchanges with the characters of the Song in William of St Thierry's commentary bears the perfection of an idealized projection whereas the audacious and somewhat clumsy construction by Rolle reveals a self violated by the damaging events of everyday life. However, it must be borne in mind that the autobiographical element that characterizes Rolle's literary contribution is made possible by his deep immersion into the Song of Songs and the subsequent production of pieces engaging with its material. While Rolle may attempt the construction of a self based on the same premises as those used by his twelfth-century predecessors, his contribution achieves something rather different. In the religious and political turmoil which marked the fourteenth century, the perception of a self grounded in a Neo-Platonic system marked by a dialogic exchange exclusively dedicated to the topic of love becomes impracticable. Rolle needs to reinvent medieval subjectivity for the construction of the dialogic exchange which he wants to imitate. Turning inward in the fourteenth century gives birth to the emergence of an awareness shaped of course by personal characteristics, which are also dependent upon the cultural, social, political and religious conditions of the period. The journey covered by Rolle turns out to be more arduous than that of his twelfth-century predecessors. Indeed, ambivalence seems to permeate almost every single line of his corpus: humility and pride, misogyny and praise of women, selfishness and altruism. However, the making of an ambitious spiritual system accessible to all his fellow Christians, and written in the vernacular for all to read and perfom, is the way to measure his final success as appropriator of the Song of Songs for the construction of his own self.

If the making of this self is at the heart of his Latin mystical treatises, where it is being offered as a model, the later writings, written in the vernacular, modulate this role and propose instead roles which become more aware of the need of a perceived audience. From the role of 'messager' or intermediary which Rolle attributes to himself in *Ego dormio*, he offers in *The Form of Living* a partnership where the anchoress Margaret Kirkby becomes the model for the solitary life. Accessibility has become the hallmark of Rolle's later writings and the continuing interest which the Middle English writings still attract today, against the neglect of his Latin writings, is a measure of the way Rolle, after having become conscious of his own self, managed to provide a system which took notice of the needs of other selves.

Notes

Introduction

1. For a significant general contribution on this topic, see J. F. Benton, 'Consciousness of Self and of Individuality', in R. L. Benson and G. Constable, with C. D. Lanham (eds.), *Renaissance and Renewal in the Twelfth Century* (1982; repr. Toronto, 1991), 263–95; see also C. M. Morris, *The Discovery of the Individual, 1050–1200* (London, 1972). Although both authors contribute significantly to our understanding of the emergence of the consciousness of the self from the twelfth century onwards, they both omit to use the commentary tradition as one of their source materials.
2. See C. Taylor, *Sources of the Self: The Making of the Modern Identity* (Cambridge, 1992), esp. 127–42 and 355–67. In the first extract Taylor demonstrates Augustine's overwhelming influence over the notion of the self and the language of inwardness. The following chapters of his magisterial book turn to Descartes, Locke and also Montaigne, without considering post-Augustinian medieval elaborations of the language of inwardness.
3. For a discussion of Augustine and the first-person standpoint, see Taylor, *Sources*, 132–4.
4. Benton devotes a small part of his article to this topic; see Benton, 'Consciousness of Self', 271–4. For a general discussion of the state of Western religion in the wake of the Fourth Lateran Council, see R. N. Swanson, *Religion and Devotion in Europe, c.1215–c.1515*, Cambridge Medieval Textbooks (Cambridge, 1995), 10–41.
5. My account of the Augustinian language of inwardness is indebted in great part to Taylor, *Sources of the Self*.
6. B. Smalley, *The Study of the Bible in the Middle Ages* (1952; repr. Oxford, 1983). For a study of the development of a medieval theory of authorship within the commentary tradition, see A. J. Minnis, *Medieval Theory of Authorship: Scholastic Literary Attitudes in the Later Middle Ages* (1984; repr. Aldershot, 1988); see also A. J. Minnis and A. B. Scott,

[7] with the assistance of D. Wallace (eds.), *Medieval Literary Theory and Criticism c.1100–c.1375: The Commentary Tradition* (1988; repr. Oxford, 1991).

[7] For a Latin version of the Song of Songs, see *Biblia sacra iuxta vulgatam Clementinam*, ed. A. Colungo and L. Turrado, Biblioteca de autores cristianos (Madrid, 1985), 614–18. All references to the Vulgate in this book are to this edition. For a Latin version of the Song of Songs with a facing English translation, see E. A. Matter, *The Voice of My Beloved: The Song of Songs in Western Medieval Christianity* (Philadelphia, 1990), xv–xxxv.

[8] Our editions of the Vulgate arrange the text as a series of exchanges involving a bride, a bridegroom, a chorus of young girls and a chorus of brothers at the end. As Matter shows in her short commentary to her own version of the Song, not only was such neat arrangement of the song not so clearly signposted in the medieval Vulgate versions, but also a great number of non-Vulgate versions were in circulation and used in parallel to the Vulgate text. See Matter, *Voice of my Beloved*, xxxiv–xxxv.

[9] Ann Astell considers four twelfth-century interpretative streams (ecclesiastical, Marian, Victorine and Cistercian) based on her discussion of the role played by the *anima* part of the soul and her engagement with four major feminine archetypes (Virgin, Mother, Medial Woman, and Hetaira) which correspond to, and characterize the four streams above. See A. W. Astell, *The Song of Songs in the Middle Ages* (Ithaca, NY, and London, 1990), 1–15.

[10] For treatments of Marian and ecclesiastical commentaries, see Astell, *Song of Songs*, 42–72; see also Matter, *Voice of my Beloved*, 86–122.

[11] For a discussion of literary form and authorial role in twelfth-century commentaries of the Song of Songs, with emphasis put on the way God controlled human authors, see Minnis, *Medieval Theory*, 42–58.

[12] For an account of the evolution of the roles of translation and hermeneutics, with emphasis on the historical situation of the interpreter as condition of interpretation, see R. Copeland, *Rhetoric, Hermeneutics and Translation in the Middle Ages: Academic Traditions and Vernacular Texts*, Cambridge Studies in Medieval Literature 11 (Cambridge, 1991), 37–62.

[13] Within her definition of the commentary as a 'secondary' or 'complex' genre borrowing and elaborating from the primary genre, represented by the Bible in our case, Matter qualifies the Song of Songs commentaries: 'Within this broad definition, I would argue that Song of Songs commentaries make up a special category, constituting a sub-genre of their own, an example of what Maria Corti has described as the "internal transformation" of one genre into another; the second participates and shares with the first but eventually develops characteristics of its own.' See Matter, *Voice of my Beloved*, 7–8.

14 For a study of those meditative pieces, see my article, 'Enclosed Desires: A Study of the Wooing Group', in W. F. Pollard and R. Boenig (eds.), *Mysticism and Spirituality in Medieval England* (Cambridge, 1997), 39–62.

Part One: Chapter 1

1 Richard of St Victor, *The Twelve Patriarchs. The Mystical Ark. Book Three of Trinity*, tr. G. A. Zinn, The Classics of Western Spirituality (New York, 1979) (hereafter *The Twelve Patriarchs* or *The Mystical Ark*). References to the Latin are from the *Patrologia latina*, 196 (hereafter *PL*), which gives the title of *Benjamin minor (B.min.)* for *The Twelve Patriarchs* and *Benjamin major (B.maj.)* for *The Mystical Ark*.
2 For a general presentation of Richard's mystical system, see *The Twelve Patriarchs*, 1–49.
3 For a brief introduction to Hugh of St Victor, with a discussion of his allegorical method, see A. J. Minnis and A. B. Scott, with the assistance of D. Wallace (eds.), *Medieval Literary Theory and Criticism c.1100–c.1375: The Commentary Tradition* (1988; repr. Oxford, 1991), 65–86.
4 See Hugh of St Victor, *The Didascalicon of Hugh of St Victor*, tr. J. Taylor (1961; repr. New York, 1991), 48–9.
5 Ibid., 49.
6 Ibid., 64.
7 For a study of the Victorine reading of the Song of Songs, regarded as a contemplative work requiring a contemplative reading, see A. W. Astell, *The Song of Songs in the Middle Ages* (Ithaca, NY, and London, 1990), 77–89. Astell notes how important the 'modus contemplativus' is for the Victorines. Such reading involves the use of four tropes, which Astell lists as parataxis, paradox, *comparatio* and *conversio*. The latter, which is translated as metaphor, is the trope I have chosen to focus on in my own elaboration of the importance of the work of contemplation in Richard of St Victor.
8 Hugh of St Victor's list of five steps in book 5 consists of the following: study, meditation, prayer, performance, and contemplation, the latter being described as the one 'in which, as by a sort of fruit of the preceding steps, one has a foretaste, even in this life, of what the future reward of good work is'. See Hugh of St Victor, *The Didascalicon*, 132.
9 See *The Twelve Patriarchs*, 68; *B.min.*, col. 11.
10 This signifies that Richard considers descriptions of hell and other infernal torments in the literal sense, whereas descriptions of the heavenly Jerusalem for instance have to be understood mystically: 'None

of the faithful who reads in holy Scripture about hell, the flames of Gehenna and the outer darkness believes that these things have been said figuratively, but he does not doubt that these things exist somewhere truly and Bodily.' *The Twelve Patriarchs*, 70.

[11] For a discussion of the chronological arrangement of the two treatises, ibid., 6.

[12] See ibid., 29. For a more extensive discussion of this tripartite division, see R. Javelet, 'Thomas Gallus et Richard de St Victor mystiques', *RTAM*, 29 (1962), 206–33; 30 (1963), 88–121.

[13] Here I am summarizing J. Châtillon, 'Les Trois Modes de la contemplation selon Richard de Saint-Victor', *Bulletin de littérature ecclésiastique*, 41 (1940), 3–26.

[14] See *The Twelve Patriarchs*, 25.

[15] *The Mystical Ark*, 204. [. . . invisibilia sunt quae mente conspicimus, et tamen ex rerum visibilium similitudine illa nobis formamus. *B.maj.*, col. 99] This kind of statement, with the implication that metaphorical language has the ability 'to name the unnamed', challenges theories of language based on a relation of naming. For philosophical discussions on the subject, see J. M. Soskice, *Metaphor and Religious Language* (1985; repr. Oxford, 1989); see also E. F. Kittay, *Metaphor: Its Cognitive Force and Linguistic Structure* (1987; repr. Oxford, 1989).

[16] For a detailed study of the Platonic influence on Richard's contemplative system, see J. A. Robillard, 'Les Six Genres de contemplation chez Richard de Saint-Victor et leur origine platonicienne', *Revue des sciences philosophiques et théologiques*, 28 (1939), 229–33; see also *The Twelve Patriarchs*, 29.

[17] *The Mystical Ark*, 233. [Tenet itaque imaginatio vicem primi coeli, ratio secundi, intelligentia vero vicem tertii. Et horum quidem primum caeterarum comparatione grossum quidem atque corpulentum, et suo quodammodo palpabile atque corporeum, eo quod sit imaginarium, atque phantasticum post se trahens, et in se retinens formas, et similitudines rerum corporalium. *B.maj.*, col. 118.]

[18] Javelet provides interesting insights on the discussion of the *excessus* by Richard of St Victor, Bernard of Clairvaux and Thomas Gallus; Richard and Bernard agree in their use of affective vocabulary when describing the *excessus*; see Javelet, 'Thomas Gallus', 30, 89. For Bernard of Clairvaux, see E. Gilson, *The Mystical Theology of St Bernard*, tr. A. H. C. Downes, Cistercian Studies Series 120 (1934; repr. Kalamazoo, 1990), esp. 119–52.

[19] *The Twelve Patriarchs*, 68. [Rationalis autem est illa, quando ex his quae per sensum corporeum novimus, aliquid imaginabiliter fingimus. Verbi gratia: Aurum vidimus, domum vidimus, auream autem domum nunquam vidimus. Auream tamen domum imaginari possumus si

volumus. Hoc utique bestia facere non potest . . . *B.min.*, col. 11.]
20 . . . invisibilia enim ipsius a creatura mundi per ea quae facta sunt intellecta conspiciuntur. See Augustine's discussion on figurative language in *On Christian Doctrine*, tr. D. W. Robertson, Jr. (London, 1958), 50–3.
21 *The Twelve Patriarchs*, 58. [Discurrite ergo imaginatio (utpote ancilla) inter dominam et servum, inter rationem et sensum; et quidquid extrinsecus haurit per sensum carnis, intus repraesentat ad obsequium rationis. Semper ergo imaginatio rationi assistit, nec ad momentum quidem ab ejus famulatu se subtrahit. Nam sensu etiam deficiente, ipsa ministrare non desinit. Nam in tenebris positus, nihil video, sed quaelibet illic imaginari possum, si volo. Sic semper et in omnibus imaginatio praeste est, et ejus obsequio ubique ratio ubi potest. *B.min.*, col. 5.]
22 *The Twelve Patriarchs*, 67. [Res enim invisibiles, per rerum visibilium formas describunt, et earum memoriam per quarumdam concupiscibilium specierum pulchritudinem mentibus nostris imprimunt. *B.min.*, cols. 10–11.]
23 See *The Twelve Patriarchs*, 67; see also A. J. Minnis, 'Langland's Ymaginatif and Late-Medieval Theories of Imagination', *Comparative Criticism*, 3 (1981), 71–103.
24 *The Twelve Patriarchs*, 56.
25 See ibid., 8.
26 Richard de Saint-Victor, *Sermons et opuscules spirituels inédits*, ed. J. Châtillon et W.-J. Tulloch (Bruges, 1951), l.
27 For a definition of the negative language, see A. Louth, *Denys the Areopagite* (London, 1989), 45–7.
28 See Javelet, 'Thomas Gallus', 29, 210, n. 15.
29 See *The Twelve Patriarchs*, 63; *B.min.*, col. 8.
30 The use of the Song of Songs's language and imagery is particularly effective in *The Mystical Ark*; see *The Mystical Ark*, 259–343; see also introductory material p. 23; for a study of the importance of love in the Ricardian system, see Javelet, 'Thomas Gallus', 29, 230.
31 See *The Twelve Patriarchs*, 65; *B.min.*, col. 9.
32 For a treatment of this topic, see Javelet, 'Thomas Gallus', 30, 93.
33 *The Twelve Patriarchs*, 65–6. [Ubi amor, ibi oculus. Libenter aspicimus quem multum diligimus. Nulli dubium quia qui potuit invisibilia diligere, quin velit statim cognoscere, et per intelligentiam videre, et quanto plus crescit Judas (affectus videlicet diligendi), tanto amplius in Rachel fervet desiderium pariendi, hoc est studium cognoscendi. *B.min.* col. 10.]
34 In *Viae Syon Lugent*, probably written by the Carthusian Hugh of Balma in the second half of the thirteenth century, the author discusses how the connection with the deity and the soul operates through the *affectus*. Hugh continues nevertheless by demonstrating how the *intellectus* finds

its food in the ravishments of the *affectus* during its journey to God; see Hugh of Balma's work under *Mystica theologia*, in *Omnia opera sancti Bonaventurae*, 8, ed. A. C. Peltier (Paris, 1866); for an English translation, see *Carthusian Spirituality: The Writings of Hugh of Balma and Guigo de Ponte*, tr. D. D. Martin, The Classics of Western Spirituality (New York, 1997); see also F. Ruello, 'Statut et rôle de l'*intellectus* et de l'*affectus* dans la *Théologie mystique* de Hughes de Balma', *Kartäusermystik und-mystiker*, Analecta Cartusiana 55/1 (Salzburg, 1981), 1–46.

35 F. Guimet, '*Caritas ordinata* et *amor discretus* dans la *Théologie trinitaire* de Richard de Saint-Victor', *RMAL*, 4 (1948), 225–36; see esp. 235.

36 See *The Mystical Ark*, 304; *B.maj.*, col. 166; see also F. A. Yates, *The Art of Memory* (London, 1966), esp. 50–104; see also Minnis, 'Langland's Ymaginatif', 90.

37 *The Twelve Patriarchs*, 66. [Cogitat per imaginationem, quia necdum videre valet per intelligentia puritatem. *B.min.*, col. 10.]

38 *The Mystical Ark*, 263–4. [Quid ibi faciat imaginatio ubi nulla est transmutatio nec vicissitudinis obumbratio? Ubi pars non est minor suo toto, nec totum universalius suo individuo, imo ubi pars toto non minuitur, et totum ex partibus non constituitur, quia simplex est quod universaliter proponitur, et universale quod quasi particulare profertur, ubi totum singula, ubi omnia unum et unum omnia. In his utique et absque dubio succumbit humana ratio, et quid faciat ibi imaginatio? Absque dubio in ejusmodi spectaculo officere potest, adjuvare omnino non potest. *B.maj.*, col. 138.]

39 For a detailed description on this point, see Javelet, 'Thomas Gallus', 29, 229.

40 See the cloud-image in *The Mystical Ark*, 179, 306, 311; for a comparison between the *Cloud*-author and the Victorines, see R. A. Lees, *The Negative Language of the Dionysian School of Mystical Theology: An Approach to the Cloud of Unknowing*, Analecta Cartusiana 107 (Salzburg, 1983), esp. 498; for a comparison between Richard of St Victor and Gallus, see Javelet, 'Thomas Gallus', 30, 89; see also Minnis et al. (eds.), *Medieval Literary Theory*, 164–73.

41 *The Mystical Ark*, 285. [Modicum in horto, modicum in vestibulo, modicum thalamo, donec tandem aliquando post multam exspectationem, post multam fatigacionem cubiculum introeat, et intimum atque secretissimum locum obtineat. Modicum in horto, dum tumultuantium turba digeritur; modicum in vestibulo, dum thalamus adornatur; modicum in thalamo, dum lectulus sternitur. Et cogitur dilectus omnibus his locis exspectare modicum et modicum, modicum ibi et modicum ibi. Ex hortulo auditur, in vestibulo videtur, in thalamo deosculatur, in cubiculo amplexatur. *B.maj.*, col. 153.]

42   See *The Mystical Ark*, 306; *B.maj.*, cols. 166–8.
43   Javelet describes the synderesis in both Richard and Thomas Gallus, the thirteenth-century Victorine, stressing how Richard, in contrast to the latter, insists on the spiritual wedding and the union, symbolized by the coitus; see 'Thomas Gallus', 30, 98. For further information on Thomas Gallus, see T. Gallus, *Commentaire du cantique des cantiques*, ed. J. Barbet (Paris and Louvain, 1972); for a general study of the Victorine school and its masters, see J. Châtillon, 'De Guillaume de Champeaux à Thomas Gallus: Chronique d'histoire littéraire et doctrinale de L'École de Saint-Victor', *RMAL*, 8 (1952), 139–62, 247–73. Apart from his commentary on the Song of Songs, Thomas Gallus (d. 1246), canon regular at the abbey of St Victor, spent more than twenty years working on the writings of Pseudo-Dionysius.
44   See *The Twelve Patriarchs*, 144; *B.min.*, col. 61.
45   See Minnis, 'Langland's Ymaginatif', 89.
46   See M.-D. Chenu, *La Théologie au douzième siècle* (Paris, 1966), 167–8.
47   M. Schumacher, 'Mysticism in Metaphor', in *S. Bonaventura 1274–1974*, 2 (Rome, 1974), 369.
48   See *The Twelve Patriarchs*, 15–16, 74–5; *B.min.*, cols. 15–16.
49   On the interpretation of a difficult literal sense, see *The Twelve Patriarchs*: 'Nevertheless in all of these, if we follow only the sense of the letter, we find nothing in them at which we may worthily marvel. But perhaps in such words this is what we so gladly embrace: that from a kind of pleasing silliness, so to speak, of the literal sense, we are forced to take refuge in spiritual understanding.' Ibid., 77.
50   Ibid., 76. [Sed quomodo dans eloquia pulchritudinis, fortassis hoc per exempla evidentius ostendimus, persuadebimus plenius. Vultis audere eloquia pulchritudinis, eloquia suavitatis, plena decore, plena dulcedine, qualia Nephtalim formare consuevit, vel qualia eum formare convenit: *Osculetur me*, inquit, *osculo oris sui* (Cant. I). *Fulcite me floribus, stipate me malis, quia amore langueo* (Cant. II). *Favus distillans labia tua, mel et lac sub lingua tua, et odor vestimentorum tuorum sicut odor thuris* (Cant. IV). Quid, quaeso, dulcius hujusmodi eloquiis libentius, quid avidius auditur? Ista verba carnale aliquid sonare videntur, et tamen spiritualia sunt quae per ipsa describuntur. Sic novit Nephtalim carnalia cum spiritualibus permiscere, et per corporalia incorporea describere, ut utraque hominis natura in ejus dictis inveniat unde se mirabiliter reficiat qui ex corporea et incorporea natura constat. Hinc est fortasse quod homini tam suaviter sapiunt, quod quodammodo, ut dictum est, utramque ejus naturam reficiunt. *B.min.*, col. 17.]
51   See Châtillon, 'Les Trois Modes', 16–7.
52   See *The Mystical Ark*, 200–1; *B.maj.*, cols. 95–9.
53   *The Mystical Ark*, 196. [Nam ut hic locus plene et sufficienter explicari

possit, proprium tractatum requirit. Tanto hic locus majori et diligentiori inquisitione eget, quanto huic ratiocinationi, tota hujus speculationis ratio incumbit. Constat autem in hac et in subsequenti speculatione maximam et pene praecipicam spiritualium virorum consolationem, nostris temporibus inesse. Nam pauci admodum sunt qui ad novissima illa duo contemplationum genera possint assurgere. *B.maj.*, col. 94.]

54 Principally by Minnis: 'Langland's Ymaginatif', 71–103; 'The Sources of *The Cloud of Unknowing*: A Reconsideration', *MMTE* 2 (1982), 63–75; 'Affection and Imagination in *The Cloud of Unknowing* and Hilton's *Scale of Perfection*, *Traditio*, 39 (1983), 323–66; see also H. White, 'Langland's Ymaginatif, Kynde and *The Benjamin major*', *MA*, 55 (1986), 241–7.

55 See *The Cloud of Unknowing: And Related Treatises on Contemplative Prayer*, Analecta Cartusiana 3, ed. P. Hodgson (Salzburg, 1982), esp. 129–45. On the translator of the Middle English *Benjamin minor*, see R. Ellis, 'Author(s), Compilers, Scribes and Bible Texts: Did the Cloud-Author Translate *The Twelve Patriarchs*?, *MMTE* 5 (1992), 193–221.

56 Schumacher, 'Mysticism in Metaphor', 369.

Chapter 2

1 *The Works of Bernard of Clairvaux*, 2, *On the Song of Songs*, 1, tr. K. Walsh, Cistercian Fathers Series 4 (Kalamazoo, 1971), 2–3. [Alioquin ante carnem disciplinae studiis edomitam et spiritui mancipatam, ante spretam et abiectam saeculi pompam et sarcinam, indigne ab impuris lectio sancta praesumitur ... Quae enim societas ei quae desursum est sapientiae et sapientiae mundi, quae stultitia est apud Deum, aut sapientiae carnis, quae et ipsa est inimica Deo? *Sancti Bernardi opera*, 1, ed. J. Leclercq, C. H. Talbot and H. M. Rochais (Rome, 1957), 4.]

2 *The Works of Bernard*, 2, 7. [Ceterum non est illud cantare seu audire animae puerilis et neophytae adhuc, et recens conversae de saeculo, sed provectae iam et eruditae mentis, quae nimirum suis profectibus, Deo promovente, in tantum iam creverit, quatenus ad perfectam aetatem et ad nubiles quodammodo pervenerit annos, – annos dico meritorum, non temporum –, facta nuptiis caelestis sponsi idonea, qualis denique suo loco plenius describetur. *Sancti Bernardi opera*, 1, 8.]

3 E. A. Matter, *The Voice of my Beloved: The Song of Songs in Western Medieval Christianity* (Philadelphia, 1990); see also A. W. Astell, *The Song of Songs in the Middle Ages* (Ithaca, NY, and London, 1990); see also D. Turner, *Eros and Allegory: Medieval Exegesis of the Song of Songs*, Cistercian Studies Series 156 (Kalamazoo, 1995); see also R. Fulton, 'Mimetic Devotion, Marian Exegesis, and the Historical Sense of

the Song of Songs', *Viator*, 27 (1996), 85–116. Some modern studies of the Song of Songs provide interesting evidence for the use of the commentary form in their investigations of this difficult biblical book; see for instance M. Falk, *Love Lyrics from the Bible: A Translation and Literary Study of the Song of Songs*, Bible and Literature Series 4 (1976; repr. Sheffield, 1982); F. Landy, *Paradoxes of Paradise: Identity and Difference in the Song of Songs*, Bible and Literature Series 7 (Sheffield, 1983); M. D. Goulder, *The Song of Fourteen Songs*, Journal for the Study of the Old Testament, Supplement Series 36 (Sheffield, 1986); O. Keel, *The Song of Songs: A Continental Commentary*, tr. F. J. Gaiser (Minneapolis, 1994); A. LaCoque, *Romance, She Wrote: A Hermeneutical Essay on Song of Songs* (Harrisburg, PA, 1998).

4 P. C. Spicq, *Esquisse d'une histoire de l'exégèse latine au Moyen Age* (Paris, 1944); see esp. his 'Table des commentaires bibliques', 397; for a detailed list of medieval writings dealing with the Bible, see F. Stegmüller, *Repertorium biblicum medii aevi*, 11 vols. (Madrid, 1950–80); for a list of commentaries of the Song of Songs to 1200, see Matter, *Voice of my Beloved*, 203–10.

5 See Matter, *Voice of my Beloved*, 20–48; see also G. R. Evans, *The Mind of St Bernard of Clairvaux* (Oxford, 1983), 116; see also L. Bouyer, *The Christian Mystery from Pagan Myth to Christian Mysticism* (Edinburgh, 1990), 149–59.

6 For an English translation of Rufinus' Latin version of Origen's commentary, see Origen, *The Song of Songs. Commentaries and Homilies*, tr. R. P. Lawson (London, 1957); see also Origen, *An Exhortation to Martyrdom, Prayer, First Principles: Book Four, Prologue to the Commentary on the Song of Songs, Homily XXVII on Numbers*, tr. R. A. Greer, The Classics of Western Spirituality (New York, 1979); see also H. Pietras, *L'Amore in Origene*, Studia Ephemerides 'Augustinianum', 28 (Rome, 1988); see J. Leclercq, 'Aux sources des sermons sur les Cantiques', in J. Leclercq (ed.), *Recueil d'études sur Saint Bernard et ses écrits*, 1 (Rome, 1962), 275–320, and 'Saint Bernard et Origène d'après un manuscrit de Madrid', in J. Leclercq (ed.), *Recueil d'études sur Saint Bernard et ses écrits*, 2 (Rome, 1966), 373–85; see also L. Brésard, 'Bernard et Origène commentent le Cantique', *CCist*, 44/2 (1982), 111–30; 44/3 (1982), 183–209; 44/4 (1982), 293–308, and 'Bernard et Origène, le symbolisme nuptial dans leurs œuvres sur le Cantique', *Cîteaux*, 36/3–4 (1985), 129–51.

7 For a brief discussion of the fourfold method derived from Cassian, see A. J. Minnis, *Medieval Theory of Authorship: Scholastic Literary Attitudes in the Later Middle Ages* (1984; repr. Aldershot, 1988), 34. Minnis's discussion repeats some of the information provided in B. Smalley, *The Study of the Bible in the Middle Ages* (1952; repr. Oxford, 1983), 28–9.

8. This is Guibert of Nogent's passage as it appears in his commentary on Genesis; quoted by Minnis, *Medieval Theory of Authorship*, 34.
9. See Matter, *Voice of my Beloved*, 49–52; see W. Riehle, *The Middle English Mystics*, tr. B. Standring (London, 1981), 35; M. D. Goulder, *The Song of Fourteen Songs*, Journal for the Study of the Old Testament, Supplement Series, 36 (Sheffield, 1986), 80.
10. H. de Lubac, *Exégèse médiévale: Les Quatre sens de l'Écriture*, 3 vols. (Paris, 1959–64); Smalley, *Study*.
11. See Matter, *Voice of my Beloved*, 3–19.
12. For a study of Julian, see G. Bouwman, *Des Julian von Aeclanum Kommentar zu den Propheten Osee, Joel und Amos* (Rome, 1958); A. Bruckner, *Julian von Eclanum: Sein Leben und seine Lehre* (Leipzig, 1897); for a perceptive study of Bede's commentary, see Matter, *Voice of my Beloved*, 97–101.
13. We have only fragments of Julian's *Libellum de amore*, transmitted to us by Bede in his own commentary on the Song; see Bouwman, *Des Julian von Aeclanum*, 6.
14. Ibid., 11–114.
15. PL 91, Bedae venerabilis, col. 1083; for a study of allegory within the commentary tradition, see Lubac, *Exégèse médiévale*, 1, 373–96, 489–548.
16. T. A. Carrol, *The Venerable Bede: His Spiritual Teachings* (Washington, DC, 1946); see esp. 67–98.
17. See Lubac, *Exégèse médiévale*, 1, 587. The authorship of this commentary on the Song of Songs, in *PL* 196, cols. 405–524, has been put into question by Ohly, although Beryl Smalley considers it to be by Richard of St Victor; see F. Ohly, *Hohelied-Studien: Grundzuge einer Geschichte der Hoheliedauslegung des Abendlandes bis zum 1200* (Wiesbaden, 1958), 221–8; see Smalley, *Study*, 106. Matter does not discuss this point, but in her list of writers of commentaries on the Song of Songs, Richard of St Victor's name is accompanied by a question mark. See Matter, *Voice of my Beloved*, 203–10. Astell, on the other hand, mentions the author as Pseudo-Richard of St Victor. I shall follow the practice of the latter in my own references to this work and its possible author. See Astell, *Song of Songs*, 27–8, 36–8.
18. *The Letters of St Bernard of Clairvaux*, tr. B. S. James (London, 1953), 229. [Ceterum, ubi ingenium aut quando otium mihi sufficiens ad id quod petis? Neque enim leve quid aut vile, et quod nos possumus, postulare videris. Minime quippe pro minimis sic instares. Nam voluntatem tuam et curam in hoc satis produnt crebrae epistolae tuae, et vehementior spiritus eas animans. Nimirum proinde quanto id curiosus velle te sentio, tanto, crede mihi, scrupulosus acquiesco. Cur hoc? Ne magna videlicet exspectanti ridiculum producam murem. *Sancti Bernardi opera*, 7, 359.]

[19] *The Letters*, 230. [Nihilominus tamen vermis iste continue rodit me *et dolor meus in conspectu meo semper*. Et quidem alias satis tribulor; sed, ut verum fatear, in nullo aeque. Vincit labores itineris, caloris incommodum, curarum anxietates. *Sancti Bernardi opera*, 7, 361.]

[20] See Leclercq, 'Aspects littéraires de l'oeuvre de S. Bernard', in J. Leclercq (ed.), *Recueil d'études sur Saint Bernard et ses écrits*, 3 (Rome, 1969), 25.

[21] *The Works of Bernard of Clairvaux*, 2, 1–2.

[22] Ibid., 6. [Istiusmodi canticum sola unctio docet, sola addiscit experientia. Experti recognoscant, inexperti inardescant desiderio, non tam cognoscendi quam experiendi. *Sancti Bernardi opera*, 1, 7.]

[23] See Minnis, *Medieval Theory of Authorship*, 51–8.

[24] *The Works of William of St Thierry*, 2, *Exposition on the Song of Songs*, tr. C. Hart, Cistercian Fathers Series 6 (Shannon, 1970), 7. [Non autem profundiora mysteria, quae in eo continentur, attentamus, de Christ.o et Ecclesia; sed cohibentes nos intra nos, et in nobismetipsis nosmetipsos metientes, de Sponso as Sponsa, de Christ.o et Christ.iana anima, sensum tantummodo moralem aliquem, in quo omnibus audere licet, pro sensus nostri paupertate perstringimus, laboris nostri non alium requirentes fructum, quam similem materiae, id est amorem ipsum. *Exposé sur le cantique des cantiques*, SC 82, ed. J.-M. Déchanet (Paris, 1962), 76.]

[25] See Spicq, *Esquisse*, 129.

[26] Astell, *Song of Songs*, 36. [Hinc est enim quod in hoc libro qui Canticum canticorum conscriptus est, amoris quasi corporei verba ponuntur, ut a corpore suo anima per sermones suae consuetudinis refricata, recalexat, et per verba amoris qui infra est, excitetur ad amorem qui supra eSt Nominantur enim in hoc libro oscula, nominantur ubera, nominantur genae, nominantur femora. In quibus verbis non irridenda est sacra Scriptura, sed amplior Dei misericordia consideranda est; quia dum membra corporis nominat, sic ad amorem vocat. *PL* 196, Richard of St Victor, *In cantica canticorum explicatio*, col. 405.]

[27] Unless indicated, translations are my own. [Anima quae Deum quaerit et ad Dei dilectionem et cognitionem plenius pertingere cupit in lectulo hunc quaerere debet, id est in quiete mentis. Richard of St Victor, *In cantica canticorum explicatio*, col. 410.]

[28] Ita mentis pax et tranquilitas lectulus est in quo sponsa quiescit. In hoc lectulo quaerit dilectum per noctem, quando scilicet sapita sunt desideria carnis, et post pugnam et labores victoria successit, et quies data est. Richard of St Victor, *In cantica canticorum explicatio*, cols. 410–11.

[29] See *PL* 196, Richard of St Victor, *In cantica canticorum explicatio*, col. 482.

[30] J. Leclercq, 'L'Attitude spirituelle de S. Bernard devant la guerre', *CCist*, 1 (1974), 195–225; see esp. 202–5; see also G. R. Evans, *The Mind of St Bernard of Clairvaux* (Oxford, 1983), 24.

31 *The Works of William of St Thierry*, 2, 18–19. [Ideo Spiritus sanctus, canticum amoris spiritualis traditurus hominibus, totum spirituale vel divinum ejus interius negotium, exterius vestivit carnalis amoris imaginibus; ut com non nisi amor plene capiat quae sunt divinae, adducendus et migraturus amor carnis in amorem spiritus, cito apprehenderet sibi similia; et cum impossibile esset verum amorem cupidum veritatis diu haerere vel quiescere in imaginibus, citius pertransiret via sibi nota in id quod imaginaretur; et quamvis spiritualis homo, tamen carnalis amoris naturales suas pro participatione carnis delicias captivatas a sancto Spiritu, in obsequium spiritualis amoris amplecteretur. Unde hic quaedam quasi ex occulto aliquo inverecundius prosiliens, nec quae, nec unde sit, nec cui loquatur edicens: 'Osculetur, inquit, me osculo oris sui.' *Exposé*, 100–2.]

32 *The Works of William of St Thierry*, 2, 19. [O Amor a quo omnis amor cognominatur, etiam carnalis ac degener, Amor sancte et sanctificans, caste et castificans, et vita vivificans, aperi nobis sanctum canticum tuum, revela osculi tui mysterium, verrasque susurri tui, quibus virtutem tuam, et suavitatis tuae delicias, incantas cordibus filiorum tuorum. *Exposé*, 102.]

33 See Blanpain, 'Langage mystique, expression du désir dans les sermons sur le Cantique des Cantiques de Bernard de Clairvaux', *CCist* xxxvi, 1 (1974), 45–68; see esp. 50; for a Modern English translation of the Rule of St Benedict, see *Western Asceticism*, ed. O. Chadwick, The Library of Christian Classics (Philadelphia, 1958), 290–337.

34 *Bernard of Clairvaux, Treatises*, 2, *The Steps of Humility and Pride, On Loving God*, tr. R. Walton, Cistercian Fathers Series 31 (Kalamazoo, 1980), 110–11.

35 See Blanpain, 'Langage mystique', 48–9.

36 W. A. Pantin, *The English Church in the Fourteenth Century* (Cambridge, 1955), 249.

37 *The Works of St Bernard*, 2, 9.

38 *The Works of St Bernard*, 3, *On the Song of Songs*, 2, tr. K. Walsh, Cistercian Fathers Series 7 (1976; repr. Kalamazoo, 1983), 134.

39 Exegetes were well informed and provided explanations for some of the biblical texts which appealed to the disposition or affections (*affectus*) of the reader. The Song of Songs and the Psalter were regarded as such; see Minnis, *Medieval Theory*, 49–50.

40 *The Works of St Bernard*, 3, 131.

41 *The Works of William of St Thierry*, 2, 26. [Ipsum etiam osculum fideli animae sponsae suae porrigit et imprimit, cum de memoria communium bonorum, privatum ei et proprium commendans gaudium, gratiam ei sui amoris infundit; spiritum ejus sibi attrahens, et suum infundens ei, ut invicem unus spiritus sint. *Exposé*, 112–14.]

42 See *The Works of William of St Thierry*, 2, 10.
43 Ibid., 2, 9. [Scibitur autem Canticum hoc in modum dramatis et stylo comico, tanquam per personas et actus recitandum; ut sicut in comoediis recitandis personae diversae, et diversi actus, sic et in hoc Cantico concurrere sibi videantur personae et affectus, ad peragendum susceptum negotium amoris, et mysticum contractum divinae et humanae conjunctionis. Personae vero quatuor sunt: Sponsus, et sodales ejus; Sponsa, et adolescentularum chorus. *Exposé*, 80; see also Origen, *Prologue*, 217.]
44 See *Exposé*, 13–16.
45 *Bernard of Clairvaux: On the Song of Songs*, 3, tr. K. Walsh and I. M. Edmonds, Cistercian Fathers Series 31 (Kalamazoo, 1979), 133. [Nimium me fortasse queratur in sui suggillatione Iudaeus, qui intellectum illius dico bovinum. Sed legat in Isaia, et plus quam bovinum audiet: '*Cognovit bos*, inquit, *possessorem suum, et asinus praesepe domini sui. Israel non cognovit me, populus meus non intellexit.*' Vides me, Iudaee, mitiorem tibi Propheta tuo. Ego comparavi te iumentis, ille subicit. *Sancti Bernardi opera*, 2, ed. J. Leclercq, C. H. Talbot and H. M. Rochais (Rome, 1958), 144.]
46 See Blanpain, 'Langage mystique', 59: 'Nous dirons que l'*affectus* dans la psychologie des auteurs spirituels du 12è siècle est comme la 'pulsion' qui incite, qui crée le désir. Le sujet subit une attraction, il est 'affecté' par une valeur qui l'attire. Le désir est mis ainsi en mouvement, il s'oriente, se concentre dans une direction, sur un objet.' See also M. Casey, *Athirst for God: Spiritual Desire in Bernard of Clairvaux's Sermons on the Song of Songs*, Cistercian Studies Series 77 (Kalamazoo, 1988), 131–243.
47 Ives: *Épître à Séverin sur la Charité*. Richard de Saint-Victor: *Les Quatre Degrés de la violente charité*, ed. G. Dumeige, Textes philosophiques du Moyen Age 3 (Paris, 1955), 115.
48 Nonne tibi corde percussus videtur, quando igneus ille amoris aculeus mentem hominis medullitus penetrat, affectumque transverberat, in tantum ut desiderii sui estus cohibere vel dissimulare omnino non valeat? Richard of St Victor, *Les Quatre Degrés*, 131.
49 For a discussion of the fourfold division of the *affectus*, appearing in Pseudo-Augustine's *Liber de spiritu et anima*, see Minnis, *Medieval Theory*, 120–2; for a study of the influence of the Victorines on Bonaventure, see G. Zinn, Jr., 'Book and Word: The Background of Bonaventure's Use of Symbols', *S. Bonaventura 1274–1974*, 2 (Rome, 1974), 143–69; see also Zinn, 'Personification Allegory and Vision of Light in Richard of St Victor's Teaching on Contemplation', *University of Toronto Quarterly*, 46 (1977), 190–214; for a study of the influence of Bonaventuran psychology on Rolle, see V. Gillespie, 'Mystic's Foot: Rolle and Affectivity', *MMTE* 2 (1982), 199–230; see also J. McLaughlin, 'St Bonaventure and the English Mystics', *S. Bonaventura 1274–1974*, 2 (Rome, 1974), 279–87.

50 Est igitur *affectus* spontanea quaedam ac dulcis ipsius animi ad aliquem inclinatio. See Blanpain, 'Langage mystique', 60, quoting from *PL* 195, *Speculum caritatis*, col. 587.

51 Affectio est ut mihi videtur spontanea quaedam mentis inclinatio ad aliquem cum delectatione. See Blanpain, 'Langage mystique', 60, quoting from *Sermones inediti*, ed. C. H. Talbot (Rome, 1952), 18; see also *DS* 1, cols. 235–46; see also B. Stoeckle, 'Amor carnis – abusus amoris. Das Verstandnis von der Konkupiszens bei Bernhard von Clairvaux und Aelred von Rieval', *Analecta monastica*, 7, Studia Anselmiana 54 (Rome, 1965), 147–76.

52 E. Auerbach, *Literary Language and its Public in Late Latin Antiquity and in the Middle Ages* (Princeton, 1965), 71.

53 Riehle talks of the wound caused by the lance of Longinus, and the notion of entering it in order to become one with Christ as being a conscious analogy between the wound of Christ and the female pudenda. Although Riehle has Franciscan texts and spirituality in mind, his comment also applies to Cistercian literature. See Riehle, *Middle English Mystics*, 44–7.

54 *Bernard of Clairvaux*: *On the Song of Songs*, 3, 147. [Enimvero non sentiet sua, dum illius vulnera intuebitur. Stat martyr tripudians et triumphans, toto licet lacero corpore; et rimante latera ferro, non modo fortiter, sed alacriter sacrum e carne sua circumspicit ebullire cruorem. Ubi ergo tunc anima martyris? Nempe in tuto, nempe in petra, nempe in visceribus Iesu, vulneribus nimirum patentibus ad introeundum. Si in suis esset visceribus, scrutans ea ferrum profecto sentiret; et dolorem non ferret, succumberet et negaret. Nunc autem in petra habitans, quid mirum, si in modum petrae duruerit. Sed neque hoc mirum si, exsul a corpore, dolores non sentiat corporis. Neque hoc facit stupor, sed amor. *Sancti Bernardi opera*, 2, 153.]

55 E. Gilson, *The Mystical Theology of Saint Bernard*, tr. A. H. C. Downes (London, 1955), 85.

56 See Blanpain, 'Langage mystique', 65.

57 See *Sancti Bernardi opera omnia*, 3, 109–54; see Gilson, *Mystical Theology*, 87–8; see also J. Hourlier, 'S. Bernard et Guillaume de Saint-Thierry dans le "Liber de amore"', *Saint Bernard théologien*, Analecta sacri ordinis cisterciensis, 9 (1953), 223–33; see also in the same volume, P. Delfgaaw, 'La Nature et les degrés de l'amour selon S. Bernard', 234–52.

58 See *Sancti Bernardi opera omnia*, 3, 140.

59 Ibid., 3, 141.

60 *Bernard of Clairvaux, Treatises*, 2, 118. [Qui enim sic amat, haud secus profecto quam amatus est, amat, quaerens et ipse vicissim non quae sua sunt, sed quae Iesu Christi, quemadmodum ille nostra, vel potius nos, et

non sua quaesivit. Sic amat qui dicit: *confitemini domino quoniam bonus.* Qui Domino confitetur, non quoniam sibi bonus est, sed quoniam bonus est, hic vere diligit Deum propter Deum, et non propter seipsum. *Sancti Bernardi opera omnia*, 3, 141.]
61 See *Sancti Bernardi opera omnia*, 3, 142.
62 *Bernard of Clairvaux*, *Treatises*, 2, 119. [Beatum dixerim et sanctum, cui tale aliquid in hac mortali vita raro interdum, aut vel semel, et hoc ipsum raptim atque unus vix momenti spatio, experiri donatum est. Te enim quodammodo perdere, tamquam qui non sis, et omnino non sentire teipsum, et a temetipsa exinaniri, et paene annullari, caelestis est conversationis, non humanae affectionis. *Sancti Bernardi opera omnia*, 3, 142.]
63 Richard of St Victor, *Les Quatres Degrés*, 110.
64 Ibid., 143.
65 Ibid., 151.
66 Ibid., 153. [Forte adhuc David in primo gradu erat, sed jam de secundo presumebat quando psallens dicebat: *Confitebor tibi, Domine, in toto corde meo.* Qui in secundo gradu est fiducialiter psallere potest: *In toto corde meo exquisivi te.* Qui tertium gradum obtinet profecto ejusmodi jam dicere valet: *Concupivit anima mea, Domine, desiderare justificationes tuas in omni tempore.* Qui quartum gradum ascendit, et Deum ex tota virtute diligit, dicere potest profecto: *Non timebo quid faciat michi homo*, eo quod sit *paratum cor* ejus *sperare in Domino; confirmatum est cor* ejus, *non commovebitur in eternum, donec despiciat inimicos suos.*]
67 Ibid.
68 Astell draws parallels between Rolle and Victorine mysticism, putting emphasis on the way the bodily component plays an unusual role in both systems; see Astell, *Song of Songs*, 108.
69 'Vulnerata caritate ego sum' (Sg. 4: 9).
70 See Richard of St Victor, *Les Quatres Degrés*, 138–41.

Chapter 3

1 For a bibliography of William of St Thierry, see *William, Abbot of St Thierry: A Colloquium at the Abbey of St Thierry*, tr. J. Carfantan, Cistercian Studies Series 94 (Kalamazoo, 1987), 261–73; for a short biography and a general study of William of St Thierry, see P. Mellet, *Notes sur le désir de Dieu chez Guillaume de Saint-Thierry* (Notre-Dame de Géronde, Switzerland, 1967); see also the introduction by J. Hourlier to William's *La Contemplation de Dieu. L'Oraison de dom Guillaume*, SC 61, ed. J. Hourlier (Paris, 1959), 7–15; the other editions of the works of William used in this research are: *Oraisons méditatives*, SC 324, ed.

J. Hourlier (Paris, 1985); *Exposé sur le cantique des cantiques*, SC 82, ed. J.-M. Déchanet (Paris, 1962); *Lettres aux frères du Mont-Dieu*, SC 223, ed. J.-M. Déchanet (Paris, 1975).

2. The 'face to face' occurs in Gen. 32: 30; Ex. 33: 11; Dt. 5: 4, 34: 10, Jg. 6: 22, Ez. 20: 35; and in 1 Cor. 13: 12. Mentions of the face of God occur in Ps. 26 (27), Ps. 13: 1, Ap. 22: 4, Num. 6: 26, Ps. 80: 4, 8, 20, 42: 3; 10: 11; 51: 11; Ex. 3: 6; 33: 23; see also *DS* 5, cols. 26–33. Occurrences of the word *facies* in other contexts are extremely numerous in the Bible, and used in contexts which cannot be discussed in this research: see however the *Novae concordantiae bibliorum sacrorum iuxta vulgatam versionem critice editam*, 2, ed. B. Fischer (Stuttgart-Bad Cannstatt, 1977).

3. The information in the remaining part of this paragraph is drawn from Hourlier's introduction to the *De contemplando Deo*; see William of St Thierry, *La Contemplation de Dieu*, 16–18.

4. For a more systematic description of the content of the treatise, Ibid., 31–6.

5. The insistence by William on the presumptuousness to desire to see the face of God is somewhat reminiscent of the tone of some of the prayers and meditations of St Anselm; see for instance 'Oratio ad Christum', in which the desire for the vision of the face of God is eloquently expressed; in *Sancti Anselmi opera omnia*, 6 vols., ed. F. S. Schmitt (Edinburgh, 1946–62), 3, 6–9; for a modern English translation, see *The Prayers and Meditations of Saint Anselm with the Proslogion*, ed. B. Ward (1973; repr. London, 1988), 93–9.

6. *The Works of William of St Thierry*, 1, *On Contemplating God, Prayer, Meditations*, tr. Sister Penelope, Cistercian Fathers Series 3 (Shannon, 1971), 39–40. [. . . et ex eo quod vel leviter sensi, vel vidi, magis accenso desiderio vix patienter expecto ut aliquando auferas manum tegentem, et infundas gratiam illuminantem; ut tandem aliquando secundum responsum veritatis tuae mortuus michi, et vivens tibi, revelata facie ipsam tuam faciem incipiam videre, et affici tibi a visione faciei tuae. Et o facies facies, quam beata facies: quae affici tibi meretur videndo te, aedificans in corde suo tabernaculum deo Iacob, et omnia faciens secundum exemplar quod ei ostenditur in monte. Hic vere et competenter cantat: Tibi dixit cor meum exquisivit te facies mea, faciem tuam domine requiram. *La Contemplation de Dieu*, 64–7.]

7. *Facies* is mentioned several times in William of St Thierry, *La Contemplation de Dieu*: 2: 2, 18, 19; 3: 35, 36, 37, 41, 42; 8: 1; 11: 126; 12: 91 (figures refer to paragraph and line).

8. *The Works of William of St Thierry*, 1, 40. [Dico enim michi in languore desiderii mei: Quis amat quod non videt? Quomodo potest esse amabile, quod non aliquatenus est visibile? *La Contemplation de Dieu*, 66.]

9. For further details on William's borrowing from John Scot Erigena, see William of St Thierry, *La Contemplation de Dieu*, 41–3.

10. My summary of the meditations is drawn from William of St Thierry, *Meditativae orationes*, tr. M.-M. Davy (Paris, 1934), 11–12.
11. See M. Simon, 'Le "Face à Face" dans les méditations de Guillaume de Saint-Thierry', *CCist*, 35/2 (1973), 121–36.
12. Vultus defines the changing expression of the face, and is also used to describe the *affectiones* of the soul; see *DS* 5, col. 29.
13. See Simon, 'Le "Face à Face"', 121; the *facies ad faciem* expression appears in III, 12, 6; III, 13, 1; VII, 10, 4; X, 9, 9 (figures refer in order to meditation, paragraph and line).
14. See William of St Thierry, *Oraisons*, 72–5.
15. *The Works of William of St Thierry*, 1, 107. [Ignosce, Domine, ignosce: amor amoris tui agit me; tu scis, tu vides. Non sum scrutator maiestatis tuae, sed pauper gratiae tuae. Obsecro te per dulcedinem tuae dulcissimae mansuetudinis, non opprimat me maiestas tua, sed sublevet gratia tua. Ignosce, inquam, quia proprium est fidei desiderium visio dei, hic in enigmate, ibi vero facie ad faciem. *Oraisons*, 72–5.]
16. *The Works of William of St Thierry*, 1, 154. [Et abundantiore fluminis impetu laetificante animam illam, videtur sibi videre te sicuti es, dum de mirabili passionis tuae sacramento cogitandi dulcedine ruminat bonum tuum circa nos, tantum quantus ipse es, vel quod ipse es; videtur sibi videre te facie ad faciem, cum summi boni facies appares ei in cruce et opere salutis tuae, et ipsa crux efficitur ei ad Deum facies mentis bene affectae. *Oraisons*, 164–7.]
17. William assimilates in a very personal way elements of the Eastern mystical tradition. The presence of a large part of the corpus of Origen in the libraries of Clairvaux and Signy in the twelfth century shows the special esteem in which Origen was held by Bernard and William. Paul Verdeyen believes that William initiated the copying of the works of Origen for the Signy library; see P. Verdeyen, *La Théologie mystique de Guillaume de Saint-Thierry* (Paris, 1990), 9–11; see also J.-M. Déchanet, *Guillaume de Saint-Thierry: Aux sources d'une pensée*, Théologie Historique 49 (Paris, 1978).
18. *The Works of William of St Thierry*, 1, 108. [Haec in Trinitate sancta nil dividit, nil compingit, sed sensum fidelem sic quando et quantum et quomodo vult Spiritus sanctus perstringit, ut orantes te vel contemplantes supergressi nonnumquam omne quod tu non es, per hoc ipsum quod tu non es, videant aliquatenus te qui es, quamvis non videant te sicuti es; sed tamen medium quid devotae mentis demulceat intuitum, quod constet nec de eis esse quae tu non es, nec etsi non sit omnino totum quod es, alienum tamen esse ab eo quod es. *Oraisons*, 74–7.]
19. *The Works of William of St Thierry*, 1, 109. [. . . in neutro conturbet solitudo vel pluralitas, sed etiam ad hoc ei valeant unitas trinitatis et trinitas unitatis, ut pio et sobrio intellectu comprehendat non

comprehendendo maiestatem divinae incomprehensibilitatis. *Oraisons*, 76–7.]

20 See William of St Thierry, *Oraisons*, 136.
21 *The Works of William of St Thierry*, 1, 140. [Et dum porrigit illa osculum iustae confessionis, tu eam excipis in osculo pacis. *Oraisons*, 136.]
22 Julian of Norwich offers the same positive outlook to sin and the passion scene; see especially ch. 10 which exploits the veil image in a fascinating way for that purpose; see Julian of Norwich, *A Revelation of Love*, ed. M. Glasscoe (1976; repr. Exeter, 1986), 11–13.
23 See Gen. 2: 7; see also N. J. Perella, *The Kiss Sacred and Profane: An Interpretative History of Kiss Symbolism and Related Religio-Erotic Themes* (Berkeley and Los Angeles, 1969), 5; see also *DS* 1, 'baiser', cols. 1203–4.
24 For more details on the eucharistic mysticism of William, see Verdeyen, *La Théologie*, 167–74; see also Verdeyen, 'Parole et sacrement chez Guillaume de Saint-Thierry', *CCist*, 49 (1987), 218–28.
25 *The Works of William of St Thierry*, 1, 142. [. . . et in novum et perpetuum salutis nostrae effectum, novo semper pietatis affectu ruminantes, rursum suaviter in ipsa recondimus memoria quid pro nobis feceris, quid fueris passus. *Oraisons*, 140–1]; for an analysis of the link between the eucharistic meeting and the understanding of the revealed word, see Verdeyen, *La Théologie*, 174–7.
26 See William of St Thierry, *Exposé*: I, 35, 10–11; I, 36, 3; I, 131, 35; I, 132, 18; II, 147, 8; II, 152, 3; II, 176, 13; II, 176, 23; II, 183, 5 (faciem tuam exquirit facies mea); II, 203, 24 (figures refer in order to song, paragraph, line).
27 See William of St Thierry, *Exposé*, 112–15.
28 Ibid., 114–15; for a diverging view on the *unitas spiritus*, see J.-M. Déchanet, '*Amor ipse intellectus est:* La Doctrine de l'amour chez Guillaume de Saint-Thierry', *RMAL*, 1 (1945), 349–74.
29 If any have not learned, let them learn; let them turn around and see; let them rouse their curiosity to experience how this drama enacts itself in the behavior and the conscience of persons who, being now converted to the Lord, walk in newness of life. *The Works of William of St Thierry*, 2, 26. [Discant qui non didicerunt; convertantur ad videndum; fiant curiosi ad experiendum, quomodo actitentur haec, in conversatione, vel conscientia eorum, qui conversi ad Dominum in novitate vitae ambulant. *Exposé*, 114–15]; for a survey of the use of the word *experire* and its substantive in monastic spiritual writings, see P. Miquel, *Le Vocabulaire latin de l'expérience spirituelle dans la tradition monastique et canoniale de 1050 à 1250*, Théologie Historique 79 (Paris, 1989); see esp. 107–18.
30 *The Works of William of St Thierry*, 2, *Exposition on the Song of Songs*, tr. C. Hart, Cistercian Fathers Series 6 (Shannon, 1970), 6–7. [Ob hoc,

epythalamium, canticum nuptiale, canticum sponsi et sponsae, aggredientes revolvendum, et inspiciendum opus tuum, sancte Spiritus, te invocamus, ut amore tuo repleamur, o amor, ad intelligendum canticum amoris; ut et nos colloquii sancti Sponsi et Sponsae, aliquatenus efficiamur participes; ut agatur in nobis quod legitur a nobis. Ubi enim de affectibus agitur, non facile, nisi a similiter affectis, capitur quod dicitur. Affice ergo nos tibi, sancte Spiritus; sancte Paraclite, sancte Consolator, consolare paupertatem solitudinis nostrae, nullum extra te solatium requirentis; illumina, et vivifica desiderium tendentis, ut efficiatur amor fruentis. Adesto, ut vere amemus; ut de fonte amoris tui prodeat quidquid sentiemus vel dicemus. Canticum amoris tui sic a nobis legatur, ut amorem ispsum in nobis accendat; ipse vero amor canticum suum per se nobis aperiat. *Exposé*, 74–7.]

31 See William of St Thierry, *Exposé*, 76–9.
32 *The Works of William of St Thierry*, 2, 8. [Agit enim de amore Dei, vel quo Deus amatur, vel quo ipse Deus Amor dicitur; qui utrum *amor* dicatur, an *caritas*, an *dilectio*, non refert, nisi quod in *amoris* nomine, tener quidam amantis indicari videtur affectus, tendentis vel ambientis; in nomine vero *caritatis*, spiritualis quaedam affectio, vel gaudium fruentis; in *dilectione* autem, rei delectantis appetitus naturalis; quae tamen omnia, in amore Sponsi et Sponsae, unus atque idem Spiritus operatur. Amori vero Sponsi et Sponsae ad cantandum canticum novum, sic serviunt omnium sanctarum virtutum affectus, ut si bene et suo ordine processerint earum profectus, omnes transeant, et terminentur in ejus effectus. Caetera quidem evacuantur, caritas numquam excidit. *Exposé*, 78–9.]
33 *The Works of William of St Thierry*, 2, 28. [Fit autem jugiter in conscientia, et corde Sponsae, quaecumque illa est, effundentis coram Domino Deo suo animam suam, et cum gaudio audientis, quid loquatur in ea Dominus Deus. *Exposé*, 118–19.]
34 This paragraph paraphrases Verdeyen, *La Théologie*, 219–21.
35 *The Works of William of St Thierry*, 2, 28–9. [. . . taedet, inquit, inanium, absente Sponso, cellariorum horum, quotidianarum promissionum harum, sacramentorum involutorum horum, parabolarum ac proverbiorum horum, speculi et aenigmatis. Mysterium regni Dei desidero, palam mihi annuntiari de Patre deposco; faciem ad faciem, oculum ad oculum, osculum ad osculum: *Osculetur me osculo oris sui*. *Exposé*, 118–21.]
36 *The Works of William of St Thierry*, 2, 29. [. . . sed sapit quod inspirat spiritus oris, vel osculi ejus; quod tunc sapiet ad plenum, cum in ipso erit gaudium meum plenum. *Exposé*, 120–1.]
37 William of St Thierry, *Exposé*, 124–5.
38 Caroline Walker Bynum notices that Bernard and William use the breast

image, which is erotic in the biblical text, to make references to abbots and other prelates as nursing and mothering the souls in their charge. The image is also used to talk about the burdens of the abbacy. See C. W. Bynum, *Jesus as Mother: Studies in the Spirituality of the High Middle Ages* (Berkeley, 1982), 117.

39 C. W. Bynum, *Holy Feast and Holy Fast: The Religious Significance of Food to Medieval Women* (London, 1987); pls. 8 –30 illustrate how visual arts adapt literary textual images into tangible objects for the satisfaction of devotional practices; see especially the detailed and sophisticated paintings describing the lactating Mary and Christ feeding from the wound on his side (pls. 24–30).

40 See William of St Thierry, *Exposé*, 276–81.

41 Ibid., 222–7.

42 For a discussion of the *unitas spiritus*, see Verdeyen, *La Théologie*, 234–52. The way in which William uses the intimacy of the carnal union as an image for the intense and mutual passion found in the trinitarian relationship is remarkable. Verdeyen sees an Origenean influence on the interpretation by William of the Pauline quotation: 'L'unité spirituelle fait participer l'âme mystique à la connaissance des Personnes divines, qui se connaissent mutuellement ainsi que toutes les créatures qui ont été faites à l'image du Fils. La connaissance mystique de l'épouse qui commence à connaitre de la manière dont elle est connue (I Cor. 13: 12) est aussi un effet de la parfaite réciprocité des relations amoureuses. Si la citation est paulinienne, elle a surement été lue et comprise selon l'interprétation origénienne. Car Guillaume attribue à l'amour l'intelligence spirituelle que l'Apôtre réserve expressement à la vie éternelle.' See Verdeyen, *La Théologie*, 241.

43 *The Works of William of St Thierry*, 2, 80. [. . . fietque osculum plenum, cum osculo ad osculum, amplexu ad amplexum plena fiet et perpetua fruitio. Tunc jam ultra nemo Sponsam *suscitabit*, vel *evigilare faciet, donec ipsa velit*; ipsa vero nequaquam volet ultra. *Exposé*, 226–7.]

44 See William of St Thierry, *Exposé*, 236–7.

45 *The Works of William of St Thierry*, 2, 103. [Sic qui ordinatae caritatis est, diligit Dominum Deum suum, et in ipso seipsum, et proximum suum sicut seipsum, ipsa qualitate, ipsa quantitate. *Exposé*, 274–5.]

46 Déchanet underestimates the fact that William's *Expositio* is didactic and supposes therefore a putative general audience which William had in mind from the onset of the composition. It is true however that William is not pressed to write this treatise; see William of St Thierry, *Exposé*, 10; see also the 'Liminaires', where William describes the spiritual meaning of the Song of Songs, having in mind three levels of soul with which the putative audience can identify. The awakening of the desire and the progression in the love of God are stressed from the outset: 'When the

soul has been converted to God and is to be espoused to the Word of God, at first she is taught to understand the riches of prevenient grace and allowed to 'taste and see how sweet the Lord is; but afterwards she is sent back into the house of her conscience to be instructed, purified in the obedience of charity, perfectly cleansed of vices and richly adorned with virtues, that she may be found worthy of access to the spiritual grace of godliness and affection for virtues which is the bridechamber of the Bridegroom.' *The Works of William of St Thierry*, 2, 10. [Conversa ad Deum anima, et Verbo Dei maritanda, primo praevenientis gratiae divitias intelligere perdocetur, et permittitur gustare quoniam suavis est Dominus; postmodum vero in domum conscientiae suae remittitur, erudienda, castificanda, in oboedientia caritatis, et perfecte mundanda a vitiis, et perornanda virtutibus, ut ad spiritualem gratiam pietatis admitti, et affectum virtutum, qui Sponsi thalamus est, digna habeatur. *Exposé*, 82–5.]

47 *The Works of William of St Thierry*, 2, 105. [Ideo quaecumque Sponsa est, hoc solum desiderat, hoc affectat, ut facies ejus faciei tuae jungatur jugiter in osculo caritatis; hoc est, unus tecum spiritus fiat per unitatem ejusdem voluntatis; forma vitae ejus formae amoris tui imprimatur vehementer, vehementia magni amoris, . . . *Exposé*, 280–1.]

48 *The Works of William of St Thierry*, 2, 106. [Abyssus haec alteram abyssum invocat; extasis ista longe aliud quam quod videt somniat; secretum hoc aliud secretum suspirat; gaudium hoc aliud gaudium imaginatur; suavitas ista aliam suavitatem praeorditur. *Exposé*, 282–3.]

49 *The Works of William of St Thierry*, 2, 106–7. [Cum enim plene revelabitur facies ad faciem, et perficietur mutua cognitio, et cognoscet Sponsa, sicut et cognita est, tunc erit plenum osculum, plenusque amplexus; cum non indigebitur laeva fulciente, sed totam amplexabuntur Sponsa delectationes dexterae Sponsi usque in finem aeternitatis infinitae. Tunc, inquam, plenum erit osculum plenusque amplexus, . . . *Exposé*, 284–5.]

50 In *Jesus as Mother,* 146–50, Bynum notes three characteristics of the use of the image of God as mother in twelfth-century Cistercian writings. Firstly, she draws attention to the fact that male figures are registered as mothers or are given maternal roles (nursing, conceiving and giving birth). Secondly, she notices that certain personality characteristics are seen by these authors as female and certain other as male. Thirdly, she points out that the breast image is much more fashionable than the giving birth or the conception images. These images speak of how the self can achieve the closest possible union with God.

51 Haec animales constituit homines, quae carnis sunt sapientes, sensibus corporis inhaerentes. Quae ubi perfectae rationis incipit esse, non tantum capax, sed et particeps rationis, continuo abdicat a se notam generis

femini, et efficitur animus particeps, regendo corpori accomodatus, vel seipsum habens spiritus. Quamdiu enim anima est, cito in id quod carnale est effeminatur; animus vero, vel spiritus, non nisi quod virile est et spirituale meditatur. William of St Thierry, *Lettre*, 306; see also J. J. Conley, 'The Eremetical Anthropology of William of St Thierry', *CSt*, 25/2 (1990), 115–30.

52. See William of St Thierry, *Exposé*, 84–5.
53. See M. M. Davy, 'L'Amour de Dieu d'après Guillaume de Saint-Thierry', *RSR*, 18 (1938), 319–46.
54. *The Works of William of St Thierry*, 2, 115. [Tunc parebit in lumine tuo quantum in intellectu tuo praecedit pietas simplicissimi amantis, prudentiam eruditissimi ratiocinantis; cum retroacta ratione amor pius ipse efficietur intellectus suus. *Exposé*, 304–5.]
55. See William of St Thierry, *Exposé*, 312–15. Déchanet believes that the purification theme is a Plotinian influence, which manifests even in the ways William quotes Paul's 2 Cor. 5: 13 and 1 Cor. 13: 12.
56. Although expressed metaphorically, the sitting posture, so characteristic of Rolle, has an antecedent.
57. Le signe aspire au signifié, l'image à l'Archétype. R. Javelet, *Image et ressemblance au douzième siècle*, 2 vols. (Paris, 1967); see esp. 2, 409–23.
58. *The Works of William of St Thierry*, 2, 124. [Jam Sponsus veniens Sponsae propior efficitur; jam etsi nondum facie ad faciem, proprioribus tamen figuris ei insinuatur. *Exposé*, 320–1.]
59. See Curtius's chapter on 'Le Symbolisme du livre', in E. R. Curtius, *La Littérature européenne et le Moyen-Age latin*, 2, tr. J. Bréjoux (Paris, 1956), 5–76.
60. Verdeyen notes that the opposition '*affectus–effectus*' appears in different contexts: 'Guillaume fait appel à deux terminologies différentes pour exprimer la même réalité. L'opposition "affectus–effectus" apparait aussi bien dans le contexte eucharistique que dans le contexte nuptial . . . Comme l'opposition "affectus–effectus" se réfère à l'antithèse "unité-altérité" de la vie trinitaire, elle est aussi apte à décrire la rencontre Christologique que la rencontre dans l'Esprit'; see Verdeyen, *La Théologie*, 174.
61. Déchanet insists on the fact that the *affectus* and the *effectus* modes complete one another. The humanity of Christ is the doorway to the knowledge and understanding of God and, within the Christian tradition, it is the most precious gift which God has offered man for his redemption. Déchanet comments: 'L'humanité du Christ est, pour notre auteur, un grand "sacrement", le premier de tous les sacrements, en ce sens que les gestes, les paroles, les actes de cet homme de chair, qui est Dieu, sont, d'après le plan providentiel, destinés à nous introduire, et vraiment (*efficaciter*), au sein du mystère de la vie de Dieu'; see William of St Thierry, *Exposé*, 320–1, n. 3.

62 See Verdeyen, *La Théologie*, 189–92.
63 William and Bernard emphasize differently the role of Christ in his humanity in their respective works. Both agree on his role as the doorway, but Bernard insists on describing the comfort which can be gained in penetrating and remaining in the womb of Christ. William's Meditation X throws light on the more elaborate views expressed in the *Expositio*. Devotion to the humanity of Christ necessitates the use of the sensual imagination: 'For since I have not yet progressed beyond the elementary stage of sensory imagination, you will allow and will be pleased if my still-undeveloped soul dwells naturally on your lowliness by means of some mental picturing.' *The Works of William of St Thierry*, 1, 152. [Cum enim sensualis imaginationis meae rudimenta necdum supergressus sim, permittes et gratum habebis ipsa mentis imaginatione circa humilia tua infirmam adhuc animam meam suam indolem exercere . . . *Oraisons*, X, 160–1.] William further insists on the necessity to penetrate into Christ in order to find God: 'For he labors who would go up some other way, but he who enters by you, O Door, walks on the smooth ground and comes to the Father, to whom no one may come, except by you. And he no longer labors to understand knowledge beyond his reach, for the bliss of a well-disposed conscience absorbs him utterly.' *The Works of William of St Thierry*, 1, 154. [Laborat enim qui ascendit aliunde. Qui vero per te intrat, o ostium, per planum graditur, et venit ad Patrem, ad quem nullus venit nisi per te, nec iam laborat in intellectu supereminentis scientiae, sed totus resoluitur in suavitate bene affectae conscientiae. *Oraisons*, X, 164–5.]
64 The Middle English text, *Book to a Mother*, uses the metaphor extensively; see *Book to a Mother: An Edition with a Commentary*, ed. A. J. McCarthy, Salzburg Studies in English Literature, Elizabethan and Renaissance Studies 92 (Salzburg, 1981), xx; the sources for the Christ-book metaphor, quoted in *Book to a Mother*, are Augustine, *De doctrina christiana*, 2, 42: see *PL* 34, cols. 64–5; see also *PL* 191, Peter Lombard, *Commentarius in Psalmos*, col. 403; Bonaventure, *Lignum vitae*, ed. Patres Collegii S. Bonaventurae (Quarachi, 1896), 218–19; Bonaventure, *Vitis mystica*, ibid., 505; see also John 10: 35–6; J. Leclercq, '*Lectio divina*: Jésus livre et Jésus lecteur', *CCist*, 48/3 (1986), 207–16; J. Leclercq, 'Mary's Reading of Christ', *Monastic Studies*, 15 (1984), 105–16; for a study of spiritual books and reading process during the late medieval period, see V. Gillespie, '*Lukynge in haly bukes: Lectio* in Some Late Medieval Spiritual Miscellanies', *Spätmittelalterliche Geistliche Literatur in der Nationalsprache*, Analecta Cartusiana 106/2 (Salzburg, 1984), 1–27.
65 See William of St Thierry, *Exposé*, 326–7.
66 *The Works of William of St Thierry*, 2, 127. [Invisibilem ergo post

parietem videre est tantum eum videre, quantum eum videre in vita ista possibile est. *Exposé*, 326–7]; see also 327, n. 7, which suggests that William might have read Gregory's *Life of Moses*, in which this idea is developed; see St Gregory, bishop of Nyssa, *The Life of Moses*, tr. A. J. Malherbe and E. Ferguson, The Classics of Western Spirituality (New York, 1978); for the influence of the Eastern fathers, see William of St Thierry, *Exposé*, 322, n. 2; 326, n. 1; 327, n. 7.

67 *The Works of William of St Thierry*, 2, 142. [Cum enim aspirabit dies, et inclinabuntur umbrae, tunc jam Sponsus et Sponsa non tam erunt sibi mutuo ad consentiendum, quam aderunt ad fruendum; nec in sterili amoenitate liliorum pascet Sponsus, sed in plena ubertate fructuum spiritus. Cum enim per aspirationem sancti Spiritus etiam in hac vita nox nostra sicut dies illuminabitur ad horam, ad tempus; et saecularium umbrae vanitatum inclinabuntur, cedentes lumini veritatis, seu magis in occasu vitae hujus, quae nox est, et non lux, et susceptione matutina alterius vitae, seu potissimum in matutino aeternitatis, in die generalis resurrectionis; tunc Sponsus et Sponsa incipient sibi non esse per fidem, sed adesse per speciem, facie ad faciem; nec pascet Sponsus Sponsam instar sterilium liliorum, in flore spei, sed in fructu rei. Et tunc omnes omnino umbrae vanitatis saeculi hujus inclinabuntur; hoc est ab aestimationis suae statu dejicientur. *Exposé*, 358–61.]

68 *The Works of William of St Thierry*, 2, 143. [Hominis enim conglorificati Deo omnes animae vires, virtutes, voluntates, intentiones, affectiones, per virtutem resurrectionis liberatae a servitute corruptionis, et subjectione vanitatis, incommutabiliter stabilientur ad plene vivendum quod sensim credebatur; ad certissime habendum quod trepide sperabaur; ad solide fruendum quod fide amabatur. *Exposé*, 360–1.]

69 For a similar hide-and-seek game, see the discussion by Tixier on the *Cloud of Unknowing* in R. Tixier, ' "Good Gamesumli Pley": Games of Love in *The Cloud of Unknowing*', *DR*, 108 (1990), 235–53.

70 *The Works of William of St Thierry*, 2, 147. [Etenim, sicut jam supra diximus, ut ex usu carnalis amoris circa spiritualem amorem, et affectum Sponsi et Sponsae aliquem sentiamus experientiae sensum . . . *Exposé*, 366–9.]

71 *The Works of William of St Thierry*, 2, 147. [videtur saepe Sponsus Sponsae quasi lasciviente amore alludere, et crebro subducere se vehementer amanti, rursumque reddere desideranti; egredi aliquando et abire tanquam non rediturus, ut ardentius requiratur; regredi aliquando et intrare ad illam quasi perpetuo mansurus, quo dulcius ad oscula invitetur; aliquando stare post parietem, et aspicere per fenestras, ut ad excitandum desiderium amantis videatur blandiens, sed non totus . . . *Exposé*, 368–9.]

72 *The Works of William of St Thierry*, 2, 162. [. . . quia, avertente Deo

faciem suam, omnia turbantur; verba non nisi verba, scripturae non nisi litterae sunt. *Exposé*, 398–9.]

73 See William of St Thierry, *Exposé*, 400–3; note that William uses the 'face to face' in the *Golden Epistle* too, his most systematic work on the spiritual life; the expression is at *Lettre*, 25, 45, 112 (figures indicate paragraphs).

Part Two: Prologue

1 See F. Ohly, *Hohelied-Studien: Grundzüge einer Geschichte der Hoheliedauslegung des Abendlandes bis zum 1200* (Wiesbaden, 1958), see E. A. Matter, *The Voice of my Beloved: The Song of Songs in Western Medieval Chrsitianity* (Philadelphia, 1990); A. W. Astell, *The Song of Songs in the Middle Ages* (London and Ithaca, NY, 1990); D. Turner, *Eros and Allegory: Medieval Exegesis of the Song of Songs*, Cistercian Series 156 (Kalamazoo, 1995).
2 See Turner, *Eros and Allegory*, 317–448.
3 See A. B. Emden, *A Biographical Register of the University of Oxford to A.D. 1500* (Oxford, 1957).
4 See *DS* 2, 86–109. The unedited treatise by John Russell is found in Lambeth Palace, MS 180. See A. B. Emden, *A Biographical Register of the University of Cambridge to 1500* (Cambridge, 1963).
5 See M. Engammare, *Qu'il me baise des baisiers de sa bouche: Le Cantique des cantiques à la Renaissance, Etude et bibliographie* (Geneva, 1993).
6 See William of St Thierry, *Lettre aux frères du Mont-Dieu*, SC 223, ed. J. Déchanet (1976; repr. Paris, 1985), 24–30.

Chapter 4

1 H. E. Allen, *Writings Ascribed to Richard Rolle, Hermit of Hampole, and Materials for his Biography* (New York, 1927).
2 N. Watson, *Richard Rolle and the Invention of Authority*, Cambridge Studies in Medieval Literature 13 (Cambridge, 1991).
3 The OED defines postil as: a marginal note or comment upon a text of scripture, or upon any passage of writing; a series of such comments, a commentary or exposition; *spec.* an expository discourse or homily upon the Gospel or Epistle for the day, read or intended to be read in the church service; a book of such homilies.
4 For an outstanding study on this topic, see J. A. Alford, 'Biblical *Imitatio* in the Writings of Richard Rolle', *ELH*, 40/1 (1973), 1–23. For a general study of the Bible as literature, see R. Alter, *The Art of Biblical*

Narrative (London, 1981) and J. B. Gabel and C. B. Wheeler, *The Bible as Literature: An Introduction* (Oxford, 1986), esp. 16–41. See also F. Kermode and A. Robert (eds.), *The Literary Guide to the Bible* (1987; repr. London, 1997).

5   Alford makes use of the most important concepts and images used by Rolle to show his dependence on biblical imagery and practice. On the Rollean triad, see Alford, 'Biblical *Imitatio*', 8.

6   Ibid., 10–12; he notes that one way of amplification is by contrast (*oppositio*), which is popular in the commentary tradition.

7   It seems that Liegey was the first to name *Melos* as a postil; ibid., 12.

8   Much of what Copeland has to say on translation as rhetorical invention in the writings of Chaucer and Gower applies also to Rolle, and not only in the Middle English writings. The production of a substitute for the original (the Bible in the case of Rolle) does not necessarily need the vernacular as medium. The Latin commentaries or postils by Rolle on the Song of Songs, although making use of Latin rhetoric, nevertheless equally 'challenge the traditional hegemony of academic discourse'. See R. Copeland, *Rhetoric, Hermeneutics and Translation in the Middle Ages: Academic Traditions and Vernacular Texts*, Cambridge Studies in Medieval Literature 11 (Cambridge, 1991), 179–220.

9   The same structure also pervades his *Contra amatores mundi*; see R. Rolle, *The Contra amatores mundi of Richard Rolle of Hampole*, tr. P. F. Theiner (Berkeley and Los Angeles, 1968); see e.g. 74. 51–6.

10 Unless indicated, the translations are taken from R. Rolle, *Biblical Commentaries: Short Exposition of Psalm 20, Treatise on the Twentieth Psalm, Comment on the First Verses of the Canticle of Canticles, Commentary on the Apocalyse*, ed. R. Boenig, Salzburg Studies in English Literature, Elizabethan and Renaissance Studies 92/13 (Salzburg, 1984), 106–7 (hereafter Boenig). However, in some cases, when Boenig does not provide felicitous renderings, I have provided my own. References to the Latin text are from the following edition, 'Richard Rolle's Comment on the Canticles: Edited from MS. Trinity College, Dublin, 153' by E. M. Murray (Fordham Univ. Ph.D. thesis, 1958), hereafter referred to as Rolle, *Super cant.*; see also 'Le Commentaire de Richard Rolle sur les premiers versets du *Cantique des Cantiques*', ed. Y. Madon, *MSR*, 7 (1950), 311–25. [Dum ego propositum singulare percepissem et, relicto habitu seculari, deo pocius quam homini deservire decrevissem, contigit quod quadam nocte in principio conversionis mee michi in statu meo quiescenti apparuit quedam iuvencula, valde pulcra, quam ante videram et que me in bono amore non modicum diligebat. Quam cum intuitus essem et mirarer cur in solitudinem ad me eciam in nocte venerat, subito sine mora vel loquele iuxta me se inmisit. Quod ego senciens et ne me ad malum alliceret

timens, dixi me velle surgere et nos signo crucis benedicere, invocata sancta trinitate. At illa tam fortiter me strinxit, ut nec os ad loquendum nec manus in me sentirem ad movendum. Quod videns, perpendi ibi non mulierem, set diabolum in forma mulieris me temptasse. Verti, ergo, me ad deum et cum in mente mea dixissem, 'O Ihesu, quam preciosus est sanguis tuus,' cruce imprimens in pectore cum digito qui quodammodo iam mobilis esse inciperet, et, ecce, subito totum disparuit et ego gracias deo egi, qui me liberavit. Rolle, *Super cant.*, 47–8.]

11 R. Rolle, *The Incendium Amoris*, ed. M. Deanesly (Manchester, 1915), 178–9. For a Modern English translation, see R. Rolle, *The Fire of Love*, tr. C. Wolters (1972, repr. London, 1988), 81–2; see also Watson, *Richard Rolle*, 129–30.

12 For an account of the importance of the role of women in Rolle's writings, see R. Rolle, *The Melos amoris*, ed. E. J. F. Arnould (Oxford, 1957), xl–lvii. The edition used for this study is R. Rolle, *Le Chant d'amour* (Melos amoris), 2 vols., ed. F. Vandenbroucke, SC 168–9 (Paris, 1971) (hereafter *Melos I* and *Melos II*).

13 Bernard makes a more or less similar allusion to the secular poets in sermon 74; he also denounces monks who boast having listened to, or composed Fin' Amor songs; see *Sancti Bernardi opera omnia*, 6 vols., ed. J. Leclercq, C. H. Talbot and H. M. Rochais (Rome, 1957–77), 1, 94; 2, 239. In view of Rolle's knowledge of secular authors (Ovid and Virgil), and his use of secular formulas to describe the ideal woman, the Virgin Mary, one wonders whether Rolle may not have been involved in the making of secular songs himself, perhaps to satisfy various patrons.

14 Presto profecto ad perturbandum inimicos nostros insonuit sermo Sapientis: *Inveni*, inquit, *amariorem morte mulierem, que est laqueus venatorum*; amariorem nimirum temporali morte mulierem invenit, quia plerosque qui vitam eternam meruisse videbantur, suis immundis obumbrans osculis, ad eternam mortem incautos deducit. Hinc et laqueus venatorum demonum dicitur, per quam iam pene totus mundus retibus rugiencium inferorumque loris illusoriis laqueatur. Rolle, *Melos I*, 112.

15 O Spiritus specialis, inspira spiramen: quemadmodum cupio carnem calcare et carere cupidine squalore cooperta, ita et integre animer amore Auctoris et ambulem ad alta ardens amore. Forma feminea non flectet firmatum nec puritas pacifica pectoris pii putredini patebit, sed [spreta] spurcicia Speciosum in splendore cernere suspiro et interna intendo [intente] intueri, audacter aspiciens ad oculos Amati. Rolle, *Melos I*, 226.

16 Knowles finds Rolle's harshness in his judgement of women to be the least attractive feature of his mysticism. See D. Knowles, *The English Mystical Tradition* (1961; repr. London, 1964), 62.

17 Hec femina quia formosa erat fictos fefellit: [iuvenes] iugulat antequam

18. iudicentur et senes subvertit ne in iustificacionem succrescant; pauperes precipitat qui precipui apparebant dum paradiso se putabant properare, et divites derisit postquam despenderit quod dederunt. Rolle, *Melos I*, 268.

18. Ergo decorem non diligas que decipit et transit, nec virginem conspicias ne forte scandalizeris in decore eius. Pinguntur enim ut parietes quia, ablato ornamento illarum, horribiles apparent nam, ut ait Poeta: *Pars minima est ipsa puella sui.* Pro odore aromatum fetore frendebunt et absinthium gustantes immundi amici meretricis monile merore mutatur, et capitum corona carnalium charorum cadit in chaos cum cunctis captivis cupidinem consummans in pessimo pavore. Hinc fuge fornicariam ne fides frangatur, nam famem et frenesim fugat fidelis vita, venenum quod vomit voluptas . . . Rolle, *Melos I*, 306. The quote (in italics) is from Ovid's *Remedia amoris.* See P. Ovidis Nasonis, *Remedia amoris*, ed. A. A. R. Henderson (Edinburgh, 1979), 12.

19. Quamobrem curabant comprehendere currentem, et lubricum et lapsum iudicaverunt, putantes quod pro puellis persisterem cum pravis, cum a nullis nimirum eram absconsus qui de amore [Auctoris] audire amabant. Sed sciant simpliciter quod sanctus subsisto; similiter singuli qui male senserunt protinus peniteant ne puniantur. Errabant utique iniquum opinantes: non fallit me femina, nec pareo puellis, neque glorior in gula que iugulat gentiles. Mens quam Maiestas a malis mundavit moratur a macula in musico melode et manet in mellifluo misterio munita. Rolle, *Melos II*, 102.

20. Boenig, 78. [. . . eciam inter feminas possumus vivere et delectacionem femineam in animo nullam sentire. Rolle, *Super cant.*, 22.]

21. See A. Wilmart 'Le Cantique d'amour de Richard Rolle', *RAM*, 20–1 (1939–40), 131–48; see also G. M. Liegey, 'The *Canticum amoris* of Richard Rolle', *Traditio*, 12 (1956), 369–91. Rolle, *Melos II*, 72, mentions Mary in the same tone as that of the *Canticum amoris*, and recollects her importance during Rolle's youth. Drawing evidence from this passage, Liegey, 'The *Canticum amoris*', 372–3, defends the view that there is no discontinuity in Rolle's devotion to the Virgin Mary. For an opposite view, see Allen, *Writings*, 90–2.

22. A. is by Watson, *Richard Rolle*, 106; B. is my own. [A. Puella pulcherima prostravit ludentem / Fronsque serenissima facit hunc languentem. / Crines auro similes carpunt conquerentem; / Gene preamabiles solantur sedentem.] [B. Erecta supercilia fulgent floris florum. / Ut rosa rubent labia; os valde decorum. / Preclari sunt oculi, perpleni amorum. / Hiis gaudent iuvenculi a loris dolorum.] Liegey, 'The *Canticum amoris*', 387, sts. 4–5.

23. For other examples of secular borrowings, see *English Lyrics of the Thirteenth Century*, ed. C. Brown (Oxford, 1932); see esp. nos. 3, 43, 60

and 63. For a study of the Wooing Group, see D. Renevey, 'Enclosed Desires: A Study of the Wooing Group', in W. F. Pollard and R. Boenig (eds.), *Mysticism and Spirituality in Medieval England* (Cambridge, 1997), 39–62.

24 For example, Ann Astell argues for an affective assimilation of the feminine in Rolle's period of maturity without paying attention to those three broad categories and the genres in which those passages are found. Moreover, she argues that the gift of *canor* gradually led him to an affective assimilation of the feminine, which enabled him to have friendships with women. If one follows Astell's argument, then *Melos amoris* – probably written before *Contra*, and therefore not so many years before the epistles, which represents a climax in the expression of the gift of *canor* – should therefore demonstrate very strongly this affective assimilation of the feminine. In fact, on the contrary, it is packed with misogynistic remarks against sexually attractive women. Watson's dating of *Melos* places it after *Contra*, therefore even closer to the epistles. Both my dating and that of Watson, together with the content of *Melos*, show that, more than affective assimilation of the feminine, it is the kind of woman discussed which shapes Rolle's psychological reaction. See A. W. Astell, 'Feminine Figurae in the Writings of Richard Rolle: A Register of Growth', *MQ*, 15/3 (1989), 117–24. For a discussion of the dating of *Melos*, see Watson, *Richard Rolle*, 273–94.

25 See Rolle, *Super cant.*, 1.

26 See for instance the careful attention paid by Rolle to his translation practice and the needs of his audience, Margaret Kirkby, in his Prologue to *The English Psalter*; see 'Richard Rolle, *The English Psalter*: Prologue', in *The Idea of the Vernacular: An Anthology of Middle English Literary Theory 1280–1520*, ed. J. Wogan-Browne, N. Watson, A. Taylor and R. Evans, Exeter Medieval Texts and Studies (Exeter, 1999), 244–9; in the same volume, see also R. Evans, 'An Afterword on the Prologue', 371–8.

27 Murray argues for the use of the term in the following way: 'Rolle's avowed intention is to employ the first two and one half verses of the *Canticle of Canticles* for a spiritual treatise on contemplation. Within that framework he glosses the text, he composes a meditation, he writes a prayer, he gives lyrical expression to his feeling, he digresses on personal experience, he discusses timely questions, and disputes in the manner of the schools. The term *postilla* thus seems most descriptive of the various titles applied to the *Canticles*'. See Rolle, *Super cant.*, lii.

28 For a study of the devotion to the Name of Jesus in medieval England, see D. Renevey, '*The Name Poured Out*: Margins, Illuminations and Miniatures as Evidence for the Practice of Devotions to the Name of Jesus in Late Medieval England', *The Mystical Tradition and the*

Carthusians, Analecta Cartusiana 130/9 (Salsburg, 1996), 127–47; see also 'Anglo–Norman and Middle English Translations of the Hymn *Dulcis Iesu Memoria*', in R. Ellis and R. Tixier (eds.), *The Medieval Translator* 5 (Turnhout, 1996), 264–83; see also 'Name Above Names: The Devotion to the Name of Jesus from Richard Rolle to Walter Hilton's *Scale of Perfection* I', in *MMTE* 6 (1999), 103–21.

29 This brief summary of the main developments of *Super canticum canticorum* is borrowed from Rolle, *Super cant.*, lii–lxxiv.

30 See Matter, *Voice of my Beloved,* 151–200. For a detailed account of the Song of Songs in the liturgy, with special emphasis on Marian commentaries, see R. Fulton, 'Mimetic Devotion, Marian Exegesis, and the Historical Sense of the Song of Songs', *Viator,* 27 (1996), 85–116.

31 See Pseudo-Richard of St Victor, *Explicatio in Cantica canticorum,* PL 196, cols. 405–524.

32 Copeland offers the following comment on the new conditions of reading created by the commentary: 'Thus in medieval commentary the incorporation of rhetorical theories of argumentation into exegesis gives the hermeneutical function a heuristic force: commentary can act productively to effect a change on the text for new conditions of reading.' See Copeland, *Rhetoric,* 65.

33 Although my aim is not to trace the sources which supported the writings of Rolle, one should bear in mind that the circulation of twelfth–century authors enjoyed great popularity in the fourteenth and fifteenth centuries. For a general discussion on the topic, see G. Constable, 'The Popularity of Twelfth-century Spiritual Writers in the Late Middle Ages', in A. Molho and J. A. Tedeschi (eds.), *Renaissance: Studies in Honor of Hans Baron,* (Dekalb, IL, 1971), 3–28; and 'Twelfth–Century Spirituality and the Late Middle Ages', in O. B. Hardison (ed.), *Medieval and Renaissance Studies: Proceedings of the Southeastern Institute of Medieval and Renaissance Studies* (Chapel Hill, NC, 1971), 27–60.

34 For a consideration of *caritas* in the visual arts, see R. Freyhan, 'The Evolution of the Caritas Figure in the Thirteenth and Fourteenth Centuries', *JWCI* (1948–9), 68–86; for a definition of *caritas* as mother of all the virtues, see 68, n. 2; for a survey of the notion of *caritas*, see *DS* 2 cols. 507–691.

35 See Chapter 3 above.

36 See J. P. H. Clark, 'Richard Rolle as a Biblical Commentator', *DR,* 104 (1986), 165–213, esp. 187.

37 *Ives: Épître à Séverin sur la charité. Richard de Saint-Victor: Les Quatres Degrés de la violente charité,* ed. G. Dumeige, Textes philosophique du Moyen Age 3 (Paris, 1955), 110–51.

38 Ibid., 153; see also my discussion of Richard of St Victor's system in Chs. 1 and 2 above.

39 Ibid., 157; see also M. Jennings, 'Richard Rolle and the Three Degrees of Love', *DR*, 93 (1975), 193–200; see esp. 195.
40 See Richard of St Victor, *Les Quatres Degrés*, 167; see Allen, *Writings*, 66–8; see also Clark, 'Richard Rolle as a Biblical Commentator', 185–6.
41 For a study of Rolle's theology, see J. P. H. Clark, 'Richard Rolle: A Theological Re-assessment', *DR*, 100 (1983), 108–39; see esp. 124–6, where Clark suggests that Rolle's degrees of love derive directly from the *De IV Gradibus*; see also Jennings, 'Three Degrees', 197–200.
42 This translation is mine; see also Boenig, 57. [Amodo igitur O virgines celo suspicite; ibi sponsum querite; cum amatoribus mundi nolite vos inquinare. Fatuas enim virgines Christus se non cogniturum asserit, quas mundialis amore vanitatis ab illo nunc expellit. Ille utique iam pompose muliercule in tortis crinibus, cornibus elatis incedentes, solo amore carnali decorari appetunt. Illam solam viam que Christo ducit odiunt et abhorrent, quia autem formam et substanciam a deo datam frustra et nequiter non curant effundere. Rolle, *Super cant.*, 2.]
43 Boenig, 59. [Fervor utique divini amoris speculacionis preit dulcorem, quia nisi Christum quis recte diligit, proculdubio in canore celestis contemplacionis non iubilabit. Contemplativa vero suavitas mortis precedit desiderium, quia tunc cum gaudio morimur quando delicias eterni amoris canentes, solam in deo delectacionem contemplamur. Foras enim mittitur omnis transitorie cupidinis delectacio, dum igne sancti spiritus veraciter inardescimus, et eternitatis gloriam incessanter desideramus. *Qui autem adheret deo*, ut ait apostolus, *unus spiritus est* cum eo. Unde et in hoc nostrum consistit gaudium, cum deus in nobis habitat, ut nos in eo vivamus. Rolle, *Super cant.*, 4.]
44 This translation is mine; see Boenig, 56. [Nimirum immundicie amatores in hiis verbis nequaquam placuerunt Christum. Rapitur autem divine contemplacionis dulcedine, ardorem incircumscripti luminis presentit veraciter, qui in hiis verbis, *Osculetur me osculo oris sui* deum recte glorificat. Rolle, *Super cant.*, 1.]
45 R. Copeland, 'Richard Rolle and the Rhetorical Theory of the Levels of Style', *MMTE* 3, (1984), 55–80; see esp. 76.
46 Riehle offers a precise overview of the use of the Song of Songs imagery in English mystical works. His study considers the use of metaphors of love from Bede's commentary to *A Talking of the Love of God*. See W. Riehle, *The Middle English Mystics*, tr. B. Standring (London, 1981), 34–55.
47 For a case study of the conceptualization of feeling, see G. Lakoff, *Women, Fire and Dangerous Things: What Categories Reveal about the Mind* (Chicago and London, 1987), 377–415.
48 Boenig, 60–1. [In hoc autem intelligimus quia incircumscriptum lumen verum est et eternum; nam, cum mentes nostras illuminat, quanto ab illo

calore medullitus exurimur, tanto suavius cum deo gloriamur. Non autem quemadmodum sol iste materialis, qui se diu considerantes pene excecat; set proculdubio, qui illum solem celestis patrie cum desiderio et diligencia non respicit, sine fine cecus erit. Eternum utique illud lumen indubitanter cognoscimus quia quanto diucius in hac vita vivimus, tanto illud veracius sentimus. Rolle, *Super cant.*, 5.]

[49] This translation is mine. [Venter saturatus venerem pocius quam Christum amplexatur. Rolle, *Super cant.*, 10]; Boenig, 66, translates: 'They have venerated the filling of their stomach rather than embraced Christ'. This translation is inaccurate, as the word *venerem* cannot stand for a third person plural in any of the tenses of the verb *venerare*. Madon, 'Le *Commentaire* de Richard Rolle', 324–5, gives the correct French translation: 'Un ventre rassasié embrasse Venus beaucoup plus que le Christ'. The Wife of Bath knows her Ovid as well, as she comments: 'And after wyn on Venus moste I thynke'; see G. Chaucer, *The Riverside Chaucer*, ed. L. D. Benson (1987; repr. Oxford, 1988), 111 (l. 464). I am grateful to the official reader of the press for pointing out this Ovidian borrowing (*Ars amatoria*, 229–44). As for Rolle's possible deep knowledge of the pagan authors, and more especially Ovid, one should recollect that the *Liber Catonianis* was the schooltext for students par excellence. It contained six classical texts: one of them, the fourth text, the *Elegiae Maximiani*, was sometimes replaced in England by Ovid's *Remedia amoris*, a work with much 'more overt "morality" and misogyny'. See M. C. Woods and R. Copeland, 'Classroom and Confession', in D. Wallace (ed.), *The Cambridge History of Medieval English Literature* (Cambridge, 1999), 376–406, esp. 382.

[50] See E. F. Kittay, *Metaphor: Its Cognitive Force and Linguistic Structure* (1987; repr. Oxford, 1989), 32; see also S. H. Phillips, 'Mysticism and Metaphor', *International Journal for the Philosophy of Religion*, 23 (1988), 17–41; see also C. Barrett, 'The Language of Ecstasy and the Ecstasy of Language', in M. Warner (ed.), *The Bible as Rhetoric: Studies in Biblical Persuasion and Credibility* (London, 1990), 205–21.

[51] See Copeland, *Rhetoric*, 83.

[52] This translation is mine; see also Boenig, 76–7. [Set et ideo languet ad osculum *quia meliora sunt ubera tua vino*. Nam si ubera Christi meliora vino non intelligeret, profecto querere osculum non auderet. Quia nisi in divinis doctrinis delectari satagimus proculdubio ad suavitatem eterne dulcedinis veraciter non suspiramus. Hoc manifestum est quandoquidem et laicus, quam cito divino amore se tactum senserit, ad audiendum et loquendum de deo, secularibus curis postpositis, vehementer inardescit. Quanto eciam magis nos qui eciam, iuvante deo, scripturas sacras intelligere possumus ad legendum et audiendum verbum dei ac aliis scribendis et docendis nos accingere debemus. Rolle, *Super cant.*, 20–1.]

Laicus, with *illiteratus, rusticus* and *idiota* were used to name the illiterate; see B. Stock, *The Implications of Literacy* (Princeton, 1983), 27.

53 This translation is mine; see Boenig, 88. [Hic igitur ab hac proteccione dei reprobus excluditur qui instabilis in prosperis cadens in adversis a demone deportatur. Sicut enim beata sunt ubera que sancti suxerunt, sic maledicta sunt ubera que peccatores nutrierunt. Set volo ut hic nichil carnale intelligas, set totum spirituale. Cum diabolus inventor sit primus et pater peccati, mali cum peccant quasi ab eo nati sunt. Illos eius ubera nutriunt, dum ad gulam et luxuriam et ad cetera vicia letantes vadunt. Rolle, *Super cant.*, 31.]

54 Gilbert of Hoyland gives an excellent description of *ruminatio* in his fifth sermon on *The Song;* see *The Works of Gilbert of Hoyland. Sermons on the Song of Songs,* 1, tr. L. C. Braceland, Cistercian Fathers Series 14 (Kalamazoo, 1978), 85–6.

55 The analogy between the wound motif and the ancient love–arrow is stressed by Riehle, *Middle English Mystics,* 47–8.

56 This translation is mine; see Boenig, 69. [*Osculetur me.* Cum sancta mens tam crebro suavia verba repetat, quid aliud insinuat nisi hoc quod ostendere nititur? Quia omnis vere electa anima amore divino vulneratur. Vulneratus autem querit medicum, et caritate tactus animus ardescit in conditorem. Liquet profecto quia huiusmodi vulnus non est livoris set amoris, non doloris set dulcoris. Osculum non cessat petere, quia eternitatis gaudium non torpet desiderare. Et dum osculum ardenter petitur, deus se totum infundit in animam et mirabiliter letificat eam, quam dum eterno amore inebriat, salubri lancea vulnerata, supra cuncta terrena desideria levat. Rolle, *Super cant.*, 13–14.]

57 In a certain way Rolle does with his own message what patristic criticism does with the Bible and theological texts: 'It addresses particular textual conditions only in so far as these aid or impede access to supra–textual meaning. The problem of difference, of linguistic and literary heterogeneity, is of course a central theme in patristic theory; but whereas Roman theory seeks to erase difference (even as it recognizes it) by foreclosing the originary claims of the source and substituting Latin for Greek, patristic criticism seeks more to resolve difference by pointing towards a communality of source and target in terms of the immanence of being.' See Copeland, *Rhetoric,* 43.

58 Boenig, 73–4. [Vere scio quod in deo magnum sentit gaudium, qui ab eo petit osculum. Unde et hoc non auderem petere, nisi scirem illum hoc me velle. Ex magna enim amoris delectacione animus ad superna rapitur et eterni luminis splendore circumfultus archana dei profunde perscrutatur ... Sic vero, dum se totam in una eterni amoris flagrancia indesinenter colligit, se intus iugiter retinens amodo ad exteriora oblectamenta cupienda nequaquam fluit. Et quia internis deliciis delicate depascitur, in

solo conditoris desiderio anhelans dissolui letaretur. Unde non mirum quia anima que tanto eterne suavitatis ardore liquefit adhuc suspirans dicit, *Osculetur me*. Rolle, *Super cant.*, 17–18.]

59 See Rolle, *Super cant.*, 18; see also Boenig, 74.
60 See Freyhan, 'Evolution', 83–5.
61 Clark notes also how Sg. 1: 2 serves in the making of the theme of Jesus as mother. See Clark, 'Richard Rolle as a Biblical Commentator', 177. For further studies on the theme of Jesus as mother, but with no reference to Rolle, see C. W. Bynum, *Jesus as Mother: Studies in the Spirituality of the High Middle Ages* (Berkeley, 1982).
62 Boenig, 86–7. [Unde et, allegorice loquendo, ad quemlibet sanctum potest dici illud quod mulier dixit in evangelio ad Christum. *Beatus venter, qui te portavit, et ubera que suxisti.* Quemadmodum namque antequam in mundum nascimur corporaliter in matris utero portamur, et priusquam ambulare vel currere vel aliquem cibum forte sumere possumus necessarie est ut lac ab uberibus matris capiamus; ita, spiritualiter, ante baptismum vel ante penitenciam, in utero Christi, id est, in paciencia sua, ne vel abortivi suffocemur, vel diversis sceleribus dampnati simus, gestamur. Cum vero per baptismum vel per penitenciam a carcere infidelitatis vel iniquitatis parturiente nos deo extracti fuerimus, opus habemus ut lac quo nutriamur sugendo ad ubera pendamus. Rolle, *Super cant.*, 29–30.]
63 See Liegey, 'The *Canticum amoris*', 370; Liegey notes that both the gospel of the feast and the gospel of the vigil are important elements of Rolle's devotion and mark many of his writings.
64 Boenig, 93. [Est itaque caritas virtutum perfectissima, nobilissima et suavissima, quam iste sanctus possidere meruit qui, de virtute in virtutem transiens, usque ad summam pervenit. Istam virtutem amantem cum amato scimus coniungere, id est, Christum cum electa anima perenniter copulare. Reformat autem in nobis caritas summe trinitatis ymaginem, et creaturam creatori facit esse simillimam. Rolle, *Super cant.*, 35.]
65 See entries in the *Dictionary of Medieval Latin from British Sources*, 2, ed. R. E. Latham (Oxford, 1981); see also J. N. Adams, *The Latin Sexual Vocabulary* (London, 1982), 179–80.
66 For a discussion of the different styles used by Rolle in accordance with the degree of love he is describing, see Copeland, 'Richard Rolle', 55–80.
67 Boenig, 93–4. [O donum caritatis quam vales pre omnibus quod solum supremum gradum tibi vendicas cum angelis, quanto enim quis de te in via plus accipit, tanto in patria sublimior et gloriosior erit. O singulare caritatis gaudium, quod tuos ligas vinculis, supra mundialia quaque usque ad celestia rapis! Qui te non habet in terris, iacet quicquid habet; qui autem in te toto posse letari nititur, supra terrena cito levatur. O cara caritas, quam bona es; que sola coram conditore apparere non formidas!

Tu audacter intras in cubiculum eterni regis; tu sola Christum rapere non vereris. Ipse est quem quesisti; ipse est quem amasti. Tuus Christus est; tene illum. Non potest te non suscipere, cui soli desiderasti obedire. Sine te, prorsus nulla Christo placent opera. Ergo tua est sedes celica; tua est societas angelica; tua est sanctitas mirifica; tua est visio dei glorifica; tua est vita sine fine permansura. Dampnabuntur omnes qui in te saluari non confidunt. O desideranda caritas, que famem relevas, extinguis sitim, frigus calefacis! Tu es vestis qua induti ad mensam Christi immobiles assistemus. Quid de tua laude dicam? Quicquid dixero, fateor, non sufficio. O quam magna es, que eciam miseros facis magnos! O quam gloriosa, que mortales facis impassibiles! Recte, ergo, dicitur: quia fortis est *dileccio* que *omnia vincit*. Rolle, *Super cant.*, 35–6 (italics are mine).] This passage is an example of what Copeland calls the 'inexpressibility topos'; see Copeland, 'Richard Rolle', 55–80. The passage in italics, *dileccio vincit omnia*, is an adaptation from Virgil's *Eclogue* (10. 69), *amor vincit omnia*, which is found on the brooch of the Prioress, one of the dubious religious characters of Chaucer's *Canterbury Tales*; see Chaucer, *The Riverside Chaucer*, 26 (l. 162).

68 See Copeland, 'Richard Rolle', 69.
69 See Watson, 'Translation', 177.
70 For a study of possible influences on Rolle, see F. J. E. Raby, *A History of Christian–Latin Poetry* (Oxford, 1953), 389–95; for a study of the influence of Howden on Rolle, see *Poems of John of Hoveden*, ed. F. J. E. Raby, Surtees Society 154 (Durham, 1939), 154; see also John of Hoveden, *Philomena*, ed. C. Blume, Hymnologische Beiträge, 4 (Leipzig, 1930); the best account on the influence of Howden on Rolle is in R. Rolle, *Richard Rolle's Expositio super novem lectiones mortuorum*, 2 vols, ed. M. R. Moyes, Analecta Cartusiana 92/12 (Salzburg, 1988), esp. 1, 47–53; see also Watson, 'Translation', 178.
71 For a thorough discussion of affectivity in Rolle's system, see V. Gillespie, 'Mystic's Foot: Rolle and Affectivity', *MMTE* 2 (1982), 199–230.
72 Boenig, 56. [Amplectitur igitur sponsas suas, que omnes una sunt sponsa, et mellifluo amoris osculo omnes et singulas saciat, eternisque amplexibus confortat. Rolle, *Super cant.*, 1.]
73 This translation is mine; see Boenig, 107. [Est itaque verus amor, castus, sanctus, voluntarius amatum pro seipso non pro suis amans, in amato se totum figens, nil extra se querens, de se contentus, flagrans, estuans, ex amato inardescens, vehemens, se in se ligans, impetuosus miro modo, omnem modum excedens, ad solum amatum se extendens, cuncta alia contempnens set et obliviscens, in amato canens, illum cogitans, illum incessanter meminens, ascendens desiderio, pergens in amato, ruens in amplexibus, absortus in osculis, totus liquescens igne ardentis amoris, ut

tibi, O bone Ihesu, merito dicatur: *Adolescentule dilexerunt te nimis.* Rolle, *Super cant.*, 49.]

74 This translation is mine; see Boenig, 126. [Et dum a priore rigore et nocivo frigore liquescit, ad amplectendum, ad osculandum dilectum eciam aliquando nec tracta nec vocata curit. Rolle, *Super cant.*, 67.]

75 It is beyond the scope of this work to study the relations between metaphors and images. However, the reproduction and interpretation through images of the whole of the Song of Songs in *La Bible moralisée* is revealing of the ways the vocabulary of love could be set into pictures; see *La Bible moralisée conservée à Oxford, Paris et Londres: Reproduction intégrale du manuscrit du xiiie siècle*, 2 (Paris, 1912), pls. 290–317 (fols. 66–93^v in Paris, Bibliothèque Nationale, MS Latin 11560).

76 The writings of an author like Margery Kempe evidences this fact forcefully; see *The Book of Margery Kempe*, ed. H. E. Allen and S. B. Meech, EETS OS 212 (1940; repr. Oxford, 1961).

77 For an adaptation of this passage and other extracts in Rolle's writings devoted to the name, see the compilation *Orationes ad honorem nominis Ihesu* in R. Rolle, *Emendatio Vitae. Orationes ad honorem nominis Ihesu: Edited from Cambridge University Library MSS Dd.v.64 and Kk.vi.20*, ed. N. Watson, Toronto Medieval Latin Texts 21 (Toronto, 1995).

78 Boenig, 96. [Tibi vero, O domina, congruit ab eterno rege osculum petere et accipere, que eciam os eius meruisti lactare, et merito, *quia meliora sunt ubera tua vino*. O beata ubera, que eternus conditor non renuit sugere, et ab illis, secundum morem infancium, lac haurire. O mater, electa et vere gloriosa, quantis affluisti deliciis cum illud os eterni patris os suum tuo applicuit, et tenellis digitis mamillas contrectavit. Consolaris flentem, set expectas alludentem. Rolle, *Super cant.*, 38.]

79 Boenig, 97. [O Ihesu pie, infunde in visceribus nostris hoc oleum; scribe in cordibus nostris nomen tuum. Cum pro nobis voluisti oleum effusum vocari nomen tuum, da nobis illud oleum ad gustandum, ad amandum, ad amplectendum. Rolle, *Super cant.*, 39.]

80 Boenig, 97. [Hoc oleum nos reficiat; hoc oleum nos perficiat; hoc oleum nos impinguet; hoc oleum delectet. Rolle, *Super cant.*, 39.]

81 See Rolle, *Super cant.*, 47–50.

82 Ibid., 51.

83 Boenig, 109–10. [Hoc nempe manifeste videtur, quando, quidem in sanctis hominibus, deus secundum capacitatem suam se infundit. Cum, igitur, deus non in se set in nobis grandescat, liquido colligere possumus quod in illa anima grandissimum se ostendit, in qua plenius et perfeccius se per suam graciam infundit. Quamobrem, cum constet omnibus sancte matris ecclesie filiis quia nemo deum in se manentem habet nisi qui caritatem habet, quoniam qui deum non amat frustra se deum habere dicit, sequitur profecto, quod qui minus deum diligit eciam minus de deo

sentit et qui maius in caritate exardet, perfeccius et habundancius deum habet. Rolle, *Super cant.*, 51.]
84   See Rolle, *Super cant.*, 54.
85   Boenig, 115–16. [Multi vocati ad fidem; pauci electi ad salvacionem, quia nisi caritate quis vestitus fuerit, nulli dubium quin a nupciis expulsus erit. Hec igitur virtus que est caritas magna est et nimis magna, quoniam illam non inveniunt aliqui nisi cari amici dei. Non metuet autem ante tribunal Christi assistere qui caritatem secum poterit portare. Multi multa tribuunt; alii magna faciunt; alii dura paciuntur; alii miranda operantur; alii misteria sciunt; alii summa predicant; set ille solus salvandus est qui caritatem habiturus est. Nulli frustra amant quamvis multi frustra agant. Hec autem caritas si vera erit maximo labore adquiritur, set vere habita inexcogitabili dulcore possidetur. Rolle, *Super cant.*, 56–7.]
86   Boenig, 117. [Et amor non est tractus, set spontaneus, seipsum libenter afficiens pro amato, eciam cum delectacione currens ad amatum. Rolle, *Super cant.*, 58.] In the *Contra amatores mundi*, Rolle is more expansive about the difficulties in talking about eternal love. He admits that the task is beyond all human intellect: 'In truth I confess that my powers fail me when I try to speak of eternal love, because I cannot express in words in what abundance I conceive the sweetness of divine love in my own mind. My tongue fails me; my mind is not up to the task, for this is beyond all human intellect.' *Contra*, 172. [Verum fateor vires meas succumbere nitens loqui de eterno amore, quia verbis exprimere nequeo quantum de divine dileccionis suavitate in mente concipio; lingua deficit; cogitacio non sufficit, nam omnem humanum superat intellectum. *Contra*, 88.]
87   Boenig, 117. [Nullus ergo ad deum trahitur, nisi is qui eciam toto affectu trahi amando conatur. Rolle, *Super cant.*, 58.]
88   I make extensive use of the introduction by Vandenbroucke for my general summary of *Melos amoris*; see Rolle, *Melos I*, 46–52.
89   Murray, li–lii, argues that the term *postilla* describes best *Super canticum*. Even if it is true that, in his commentary, Rolle offers material which is not strictly exegetical, I believe it is best to keep that term for *Melos amoris*.
90   See Arnould, *Melos amoris*, lxviii–lxxi; see Watson, *Rolle*, 286–93.
91   Arnould, *Melos amoris*, lxviii.
92   Urget igitur amoris habundancia ut audeam aperire eloquium ad informacionem aliorum, ostendens altitudinem amancium ardentissime iusticiamque iubilancium iocunde in Iesu ac charitatem canencium in conformitate celica, necnon et claritatem conscienciarum capacium increati caloris et delectacionis indeficientis. Rolle, *Melos I*, 98.
93   For a different approach to *Melos*, regarded as the climax of Rolle's career as an *auctor*, see Watson, *Rolle*, 171–91.

[94] See R. Rolle, *The Fire of Love* (London, 1988), 93–4; for the Latin version, see R. Rolle, *The Incendium amoris*, ed. M. Deanesly (Manchester, 1915), 42–3.

[95] See Arnould, *Melos amoris*, lvii–lx; see Rolle, *Melos I*, 53–8; see Watson, *Rolle*, 174; see also S. de Ford, 'The Use and Function of Alliteration in the *Melos amoris* of Richard Rolle', *MQ*, 22 (1986), 59–66.

[96] See Gillespie, 'Mystic's Foot', 214–16, which emphasizes the contrast between earthly song and spiritual song in *The Form of Living*, *Melos amoris* and *Contra amatores mundi*; for evidence of the use of musical vocabulary in *Melos*, see Rolle, *Melos II*, Table des Thèmes: Chant, 284–6.

[97] Music is a significant element in his mysticism. A substantial study on that aspect has been carried on in Germany by F. Schulte, 'Das musikalische Element in der Mystik Richard Rolles von Hampole' (Univ. of Bonn Ph.D. thesis, 1951), which is unfortunately not easily available.

[98] In istis itaque internis occupatus liber animus solaciis, mundiales expurgans maculas, in supernam curiam nititur transcurrere, et dilectissima Deo [anima] ab eterno Conditore osculum se [promit] postulare. In hoc autem [incunctanter] signum clemencie excipitur, dum per concordantes mentes labia coniunguntur, hanc quippe unionem invisibilem [esse] ac spiritalem in divulgando [dulcedinem] dilectis Dei ostendimus. Nam irrepercussa mentis acie in illud lumen plane iocundissimum rapi [congaudemus]. See Rolle, *Melos I*, 108.

[99] Epulantes utique in solaciis simphonie celice assistunt diviciis virtutum virore vernantibus, in canticis charitatis [concenter] cum celigenis concinunt, et melle Maiestatis mirifice molliti, omnium peccatorum rubiginem calore increato continue consumunt. Ibid.

[100] For a discussion of memory in medieval culture, see M. Carruthers, *The Book of Memory: A Study of Memory in Medieval Culture*, Cambridge Studies in Medieval Literature 10 (1990; repr. Cambridge, 1993); on synaesthesia, see esp. 78–9.

[101] Vivunt in gloria, invisibilis vite fruuntur melodia. O dulce, delectabile et desiderandum osculum quod tantum confert gaudium, gignit devotos, nutrit ferventes, perficit pios! Dum enim intra nos eterni amoris delicias canentes supra nos rapimur, secundum affluenciam divinitus degustatam, in miro amoris gaudio granditer gratulamur. Et hec sunt cantica canticorum et gaudia gaudiorum. Rolle, *Melos I*, 110.

[102] See Copeland, 'Richard Rolle', 72.

[103] Rolle mentions *ruminatio* a bit further in *Melos*: 'Verum, si invenerit hunc canticum quisquam, manet medullitus mente mutata nec recedit revera: nam recte ruminatur iugi in iubilo, donec representet reddatque raptum Regi regnanti, ut semper subsistat in solio solempni et sedeat

cum summis, ut Seraphyn succensus'. See *Melos I*, 132. For a study of *ruminatio*, see J. Leclercq, *Études sur le vocabulaire monastique du Moyen Age*, Studia Anselmiana 48 (Rome, 1961), 35; see also J. Leclercq, *L'Amour des lettres et le désir de Dieu: Initiation aux auteurs monastiques du Moyen Age* (1957; repr. Paris, 1990), 72.

104 Itaque aiebat in exordio oraculum amancium: *Osculetur me osculo oris sui*. Hec verba vitalem virorem iocundamque iubilacionem emanant, in quibus eciam et mistica et mirifica memorantur. Rolle, *Melos I*, 130.

105 Divinum itaque osculum est solacium sentire eterni amoris. Ibid., 144.

106 Hanc amavi et exquisivi a iuventute mea, quesivi sponsam michi eam accipere, *et factus sum amator forme illius*, ... Ibid., 154.

107 For a discussion of *The Twelve Patriarchs*, see ch. 1.

108 Sanctus solitarius, quia pro Salvatore suo sedere sustinuit in solitudine, sedem in celestibus accipiet auream et excellentem inter ordines angelorum. Et quia vilibus vestibus pro amore Autoris induebatur, *tunicam talarem* et eternam in claritate Conditoris confectam induet, pallium quoque pulcherrimum lapidibus preciosis intextum inter paradisicolas potestates portabit in perpetuum. Rolle, *Melos II*, 140–2. There is an even more forceful use of the cloak in Rolle, *Melos I*, 314: 'Sed puto sine pravitate quod Potentissimus, pro quo pati potueram in paciencia, me perficiens, pallium preciosissimum inter paradisicolas principes in populis perfectis ad perpetuam possessionem michi paravit, et *tunicam talarem* tradet Trinitas quam tenui *inconsutilem* utique propter charitatem que non cadet et contextam per claritatem desuper per totum *descendentem* denique *A Patre luminum*'; see also 314, n. 4, which suggests 1 Cor. 15: 53–4; Gen. 37: 23; 2 Kings 13: 18; John 19: 23 and James 1: 17 as the biblical sources for this theme; see also Rolle, *Melos II*, Table des Thèmes, 319–20. The cloak image recurs in many devotional and mystical texts. The description of Haukyn the Actif Man is a well known example: 'I took greet kepe, by Crist, and Conscience bothe, Of Haukyn the Actif Man, and how he was yclothed. He hadde a cote of Cristendom as Holy Kirke bileveth; Ac it was moled in many places with manye sondry plottes – Of pride here a plot, and there a plot of unbuxom speche, Of scornyng and of scoffyng and of unskiful berynge'; see W. Langland, *The Vision of Piers Plowman: A Critical Edition of the B–Text based on Trinity College Cambridge MS B. 15. 17*, ed. A. V. C. Schmidt (London, 1984), passus XIII, ll. 271–6; see also J. Simpson, *Piers Plowman: An Introduction to the B–Text* (London, 1990), 157–61.

109 Inde enim accipiemus animam adornatam habitu albissimo, et circumfulta felicitate infallibi illustratur lumine splendentis speciei. Protinus ponetur in spera in gradu grandescens usque ad globam gloriosam et, obumbrata osculis optatis Dilecti dantis donum dignissimum, ... Rolle, *Melos I*, 180.

[110] It is the result again of an association of biblical references between Sg. 1: 1 and 2: 3 (*Sub umbra illius quem desiderabam sedi et [fructus] eius dulcis gutturi [meo]*.) Rolle, *Melos II*, 80–2, describes almost indifferently the Lover and the Tree of Joy and therefore throws light on the expression *obumbratio osculum*. See also *ombre* in Rolle, *Melos II*, Table des Thèmes, 309–10. For the use of the kiss–shadow cluster in *Melos*, see Rolle, *Melos I*, 244, 276, 290; *Melos II*, 80, 82, 92, 174, 214.

[111] Et unde hoc accidet anime electe nisi quod obumbratur itaque auxiliis Auctoris sedetque similiter sub cella salutis et muro magnifico a malis munitur, roris refrigerio recte respirans? Plane perspicimus hanc non posse perferri a pravitate pungente ut a tribulante non torreatur et in pacem putari per pugnam probata nisi quia gaudium gratis gustavit sermonis sequentis: *Et fructus eius dulcis gutturi meo*. Apparet exinde quod habet amorem et estuat amplexibus et osculum optatum sub arbore accepit lignumque leticie se latenter linivit et sustulit a scelere et erroribus iniquis, ac fructus eferbens ex flore felici fantasmata fugavit et funeris furorem Dei dilectam devotam ac dignam dulcissime depascens. Rolle, *Melos II*, 92.

[112] The significance of biblical references to describe mystical union is discussed by de Ford, 'Mystical Union', 173–201; esp. 181–2.

[113] See Rolle, *Melos II*, 92, n. 1.

[114] See Liegey, 'The *Canticum amoris*', 376–9; Liegey asserts that Rolle was familiar with the tradition of secular love poetry and stresses especially that Rolle shows 'complete familiarity with conventional languishings of the unfortunate lover of "La Belle Dame sans merci"'.

[115] Deinde a doloribus, dulcedine divina, digne discedens et, doctus disciplina, dicit per verba Veritatis, in virtute virescens: *Sagitte Domini in me sunt quarum indignacio ebibit spiritum meum*. Per penitenciam profecto precordia pectoris penetrantur et purgatis penetralibus paciencia preparatur. Siquidem sauciati sagittas ex superis senciunt sufflatas, ut nimirum non nesciant se necti cum nobilibus a naufragio et nominaliter nasci ad subsistendum cum sanctis. Rolle, *Melos I*, 202. The secular influence does not necessarily bring new imagery, but rather an alternative for the treatment and elaboration of the love motif. In the case of this quote, the passage in italics is a borrowing from Job 6: 4.

[116] Devotional treatises of the fourteenth and fifteenth centuries make abundant use of the wound and the blood motifs in their defence of the mixed life; see for instance *The Prickynge of Love*, ed. H. Kane, Salzburg Studies in English Literature, Elizabethan and Renaissance Studies 92/10 (1983), 8–10, 19–22, 69, *et passim*; for further examples of such texts, see V. Gillespie, 'Strange Images of Death: The Passion in Later Medieval English Devotional and Mystical Writing', *Zeit, Tod und Ewigkeit in der Renaissance Literatur*, Analecta Cartusiana 117/3 (Salzburg, 1987), 111–59.

117 See Rolle, *Melos I*, 204.
118 Ibid., 309–10.
119 Itaque et honor refertur Regnanti ut habeat amicam pulcherimam et puram, que donis et deliciis decora ditetur, dissipans demonia ne dire dominentur. Coronam in capite percipiet preclaram et dignum diadema plaudens portabit, in lumine lavabitur liquide letando, que nunc amore languens in laude ludiflua liquescit libenter et, rediens ad requiem, rata regina in sponsi amplexus ruet reverenter, assistens cum angelis in sede suprema ubi excellens amet ardenter sicuti Seraphin proxima Dilecto. Vestem lucidissimam induet ibi et in precioso lapide decor dulcescet. Non ut picta paries ad punctum [parebunt], sed eternus erit ornatus illarum: fulgebunt feliciter in hoc sine fine facie Factoris famosissimi fruentes. Rolle, *Melos I*, 310–12.
120 Ibid., 312. The *Lyfe of Soule*, a fourteenth-century religious manual preoccupied with the ten commandments and the Bible, also uses the clothing imagery in association with the virtues and the wedding: 'I preye the that thou write to me more opunliche of the liflode of my soule to kele the hungur and the thrist of my soule, and telle me opunlyche the virtues that Crist techith to clothe with my soule, that I be not naked in the comyng of my Lord, but be wel iclothed in my weddyng cloth.' *The Lyfe of Soule*, ed. H. Moon, Salzburg Studies in English Literature, Elizabethan and Renaissance Studies 75 (Salzburg, 1978), 20. The description of the celestial court in *Pearl* is based on similar premisses as in Rolle; for a comparison, see *The Poems of the Pearl Manuscript: Pearl, Cleanness, Patience, Sir Gawain and the Green Knight*, ed. M. Andrew and R. Waldron (1978; repr. Exeter, 1987), Stanza Group XIX, ll. 1093–1152.
121 Crines quoque colli cordis cogitaciones charitate crassati consociato canore... Rolle, *Melos I*, 324.
122 See Rolle, *Melos*, 38–9.
123 Although a common secular love topos, it is more likely that Rolle borrowed the nightingale image from John of Howden's *Philomena* and John Pecham's *Philomela*; see Watson, *Richard Rolle*, 121–2, 139, 172, 254.
124 ... unde hoc accidit in mente amante quod clare consurgo in canticum charorum et ad finem feliciter cum fervore festinans liquidus elevor Letificanti, languore ligante. Perfruens Factore sic funditus affectus fio ut philomena que concinens continue usque ad mortem in melos diligit dulcissime quia hec demum moritur melum amando et mesticia amati deducta deficit, ut dicitur, pre dileccione. Languent sic siquidem viscera virorum qui vadunt in hac via per callem [amoris] et charitas Creantis cremat in corde, ac melos mellifluum mentem demulcet, auribusque intrinsecus organum resultat laudancium Deum. Rolle, *Melos II*, 236; see also *Melos I*, 46, n. 4.

Chapter 5

1. R. Rolle, *The Contra amatores mundi*, ed. P. F. Theiner (Berkeley and Los Angeles, 1968), 39–41 (hereafter *Contra*). Theiner defends the assumption that the *Contra* is a mature work on the grounds that Rolle refers to his 'many little works' in the fourth chapter of the treatise, and that the expression refers literally to his other works; see also N. Watson, *Richard Rolle and the Invention of Authority*, Cambridge Studies in Medieval Literature 13 (Cambridge, 1991), 278, 293–4.
2. See Rolle, *Contra*, 6–28.
3. Watson's evidence for this chronology is supported by only one extract. The evidence used for his demonstration is the sentence 'et hoc audeo annuere' (most MSS read 'annectere') in *Melos*, which he claims to be evidence of an addition for the new context of *Melos*; see Watson, *Rolle*, 293–4. But the reverse could be argued as convincingly: *Contra*, less inflated with self-referential comments, omits this sentence in which his *persona* is part of the claim.
4. For a view on the transference from one genre into another by Rolle, see J. A. Alford, 'Biblical *Imitatio* in the Writings of Richard Rolle', *ELH*, 40/1 (1973), 10.
5. On the tension created by the necessary rejection of the things of the world, see Rolle, *Contra*, 9–11.
6. Theiner argues that Rolle writes here 'through himself' rather than of himself or for himself; see Rolle, *Contra*, 20.
7. Ibid., 23.
8. For a study of *Contra*, with reference to what Watson considers to be the prologue of the work, see Watson, *Rolle*, 159–70.
9. The opposition *caritas/cupiditas* (or *concupiscentia*) is a major structural device in other works too; see Alford, 'Biblical *Imitatio*', 13.
10. See Watson, *Rolle*, 160. Theiner demonstrates the effects of this in his analysis of a passage dealing with the lover leaving the nuptial bed and letting the beloved languish in sorrow: 'It is not difficult to see that this metaphor partakes of implicit contradictions which must inevitably lead to paradox; when the very work of art in which the metaphor must operate is sharply divided into two contrasting elements, one of which – *Contra amatores mundi* – is wholly devoted to the castigation and denigration of the kind of love which must then serve as the means by which the exaltation of the second element – *de amore de* – is effected, the paradox is brought into sharp focus.' See Rolle, *Contra*, 25.
11. See H. E. Allen, *Writings Ascribed to Richard Rolle, Hermit of Hampole, and Materials for his Biography* (New York, 1927), 208; see also 203–9. Allen stresses that the three attributes of ecstasy are mentioned and that 'the devotion to the Holy Name of Jesus does appear explicitly in this

work'. She believes that *Contra* is a rather mature work, although in her chronology it precedes *Incendium amoris*. For evidence that the reprimands found in *Contra* would as well apply to individuals in the religious orders, see the fourteenth-century account of the nunnery of Hampole, which was not devoid of sexual scandals, as well as other embarrassments caused by the ornate clothing of certain nuns; see *VHCE* 3, *A History of Yorkshire* (London, 1974), 164.

12. See Rolle, *Contra*, 101.
13. Heu michi misero; quia qualicumque solitario, ita fit in meis temporibus quod nec unum invenio qui cupit mecum currere, ac sedendo et tacendo eterni amoris delicias [desiderare]. Rolle, *Contra*, 86.
14. Ibid., 74.
15. See N. Watson, 'Richard Rolle as Elitist and as Popularist: The Case of *Judica me*', in M. G. Sargent (ed.), *De cella in seculum: Religious and Secular Life and Devotion in Late Medieval England* (Cambridge, 1989), 123–44; Watson provides interesting comments on Rolle's concern for the status of the solitary life.
16. For an account of Rolle's conversion, see *The Officium and Miracula of Richard Rolle of Hampole*, ed. R. Woolley (London, 1919).
17. Quia vero oblitis aliis rebus amorem Christi canere, sive in ecclesia sive in villa, aut alibi cogitare non desinit, huic solomodo intentus, nonnulli videntes putant quod insanit, dicentes illum irreverenciam deo facere et statuta ecclesie non observare. Rolle, *Contra*, 69.
18. For other examples where the body becomes a book to be read and glossed, see D. Renevey, 'Margery's Performing Body: The Translation of Late Medieval Discursive Religious Practices', in D. Renevey and C. Whitehead (eds.), *Writing Religious Women: Female Spiritual and Textual Practices* (Cardiff and Toronto, 2000), 197–216; see also M. Camille, 'The Image and the Self: Unwriting Late Medieval Bodies', in S. Kay and M. Rubin (eds.), *Framing Medieval Bodies* (Manchester, 1994), 62–99.
19. For a detailed study of *canor* in the *Melos*, see N. Watson, 'Translation', 167–80; Watson, *Rolle*, 171–91; V. Gillespie, 'Postcards from the Edge: Interpreting the Ineffable in the Middle English Mystics', in P. Boitani and A. Torti (eds.), *Interpretation: Medieval and Modern. The J. A. W. Bennett Memorial Lectures. Eighth Series* (Cambridge, 1993), 137–65. I am also grateful to Sister Maggie Ross who, in private communication, has drawn my attention to the apophatic in Rolle.
20. See Rolle, *Contra*, 71; for another important discussion of *canor*, see chs. 31–3 of *Incendium amoris*.
21. See Rolle, *Contra*, 71.
22. See Watson, 'Translation', 171.
23. Rolle, *Contra*, 153. [Quoniam ego heremita vocor, et intencione utique

degener non existo, laudo quidem bonitatem dei mei, qui me de mundo transtulit et usque ad cantibiles eterni amoris delicias clemens sublevavit. Illum igitur verum heremitam quisque diceret, qui pro amoris divini magnitudine ac spirituali dulcifluoque canore ad heremum; id est, ad locum solitudinis, evolaret. Rolle, *Contra*, 71.]

24 Sed iam vere scivi per experimentum quod vera est dileccio apud deum. Ibid., 72.

25 For a discussion on the importance of the Pseudo-Denys in Western mysticism, see J. Leclercq, 'Influence and Noninfluence of Dionysius in the Western Middle Ages', *Pseudo-Dionysius: The Complete Works*, tr. C. Luibheid, The Classics of Western Spirituality (New York, 1987), 25–32; for discussions of the cataphatic and apophatic modes, see A. Louth, *Denys the Aeropagite* (London, 1989), 87–8; see also Guigues du Pont, *Traité sur la contemplation*, ed. P. Dupont, Analecta Cartusiana 72, 2 vols. (Salzburg, 1985); see esp. 1, 35–39, 51–66.

26 Of related interest to this passage, see Clark's discussion of ch. 7 of *Incendium amoris*; see J. P. H. Clark, 'Richard Rolle: A Theological Re-Assessment', *DR*, 100 (1983), 115.

27 Rolle, *Contra*, 155. [De eterna igitur dileccione tractare ad confusionem et despeccionem amoris temporalis compellor; immo et delector. Rolle, *Contra*, 73.]

28 Rolle, *Contra*, 155. [Nam et hoc conscienciam meam a morsu immortalis vermis prorsus liberat et celesti dulcedine affectum suaviter obumbrat. Rolle, *Contra*, 73.]

29 Rolle, *Contra*, 156. [... omnes namque superflue mundi gaudiis se exhibent, et, infirmata languore visibilis speciei mentali acie, interioris hominis precordia celestibus amplectendis non assurgunt. Et hoc quidem quia nequaquam aliquando surgere conantur dum poterant, in maliciis obstinati deum non querunt. Rolle, *Contra*, 74.]

30 Julian of Norwich solves this question of gender for the soul by describing it as a genderless child; see C. W. Bynum, ' " ... And Woman his Humanity": Female Imagery in the Religious Writing of the Late Middle Ages', in C. W. Bynum et al. (eds.), *Gender and Religion: On the Complexity of Symbols* (Boston, 1986), 271; see Julian of Norwich, *A Revelation of Love*, ed. M. Glasscoe (1976; repr. Exeter, 1986), 61, where God is described as father, mother and spouse, while Christ is our brother and Jesus our saviour; the soul here is defined as beloved wife of God; see further, ibid., 75, where the soul is then described as a child.

31 Rolle, *Contra*, 157. [Venite mecum; audite dileccionem; amare concupiscite; sed eternum qui vivificat, non temporalem qui occidit, amorem gustate. Quoniam adhuc et ego iuvenis amator, tamen mirabilis, quia dilectam meam continue cogito, et ab eius amplexibus non recedo. Hec est dilecta mea sapiencia increata, vere amabilis et in amore gratissima. Rolle, *Contra*, 74.]

32 Rolle, *Contra*, 157. [Amorem mundi et visibilis speciei contempnite; ad dileccionem invisibilis conditoris mecum evolate! Rolle, *Contra*, 75.] Rolle may possibly echo Richard of St Victor, *De IV Grad.*, 158–61.
33 See Rolle, *Contra*, 78.
34 Rolle, *Contra*, 160. [. . . verum absorpta dulcedine incomprehensibilis caritatis graciis quoque inspirata sempiternis celesti leticia plenissime, ut mortales possunt perfruitur; ac visibilia cuncta transcendens ad suavitatem cantus iubilei sanctissime sublevatur. Rolle, *Contra*, 78.]
35 According to Rolle, song is beyond words and cannot be expressed. However, Rolle cannot reproduce that heavenly song, and it remains embedded in the metaphorical language which serves to convey the impression of what it could be. On the impossibility of separating images and meaning in visionary utterances, see C. Barrett, 'The Language of Ecstasy and the Ecstasy of Language', in M. Warner (ed.), *The Bible as Rhetoric: Studies in Biblical Persuasion and Credibility* (London, 1990), 205–21, esp. 218–19.
36 Rolle, *Contra*, 161. [Quippe manus dei deducens quomodo erraret? Rolle, *Contra*, 79.]
37 In *Contra*, Rolle [80. 102–17 (162. 120–163. 137)] contrasts spiritual song with the melody of the *mundanes* accompanied on musical instruments. In *Contra*, *canor* is dissociated from all images bearing an association with musical instruments and musical activity in general, whereas those images were abundantly used in the *Melos amoris*, such as this passage describing the joy of contemplation: 'They listen to the mystical organs and perceive the concert of *harps*. *In a quiet* full of wonders, always accompanied by the *cithara* and the cymbal, they linger deeply over this melody and never move away from a service sweet as honey.' [Audientes organica neupmata nimirum ac sonum suscipiunt *citharedorum* ac *sedent* suaviter *citharam* ac cimbalorum a se non sperantes, morantur medullitus in melodia et a ministerio mellifluo non sunt mutati.' Rolle, *Melos II*, 114]; see also Rolle, *Melos II*, 112–37.
38 See Alford, 'Biblical *Imitatio*', 8–9; Alford notes that Rolle is indebted to Apoc. 2: 17 for the description of *canor*.
39 Rolle, *Contra*, 163. [Vero nemo hominum hoc donum novit, nisi qui accepit. Rolle, *Contra*, 80.]
40 Rolle, *Contra*, 163. [Unde apostolus ait quia *raptus in* tercium celum, *audivit archana* dei, *que non licet homini loqui* (cf. 2 Cor. 12: 2–4). Rolle, *Contra*, 81.]
41 Rolle, *Contra*, 172. [Verum fateor vires meas succumbere nitens loqui de eterno amore, quia verbis exprimere nequeo quantum de divine dileccionis suavitate in mente concipio; lingua deficit; cogitacio non sufficit, nam omnem humanum superat intellectum. Rolle, *Contra*, 88.]
42 Rolle, *Contra*, 172. [Aperui os meum ad deum meum, et infusa est in me

tanta iocunditas, ut meipsum obliviscerer; nec sensi ubi fui, dei solius memorans: vel ad celum raptus fui vel ad me melos celicum condescendit. Rolle, *Contra*, 88.]

43 Watson emphasizes Rolle's inconsistencies in defining the state of *canor* – *Incendium amoris*, ch. 15, made clear that it descended from heaven; see Watson, *Rolle*, 167.

44 Occurrences of the 'face to face' expression are rare in the Latin treatises by Rolle considered so far. It appears twice in *Super cant.* (1, 61). The expression is not used at all in *Melos*. The 'face to face' is mentioned twice in *Contra* (p. 90), in a discussion on the beatific vision. *Facies* and *vultus* do appear in the three treatises, but the contexts in which they are set are either extraneous to the beatific vision or only distantly related to it; see *Super cant.*, 10, 12; *Melos I*, 136, 206, 314, 362; *Melos II*, 12, 14, 36, 40, 42, 54, 174, 208, 216, 236, 266; *Contra*, 69, 89, 93, 109.

45 Rolle, *Contra*, 172. [Est autem hec enigmatica visio et speculativa, non clara et perspicua, quia dum per fidem currimus eciam *per speculum et in enigmate videmus*. Rolle, *Contra*, 88.]

46 Rolle, *Contra*, 173. [Sicut enim si quis inter solem et seipsum pannum spissum et nigrum teneret, nequaquam solem videret propter obstaculum quod oculos eius claudit, licet forsitan de sole sentire possit. Rolle, *Contra*, 89.]

47 See William of St Thierry, *Exposé sur le cantique des cantiques*, SC 82, ed. J.-M. Déchanet (Paris, 1962), 326–33.

48 Rolle makes reference to Exod. 33: 20; John 1: 18; Ps. 17: 12, 98; see Rolle, *Contra*, 89.

49 Rolle, *Contra*, 174. [. . . quia valde delectabile est quod sentitur, adhuc tamen obscurum et nubilosum est quod videtur. Rolle, *Contra*, 89.]

50 Rolle, *Contra*, 174. [Paulus vero, qui raptus fuit usque ad tercium celum, non dixit quod vidit deum facie ad faciem, aut cives celestes, sed quod audivit archana dei. Et postea dixit, *videmus nunc per speculum in enigmate, tunc autem facie ad faciem*. Rolle, *Contra*, 90.]

51 Rolle, *Contra*, 174. [Unde audeo dicere quod nullis sanctorum conceditur in hac vita perfecta visio eternorum, nisi ex aliqua spirituali causa, ut aliquis convertatur. Rolle, *Contra*, 90.]

52 Rolle, *Contra*, 179. [. . . ego vero parvus sum, et in comparacione illorum minor . . . Rolle, *Contra*, 91.]

53 Rolle, *Contra*, 176. [Et quod credo nunc, sciam tunc; et quod spero nunc, videbo tunc; et quod desidero nunc, habebo tunc; sed et quem amo nunc, amabo sine fine. Caritas enim non cadit, sed manet in eternum. Rolle, *Contra*, 91.]

54 Translation is lacking from 92. 326 to 92. 338. [Hec est de qua loqui conor, ad quam et propter quam omnia refero. Rolle, *Contra*, 92.]

55 Qui vero hanc non habet nichil ei prodest quicquid habet, et qui eam

habet perfeccius, quamvis non habeat propheciam, nec misteria noverit, nec miranda agere videatur, vero audeo dicere quod sanctissimus, beatissimus, et excellentissimus est, et deo vicinior, propior, et similior erit in eternum. Rolle, *Contra*, 92.

56 Rolle, *Contra*, 176. [Hanc caritatem querite, et in mente tenete, fratres. Hec virtus, carissimi, non in laborantibus, non in stantibus, non in currentibus et discurrentibus, nec in loquentibus, sed in quiescentibus, et in sedentibus et tacentibus plenissima esse consuevit. Rolle, *Contra*, 92.]

57 On the verbal or thematic biblical associations devised by Rolle, see Alford, 'Biblical *Imitatio*', 14.

58 Rolle, *Contra*, 176. [Unde et sponsa, sponsi amplexus et oscula desiderans, ait, *lectus noster floridus* (Cant. I, 15). Qui ad lectum vadit quietem cupit, sed si durum habeat cubile, licet sponsa sit pulcra, multo cicius surgeret et abiret. Rolle, *Contra*, 92.]

59 See J. Leclercq, *Otia monastica: Études sur le vocabulaire de la contemplation au Moyen Age*, Studia Anselmiana 51 (Rome, 1963), 102–34.

60 *The Works of William of St Thierry*, 2. *Exposition on the Song of Songs*, tr. C. Hart, Cistercian Fathers Series 6 (Shannon, 1970), 77. [Lectulus floridus est amoena conscientia, et gaudium in ea Spiritus sancti, et in ipso fonte suo jugis fruitio veritatis. *Exposé*, 220–1.]

61 Rolle, *Contra*, 176–7. [Devota igitur et sancta anima, continuam in Christo dulcedinem desiderans, lectum dilecto floridus redolentem suavique placentem mollicie preparatum insinuat, ut veniens Christus, quem diligit, quem cupit, in cuius desiderio solomodo anhelans, a lecto suo nunquam recedat, sed illam continua unione letificet, que in eius amplexibus iugiter immorari gaudet. Rolle, *Contra*, 92.]

62 See J. Leclercq, *Études sur le vocabulaire monastique du Moyen Age*, Studia Anselmiana 48 (Rome, 1961), 117–21, where the equivalence between contemplation and desire is shown to pervade the medieval period; see also by J. Leclercq, *L'Amour des lettres et le désir de Dieu: Initiation aux auteurs monastiques du Moyen Age* (1957; repr. Paris, 1990), 30–52.

63 Rolle, *Contra*, 177. [Adhuc desiderio suspiro et amore langueo, quia non video faciem dei mei; verumptamen tale gaudium opto in celo, quale in carne sedens gusto et sencio. *Contra*, 93.]

64 See William of St Thierry, *Exposé*, 218–19, n. 3.

65 Ibid., 216–21.

66 See *William of St Thierry*, 2, 77. [In visione vero Dei ubi solus amor operatur, nullo alio sensu cooperante, incomparabiliter dignius ac subtilius omni sensuum imaginatione, idem agit puritas amoris ac divinus affectus, suavius afficiens, fortiusque attrahens, et dulcius continens sentientem, totumque et mente et actu in Deum transfundens fideliter amantem, et confortans et conformans, et vivificans ad

fruendum. Idcirco de fruitione statim subjungit ac dicit: *Lectulus noster floridus. Exposé*, 218–21.]

67 For a study of the strong Augustinian component in William's writings, see D. N. Bell, *The Image and Likeness: The Augustinian Spirituality of William of St Thierry*, Cistercian Studies Series 78 (Kalamazoo, 1984), esp. 125–65.

68 For accounts of contemporary discussions on the beatific vision during the pontificates of John XXII (7 Aug. 1316–4 Dec. 1334) and Benedict XII (20 Dec. 1334 –25 April 1342), see *DTC* 2, cols. 657–8. For an account of Thomas Waleys, the Oxford Dominican friar involved in this theological debate, see *DTC* 2, cols. 653–7.

69 Rolle, *Contra*, 177. [Nec volo ut alia gloria michi detur, sed ut aliter detur michi; videlicet, clare et perspicue videndo deum meum in decore suo. Et volo quod amoris gaudium, quod in me in hac vita incipitur, in regno dei mei plene perficiatur. Rolle, *Contra*, 93.]

70 Rolle, *Contra*, 195. [O amor vehemens, flagrans, fortis, rapiens! qui totum quod sumus in tua servituter edigis, et aliud preter te cogitari non sinis, tibi vendicans omne quod vivimus, omne quod sapimus, et omne quod sumus . . . O amor inseparabilis et insaciabilis, insuperabilis, violentus et impetuosus! Rolle, *Contra*, 108.]

Chapter 6

1 Estimo hoc ab eis ideo fieri, quia putabant tam gloriosum munus omnibus communiter non debere conferri; unde apostolus ait quia *raptus in* tercium celum, *audivit archana* dei, *que non licet homini loqui* (cf. *2 Cor. 12:* 2–4). R. Rolle, *The Contra amatores mundi*, ed. P. F. Theiner (Berkeley and Los Angeles, 1968), 81. [I think that they acted this way because they felt that such a glorious gift ought not to be conferred upon all men in common; whence the apostle says that 'caught up into the third heaven, he heard the secrets of God, which it is not granted to men to utter'. Rolle, *Contra*, 163.]

2 See Rolle, *Contra*, 108; see also also N. Watson, *Richard Rolle and the Invention of Authority*, Cambridge Studies in Medieval Literature 13 (Cambridge, 1991), 322–3, n. 27.

3 Copeland makes this distinction: 'Primary translations . . . operate according to the terms of exegesis: they give prominence to an exegetical motive by claiming to serve and supplement a textual authority, but they actually work to challenge and appropriate that textual authority. Secondary translations, on the other hand, give precedence to rhetorical motives, defining themselves as independent productive acts: characteristically they suppress any sign of exegetical service to a specific source, even though they produce themselves through such exegetical

techniques.' R. Copeland, *Rhetoric, Hermeneutics and Translation in the Middle Ages: Academic Traditions and Vernacular Texts*, Cambridge Studies in Medieval Literature 11 (Cambridge, 1991), 177.

4   Copeland discusses differences between Augustine's sacred rhetoric and classical rhetoric. She emphasizes how much the reader is given power of invention in sacred rhetoric: 'It gives reading and interpretation – the traditional province of the grammarian – a new status, as textual power shifts from authorial intention to "affective stylistics," to what the reader can do with the text. In practice it transfers responsibility for making meaning from the writer to the reader.' Ibid., 158. Copeland discusses at length Rolle's peculiar rhetorical strategies, especially the theory of the levels of style, which shows how the classical rhetorical tradition is blended with Augustine's sacred rhetoric in his writings: 'Rolle's aims are similar to those of Augustine, in that, for both, the spiritual state of the audience determines the function or task of oratory (rhetoric). But Rolle's realization of this aim is distinguished from Augustine's rhetorical model in that to the same audience, and within the same text, Rolle will speak in subdued, sublime, or moderate terms, depending on the nature of his immediate contextual concern, that is, his subject, the degree of love in question'. See R. Copeland, 'Richard Rolle and the Rhetorical Theory of the Levels of Style', *MMTE* 3 (1984), 55–80, esp. 76.

5   For an assessment of the audience for the Middle English mystics, with emphasis on Rolle's epistles, see S. S. Hussey, 'The Audience for the Middle English Mystics', in M. G. Sargent (ed.), *De cella in seculum: Religious and Secular Life and Devotion in Late Medieval England* (Cambridge, 1989), 109–22, esp. 110–12.

6   For a discussion of Rolle's use of languages and the recipients of his works, see R. Rolle, *The English Writings*, tr. R. S. Allen, The Classics of Western Spirituality (London, 1989), 32–41.

7   In his prologue to the *Breviloquium*, Bonaventure presents the traditional four levels of meaning: 'Finally, Scripture has depth, which consists in its having several mystical understandings. For, besides its literal meaning, in many places it can be interpreted in three ways, allegorically, morally, and anagogically.' See A. J. Minnis et al. (eds.), *Medieval Literary Theory and Criticism c.1100–c.1375: The Commentary Tradition* (1988; repr. Oxford, 1991), 233.

8   Ibid., 234.

9   Ibid., 373–519.

10 For a discussion of each element of this triad, and the inversion in their order of presentation (and possible importance), see chs. 7 (*oratio*), 8 (*meditatio*) and 9 (*lectio*) in *Emendatio vitae. Orationes ad honorem nominis Ihesu: Edited from Cambridge Univ. Library MSS Dd.v.64 and Kk.vi.20*, ed. N. Watson, Toronto Medieval Latin Texts 21 (Toronto, 1995), see also Watson, *Rolle*, 65 and 308, n. 13.

11 See R. Rolle, *The Fire of Love and The Mending of Life or The Rule of Living*, ed. R. Harvey, EETS OS 106 (1896); R. Rolle, *Prose and Verse*, ed. S. J. Ogilvie-Thomson, EETS 293 (1988); for a Modern English translation of Rolle's Middle English writings, see *The English Writings*, tr. Allen. All references (page and line) to the Middle English writings are taken from Ogilvie-Thomson's edition and given at the end of each passage. References to *Emendatio vitae* are from Watson's edition; unless indicated, translations are my own.

12 See J. P. H. Clark, 'Richard Rolle as a Biblical Commentator', *DR*, 104 (1986), 165–213; see also his 'Richard Rolle: A Theological Reassessment', *DR*, 101 (1983), 108–23.

13 The colophon in Cambridge University Library, MS Dd.v.64, indicates that this epistle was written for a nun of Yedingham; see R. Rolle, *English Writings of Richard Rolle, Hermit of Hampole*, ed. H. E. Allen (Oxford, 1931), 72 (hereafter Allen, *English Writings*); for a view on the authority of the colophon, see Rolle, *The English Writings*, 213–14, n. 16; I agree with Watson's view that the colophon of MS Dd.v.64 is not in conflict with Longleat 29, the latter of which Watson regards as a Southern copy of a collection presented to Margaret Kirkby on her enclosure. *Ego dormio*, originally written for a nun of Yedingham, was later included by Rolle as part of this collection, which formed a sort of anthology on the spiritual life; see Watson's review, *MQ*, 18/1 (1992), 33–5; see also Watson, *Rolle*, 330, n. 22.

14 Watson provides convincing evidence for the fact that the recipient of *Ego dormio* is a nun rather than a laywoman, as it was argued by Allen; see Watson, *Rolle*, 226–8.

15 For a study of biblical influence on his writings, see J. A. Alford, 'Biblical *Imitatio* in the Writings of Richard Rolle', *ELH*, 40/1 (1973), 1–23.

16 Some of the Middle English lyrics may have been written before *Ego dormio*, although the evidence offered in this chapter seems to suggest Rolle would not have written in Middle English without his knowledge of a readership requiring material in the vernacular. It is likely therefore that the earliest Middle English lyrics must have been written during the period of composition of *Ego dormio*, at a time when Rolle had already made acquaintance with the recipients of his later writings; see Watson, *Rolle*, 273–8.

17 Copeland, *Rhetoric*, 92.

18 See entry 'messagier' in the *Etymologishes Wörterbuch der Französischen Sprache*, ed. E. Gamillsheg (Heidelberg, 1969); see also *Altfranzösisches Wörterbuch*, ed. A. Toblers and E. Lommatzsch (Wiesbaden, 1963).

19 The relevant definitions for the word 'messager' are: (a) one who carries written or oral messages; professional messenger, courier; also used for a

dove; (b) one who conveys the messages, proclamations, or summons of a king or lord; an official messenger or courier; an envoy or ambassador; an ecclesiastical envoy; a papal legate; see *MED* 7.

[20] et dicitur interpres qui diversa genera linguarum novit. Scilicet quod unam linguam exponit per aliam vel unam linguam transfert per aliam. Et dicitur sic quia mediator est inter unam linguam seu loquelam et aliam . . . Quia interpres sit medius duarum linguarum [c]um transfert vel exponit unam linguam per aliam[.] Sed qui inter deum interpretatur et homines quibus divina indicat misteria interpres vocatur. Copeland, *Rhetoric*, 90; from Joannes Balbus, *Catholicon*, s.v. *interpres* (Mainz, 1460; repr. Westmead, Farnborough, Hants, 1971). For Isidore of Seville's own definition of the term, see also Copeland, *Rhetoric*, 89.

[21] See my 'Encoding and Decoding: Metaphorical Discourse of Love in Richard Rolle's Commentary on the First Verses of the Song of Songs', in R. Ellis and R. Evans (eds.), *The Medieval Translator* 4 (Exeter, 1994), 200–17.

[22] Rolle may refer also to other biblical referents when shaping this role. In the apologia to St Paul's second letter to the Corinthians (2 Cor. 11: 2), the idea of mediation between Christ and the Corinthians is registered in a passionate language similar to what Rolle does in *Ego dormio*: 'Aemulor enim vos Dei aemulatione despondi enim vos uni viro virginem castam exhibere Christo' [You see, the jealousy that I feel for you is God's own jealousy: I arranged for you to marry Christ so that I might give you away as a chaste virgin to this one husband]; see also Rolle, *The English Writings*, 212, n. 1. Another passage of this letter (2 Cor. 12: 1–10) shows St Paul boasting of his out-of-the-body exploits and makes the core of the important discussion on Rolle's mystical claims in ch. 5 of *Contra amatores mundi*. Rolle may have found consolation at this point of his career in finding parallels of self-referentiality in such an important figure. In addition, one should take note that both authors use the epistolary genre to encourage conversion and speak of the rewards which ensue.

[23] See Watson, *Rolle*, 226–36; because Watson fails to recognize the biblical voices and the liturgical associations, he exaggerates what he calls the 'mystical-cum-sexual' fantasy of *Ego dormio*.

[24] The mention of the excessive number (five or six) of garments (30. 163–4) she owns is more evidence of familiarity between sender and recipient.

[25] In *Contra amatores mundi*, in terms of spiritual exploits, the divide and the distance which the narrative voice puts between itself and the reader is very significant: 'Sed admoneo pium lectorem, ne me aut arrongantem aut superbum iudicet, ubi ardua et incognita me loquentem videt. Non enim propter me loquor, sed propter gloriam et laudem dei, et lectorum utilitatem. Nam et ipsi si eternum regem veraciter cupiunt diligere, hec et

maiora forsitan post modicum audebunt enarrare. Igitur, quamvis lector in se hec omnia non senciat, tamen non contempnat nec diffidat. Rolle, *Contra*, 93. [But I admonish the pious reader, that he not judge me either arrogant or proud when he sees me speaking of such difficult and unheard of things. For I speak not for my own sake, but for the glory and praise of God and the profit of my readers. For if they truly wish to love the eternal King, perhaps after this slight bit they will make bold to speak of these and even greater things. Therefore, although the reader may not feel all these things in himself, nevertheless let him not despise or mistrust them. Rolle, *Contra*, 178.]

[26] The Middle English pieces present clues to our perceptions of the devotions which led Rolle to the achievements described in the Latin pieces. Even from as early a work as *Incendium amoris*, we know for instance that the devotion to the Name of Jesus, such an important element in the epistles, was practised by Rolle and led him to the experience of the fire of love; see R. Rolle, *The Fire of Love*, 83. Although absent from the Latin treatises, it is very likely that meditations on the passion were part of devotions which Rolle practised before his experiences crystallized in the language that makes him so original. The spiritual programme set out within the frame of the degrees of love may be the model which allowed Rolle to reach such a high spiritual state. See W. F. Hodapp, 'Richard Rolle's Passion Meditations in the Context of his English Epistles: *Imitatio Christi* and the Three Degrees of Love', *MQ*, 20/3 (1994), 96–104.

[27] For a study of the liturgical feast of the Holy Name in late medieval England, see R. W. Pfaff, *New Liturgical Feasts in Later Medieval England* (Oxford, 1970), 62–83; see also *DS* 8, cols. 1109–26. For evidence of the importance of this devotion in Rolle's corpus, see for instance, Rolle, *Prose and Verse*, 39. 214–24, 18. 610–25, 30. 157–9; see also R. Rolle, *The English Psalter*, ed. H. R. Bradley (Oxford, 1884), 21. 6–10; 28. 10–16; 32. 30–5; 90. 7–11; see also Watson, *Rolle*, 104, 237, 243, 246, 306–7.

[28] See *Sancti Bernardi opera*, 1, *Sermo 15*; see also J. A. W. Bennett, *Middle English Literature*, ed. and completed by D. Gray (Oxford, 1990), 307. For a study of the use of the name Jesus in the East, see Bishop Kallistos of Diokleia, *The Power of the Name: The Jesus Prayer in Orthodox Spirituality*, Fairacres Publication 43 (1977; repr. Oxford, 1982); see also I. Hausherr, *The Name of Jesus*, tr. C. Cummings, Cistercian Studies Series 44 (Kalamazoo, 1978).

[29] For a general survey of the vernacular literacy of the fourteenth-century English audience, see J. Coleman, *English Literature in History: Medieval Readers and Writers* (London, 1981), 18–57; see also M. T. Clanchy, *From Memory to Written Record: England 1066–1307* (1979; repr. Oxford, 1993), esp. 1–23, 109–113, and 283–93.

30 See Copeland, *Rhetoric*, 125.
31 Rolle borrows extensively from *Super canticum*, *Melos* and *Incendium amoris* when describing the third degree. For details of such passages and their sources, see Allen, *English Writings*, 160.
32 See Watson, *Rolle*, 209; for a discusssion on this enigmatic William, see H. E. Allen, *Writings Ascribed to Richard Rolle, Hermit of Hampole, and Materials for his Biography* (New York, 1927), 230–1; see also Watson, *Rolle*, 325, n. 8.
33 For a general presentation of the work, ibid., 209–21.
34 Quid enim est conuersio ad deum nisi auersio a mundo et a pecato, a diabolo et a carne? Quid eciam est auersio a Deo nisi conuersio ad bonum commutabile, ad delectabilem speciem creature, ad opera/ diaboli, ad voluptates carnis et mundi? Non enim incessu pedum ad deum conuertimur, sed mutacione affectuum et morum. Rolle, *Emendatio*, 34.
35 For a discussion pertinent to this point, see V. Gillespie, '*Lukynge in haly bukes*: *Lectio* in Some Late Medieval Spiritual Miscellanies', *Spätmittelalterliche Geistliche Literatur in der Nationalsprache*, Analecta Cartusiana 106/2 (Salzburg, 1984), 1–27, esp. 9–10.
36 See V. Gillespie, 'Mystic's Foot: Rolle and Affectivity', *MMTE* 2 (1982), 212–14.
37 Tunc enim veraciter oramus cum de alio non cogitamus, sed tota nostra intencio ad summa dirigitur, et animus noster igne Sanctis Spiritus inflammatur. Sic profecto in nobis mira affluencia bonitatis diuine inuenitur, quia ex intimis medullis cordis nostri exurget amor Dei, et tota oracio nostra cum affectu et effectu erit; ut iam non uerba in oracione transcurramus, sed omnes eciam pene sillabas,/cum clamore valido et desiderio incenso, Deo nostro offeremus. Incenso enim corde nostro amore feruido, eciam oracio ipsa incenditur, et in odorem suauitatis ex ore nostro in conspectu Dei adoletur, vt magna iocunditas sit orare, quia dum in oracione ineffabilis dulcor oranti infunditur, ipsa oracio in iubilum commutatur. Rolle, *Emendatio*, 50–1.
38 For a detailed study of *canor* in *Melos amoris*, see N. Watson, 'Translation and Self-Canonization in Richard Rolle's *Melos amoris*', in R. Ellis (ed.), *The Medieval Translator: The Theory and Practice of Translation in the Middle Ages* (Cambridge, 1989), 167–80.
39 Omnis tamen quia ab vno fonte procedunt ad vnum finem tendunt et ad unam beatitudinem perueniunt uel ducuntur; sed diuersis uiis per unam caritatem, que maior est in vno quam in alio. Rolle, *Emendatio*, 52.
40 For a discussion of Rolle's English Psalter, with focus on the role played by the Latin and vernacular languages, see R. Morse, *Truth and Convention in the Middle Ages: Rhetoric, Representation and Reality* (Cambridge, 1991), 204–7. Morse insists on the central importance of the

Latin in this work: 'What in effect Rolle has done is to assemble a bilingual Psalter with English Commentary, so that the devout, but unlearned, reader (not imagined as female reader, nor as a collection of female readers, as will be obvious from the pronouns) can meditate upon the Latin, sentence by sentence.' Ibid., 206.

41 For a general but however illuminating discussion on this topic, see J. A. Zimmerman, *Liturgy as Language of Faith: A Liturgical Methodology in the Mode of Paul Ricoeur's Textual Hermeneutics* (London, 1988).

42 O bone Ihesu, quis michi det ut senciam te, qui nunc sentiri et non uideri potes? Infunde te in uisceribus anime mee. Ueni in cor meum, et reple illud dulcedine tua preclarissima. Inebria mentem meam feruenti vino dileccionis dulcissone; vt, omnia mala omnesque circumscriptas uisionis illusorias ymagines obliuiscens, ac te solum complectens, exultem, iubilem in Deo Ihesu meo. Rolle, *Emendatio*, 57.

43 See G. Chaucer, *The Riverside Chaucer*, ed. L. D. Benson (1987; repr. Oxford, 1987), 161. 1807–12; see also explanatory notes, 888.

44 Ure igne tuo renes meos et cor meum, qui in altari tuo ardebit ineternum. Ueni, precor te, O suauis et vera gloria! veni, dulcedo desideratissima! veni, dilecce mi, qui es tota consolacio mea! Anime languenti pro te et ad te dulcifluo ardore illabere. Calore tuo penetralia cordis mei incende; et, intima quoque tua luce illuminando, mellifluo amoris iubilo cuncta pro captu mentis et corporis depasce. Rolle, *Emendatio*, 57.

45 Est autem caritas uirtutum nobilissima, excellentissima et suauissima, quam amatum cum amato scimus coniungere, et Christum cum electa anima perpetuo copulare. Reformat in nobis summe trinitatis ymaginem, et creaturam creatori facit simillimam. Rolle, *Emendatio*, 60.

46 See the *Oxford Latin Dictionary*, ed. P. G. W. Glare (1968; repr. Oxford, 1992).

47 Tu audacter intras cubiculum regis eterni, tu sola Christum rapere non vereris. Rolle, *Emendatio*, 60.

48 . . . in amato iubilans, ipsum cogitans, ipsum incessanter reminiscens, ascendens in desiderio, ruens in dilecto, pergens in amplexibus, absortus in osculis, totus liquefactus in igne amoris. Rolle, *Emendatio*, 61.

49 In hiis eciam et huiusmodo meditacionibus delecteris ut quandoque ad medullam amoris ascendas. Rolle, *Emendatio*, 57.

50 For Rolle's adaptation of the Augustinian oratory, R. Copeland, 'Richard Rolle and the Rhetorical Theory of the Levels of Style', *MMTE* 3 (1984), 55–80. Rolle provides five definitions of contemplation, some of them borrowed from Prosper of Aquitaine (Julius Pomerius), Hugh and Richard of St Victor; see Watson, *Rolle*, 219.

51 Michi uidetur quod contemplacio sit iubilus divini amoris, susceptus in mente suauitate laudis angelice. Hec est iubilacio, que finis est oracionis perfecte et deuocionis summe in via. Hec est exultacio mentis habita pro eterno dilecto in spirituali canora uoce prorumpens. Rolle, *Emendatio*, 63.

52 See Watson, *Rolle*, 278–86; see also Rolle, *The English Writings*, 48–9.
53 For a general analysis of this epistle, see Watson, *Rolle*, 237–9; see also Rolle, *The English Writings*, 143.
54 On the hypothesis that the nun was possibly from Hampole, and that she was Margaret Kirkby to whom *The Form* was addressed, see Allen, *English Writings*, 143.
55 In fact, both for this epistle and the more ambitious *Form of Living*, Rolle borrows liberally from *Emendatio vitae* and other works. The *Compendium theologicae veritatis*, *Emendatio vitae*, *Super canticum canticorum* and the pseudo-Bernardine *Meditationes piissimae* are identified by Watson as sources for *The Commandment* and *The Form of Living* ; see Watson, *Rolle*, 237–8.
56 This idea of the tower of love evoked here recalls the allegorical sieges described in the *Roman de la Rose*, *The Castle of Perseverance* and *Piers Plowman*, among other works; see J. A. Burrow, *Medieval Writers and their Work: Middle English Literature and its Background 1100–1500* (Oxford, 1982), 93; see also the fine study by R. D. Cornelius, 'The Figurative Castle' (Univ. of Bryn Mawr Ph.D. thesis, 1930).
57 The Name of Jesus in *The Commandment* (39. 214–24) is an adaptation from *Super canticum* (43. 8–23); see Watson, *Rolle*, 237.
58 In most manuscripts, *The Form of Living* appears with a twelve-chapter division, possibly in imitation of the authoritative *Emendatio vitae*. Noetinger, who studied such versions of *The Form*, is led erroneously to make the statement that *Emendatio* is a recasting of *The Form*; see R. Rolle, *Le Feu de l'amour. Le Modèle de la vie parfaite. Le Pater*, tr. D. M. Noetinger (Solesmes, 1928), 279.
59 See Allen, *English Writings*, 82–4; Allen, *Writings*, 267–8; see also Richard Rolle, *The English Writings*, 152. For an account of Margaret Kirkby, see Allen, *Writings*, 502–11.
60 See S. A. Weber, *Theology and Poetry in the Middle English Lyric: A Study of Sacred History and Aesthetic Form* (Columbus, OH, 1969), esp. 3–25, 204–12.
61 See Rolle, *Super cant.*, 47–8.
62 The first lines of this passage (162–7) echo a passage of Cassian's *Collationes* (*PL* 49, col. 1025); quoted in Rolle, *Prose and Verse*, 194, and Rolle, *English Writings*, 216, n. 13.
63 See Rolle, *Prose and Verse*, 1. 1, 1. 18–9, 1. 21–2, 5. 106, 7. 161–2, 15. 491–2, 15. 502, 17. 586, 21. 722–4, 24. 849, 25. 875.
64 For a study of ineffability in the Middle English mystics, see V. Gillespie, 'Postcards from the Edge: Interpreting the Ineffable in the Middle English Mystics', in P. Boitani and A. Torti (eds.), *Interpretation: Medieval and Modern: The J. A. W. Bennett Memorial Lectures. Eighth Series* (Cambridge, 1993), 137–65.

65 For a discussion of a possible direct borrowing of Richard of St Victor's degrees of love from Rolle, see Clark, 'Richard Rolle: A Theological Re-Assessment', 124–6.

66 *The Works of Bernard of Clairvaux*, 2, *On the Song of Songs*, 1, tr. K. Walsh (Shannon, 1971), 6–7. [Non est strepitus oris, sed iubilus cordis; non sonus labiorum, sed motus gaudiorum; voluntatum, non vocum consonantia. Non auditur foris, nec enim in publico personat: sola quae cantat audit, et cui cantatur, id est sponsus et sponsa. Est quippe nuptiale carmen, exprimens castos et iucundoque complexus animorum, morum concordiam, affectuumque consentaneam ad alterutrum caritatem. *Sancti Bernardi opera*, 1, ed. J. Leclercq, C. H. Talbot and H. M. Rochais (Rome, 1957), 7–8.]

67 This is a paraphrase of Richard Rolle's *Incendium amoris*.

68 See Watson, 'Translation', 167–80; I disagree with Watson's contention that Rolle implies his writing and heavenly song are equivalent in status. Rolle, in *The Form*, 17. 574–8, makes clear distinctions between heavenly song, which he calls *canor*, and texts written under its inspiration.

69 The fourteenth-century sermon, *Surge et ambulat*, extant in British Library, MS Harley 505 (fol. 83^v), uses the image of the nightingale to express the corruption of those who have taken part in lustful activities. It was believed indeed that the nightingale sang sweet melodies while building its nest, but its song changed to sighing after mating. In the *exemplum*, the nightingale stands as symbol of a loss of perfection; quoted by S. Wenzel, *Preachers, Poets, and the Early English Lyric* (Princeton, 1986), 238–9. For a study of the multiple, and sometimes contradictory, symbolic functions of the nightingale, see J. L. Baird's introductory essay on the nightingale tradition in *Rossignol: An Edition and Translation*, ed. J. L. Baird and J. R. Kane (Kent, OH, 1978), 1–53.

70 Three manuscripts, National-Bibliothek, Vienna MS 4483, Prague University MS 814 and Lincoln Cathedral MS 218, contain compilations which integrate Bernard and Rolle's interpretations into a whole; see Allen, *Writings*, 66–7, 39–43. On the nightingale standing as a figure of the contemplative, see the following passage by Alexander Neckam (1157–1217): ' "The nightingale sings more sweetly in her accustomed bushes." And in the same way the contemplative man has leisure time for the sweetness of contemplation more lovingly in those places set aside for the study of fruitful meditation. And if we may speak poetically, the bird was silent as long as she remained mindful of the wrongs of Tereus, but afterward when she was changed into a bird, she was considered to be superior to all other birds in the variety of her sweet melody. Hence Martial says: "she who was mute as a girl became a garrulous bird." Just so whoever nourishes the rancor of fraternal hatred in his heart grows silent in his praises to God, but after he has been given wholly over to the

tranquillity of the contemplative life, he opens his mouth gladly in divine praises.' Quoted in *Rossignol*, 27.
71 In *Piers Plowman*, the poet answers this point in a way which throws light on the role of the act of writing as part of the spiritual quest; W. Langland, *The Vision of Piers Plowman: A Critical Edition of the B-Text based on Trinity College Cambridge MS B. 15. 17*, ed. A. V. C. Schmidt (London, 1984), passus XII, ll. 16–28.

Afterword

1 See J. F. Benton, 'Consciousness of Self and Perceptions of Individuality', in R. L. Benson and G. Constable, with C. D. Lanham (eds.), *Renaissance and Renewal in the Twelfth Century*, 2nd edn. (Toronto, 1991), 294.
2 See E. A. Matter, *The Voice of my Beloved: The Song of Songs in Western Medieval Christianity* (Philadelphia, 1990), 123–50.
3 See Benton, 'Consciousness of Self', 288.

Bibliography

Primary Texts

Anselm of Canterbury, *Sancti Anselmi opera omnia*, 6 vols., ed. F. S. Schmitt (Edinburgh, 1946–62).
—, *The Prayers and Meditations of Saint Anselm with the Proslogion*, ed. B. Ward (1973; repr. London, 1988).
Augustine, *De doctrina christiana*, *PL* 34; *On Christian Doctrine*, tr. D. W. Robertson, Jr. (London, 1958).
Benedict, The Rule of St Benedict, in *Western Asceticism*, ed. O. Chadwick, The Library of Christian Classics (Philadelphia, 1958), 290–337.
Bernard of Clairvaux, *The Works of Bernard of Clairvaux*, 2, *On the Song of Songs* 1, tr. K. Walsh, Cistercian Fathers Series 4 (Kalamazoo, 1971).
—, *The Works of Bernard of Clairvaux*, 3, *On the Song of Songs* 2, tr. K. Walsh, Cistercian Fathers Series 7 (1976; repr. Kalamazoo, 1983).
—, *Bernard of Clairvaux: On the Song of Songs*, 3, tr. K. Walsh and I. M. Edmonds, Cistercian Fathers Series 31 (Kalamazoo, 1979).
—, *Bernard of Clairvaux: On the Song of Songs*, 4, tr. I. M. Edmonds, Cistercian Fathers Series 40 (Kalamazoo, 1980).
—, *Bernard of Clairvaux, Treatises*, 2, *The Steps of Humility and Pride, On Loving God*, tr. R. Walton, Cistercian Fathers Series 31 (Kalamazoo, 1980).
—, *Sancti Bernardi opera*, 8 vols., ed. J. Leclercq, C. H. Talbot and H. M. Rochais (Rome, 1957–77).
—, *The Letters of St Bernard of Clairvaux*, tr. B. S. James (London, 1953).
Biblia sacra iuxta vulgatam Clementinam, ed. A. Colungo and L. Turrado, Biblioteca de autores cristianos (Madrid, 1985).
Bonaventure, *Lignum vitae*, ed. Patres Collegii S. Bonaventurae (Quarachi, 1896).
—, *Vitis mystica*, ed. Patres Collegii S. Bonaventurae (Quarachi, 1896).
Book to a Mother: An Edition with a Commentary, ed. A. J. McCarthy, Salzburg Studies in English Literature, Elizabethan and Renaissance Studies 92 (Salzburg, 1981).

Brown, C. (ed.), *English Lyrics of the Thirteenth Century* (Oxford, 1932).
Carthusian Spirituality: The Writings of Hugh of Balma and Guigo de Ponte, tr. D. D. Martin, The Classics of Western Spirituality (New York, 1997).
Chaucer, G., *The Riverside Chaucer*, ed. L. D. Benson (1987; repr. Oxford, 1988).
Gallus, T., *Commentaire du cantique des cantiques*, ed. J. Barbet (Paris and Louvain, 1972).
Gilbert of Hoyland, *The Works of Gilbert of Hoyland. Sermons on the Song of Songs*, 1, tr. L. C. Braceland, Cistercian Fathers Series 14 (Kalamazoo, 1978).
Gregory, bishop of Nyssa, *The Life of Moses*, tr. A. J. Malherbe and E. Ferguson, The Classics of Western Spirituality (New York, 1978).
Guigues du Pont, *Traité sur la contemplation*, ed. P. Dupont, Analecta Cartusiana 72, 2 vols. (Salzburg, 1985).
Hugh of St Victor, *The Didascalicon of Hugh of St Victor*, tr. J. Taylor (1961; repr. New York, 1991).
John of Howden, *Philomena*, ed. C. Blume, Hymnologische Beiträge, 4 (Leipzig, 1930).
—, *Poems of John of Hoveden*, ed. F. J. E. Raby, Surtees Society 154 (Durham, 1939).
Julian of Norwich, *A Revelation of Love*, ed. M. Glasscoe (1976; repr. Exeter, 1986).
La Bible moralisée conservée à Oxford, Paris et Londres: Reproduction intégrale du manuscrit du xiiie siècle, vol. 2 (Paris, 1912).
Langland, W., *The Vision of Piers Plowman: A Critical Edition of the B-Text based on Trinity College Cambridge MS B. 15. 17*, ed. A. V. C. Schmidt (London, 1984).
Medieval Literary Theory and Criticism c.1100–c.1375: The Commentary Tradition, ed. A. J. Minnis and A. B. Scott with assistance of D. Wallace (1988; repr. Oxford, 1991).
Omnia opera sancti Bonaventurae, 15 vols., ed. A. C. Peltier (Paris, 1864–71).
Origen, *An Exhortation to Martyrdom, Prayer, First Principles: Book Four, Prologue to the Commentary on the Song of Songs, Homily XXVII on Numbers*, tr. R. A. Greer, The Classics of Western Spirituality (New York, 1979).
—, *The Song of Songs: Commentaries and Homilies*, tr. R. P. Lawson (London, 1957).
Richard de Saint-Victor, *Benjamin minor*, *PL* 196, cols. 1–63. *Benjamin major*, *PL* 196, cols. 64–202.
—, *Ives: Épître à Séverin sur la charité. Richard de Saint-Victor: Les Quatre Degrés de la violente charite*, ed. G. Dumeige, Textes philosophiques du Moyen Age 3 (Paris, 1955).
—, *Sermons et opuscules spirituels inédits*, ed. J. Châtillon et W.-J. Tulloch (Bruges, 1951).

—, *The Twelve Patriarchs. The Mystical Ark. Book Three of Trinity*, tr. G. A. Zinn, The Classics of Western Spirituality (New York, 1979).
—, Pseudo, *In cantica canticorum explicatio*, *PL* 196, cols. 405–524.
Rolle, R., *Biblical Commentaries: Short Exposition of Psalm 20, Treatise on the Twentieth Psalm, Comment on the First Verses of the Canticle of Canticles, Commentary on the Apocalypse*, ed. R. Boenig, Salzburg Studies in English Literature, Elizabethan and Renaissance Studies 92/13 (Salzburg, 1984).
—, *Emendatio Vitae. Orationes ad honorem nominis Ihesu: Edited from Cambridge University Library MSS Dd.v.64 and Kk.vi.20*, ed. N. Watson, Toronto Medieval Latin Texts 21 (Toronto, 1995).
—, *English Writings of Richard Rolle, Hermit of Hampole*, ed. H. E. Allen (Oxford, 1931).
—, *Le Chant d'amour* (Melos amoris), 2 vols., ed. F. Vandenbroucke, SC 168–9 (Paris, 1971).
—, 'Le Commentaire de Richard Rolle sur les premiers versets du *Cantique des Cantiques*', ed. Y. Madon, *MSR*, 7 (1950), 311–25.
—, *Le Feu de l'amour. Le Modèle de la vie parfaite. Le Pater*, tr. D. M. Noetinger (Solesmes, 1928).
—, *Prose and Verse*, ed. S. J. Ogilvie-Thomson, EETS 293 (Oxford, 1988).
—, 'Richard Rolle's Comment on the Canticles: Edited from MS. Trinity College, Dublin, 153', ed. E. M. Murray (Fordham University Ph.D. thesis, 1958).
—, *Richard Rolle's Expositio super novem lectiones mortuorum*, 2 vols., ed. M. R. Moyes, Analecta Cartusiana 92/12 (Salzburg, 1988).
—, 'The *Canticum amoris* of Richard Rolle', ed. G. M. Liegey, *Traditio*, 12 (1956), 369–91.
—, *The Contra amatores mundi of Richard Rolle of Hampole*, ed. P. F. Theiner (Berkeley and Los Angeles, 1968).
—, *The English Psalter*, ed. H. R. Bradley (Oxford, 1884).
—, *The English Writings*, tr. R. S. Allen, The Classics of Western Spirituality (London, 1989).
—, *The Fire of Love and The Mending of Life or The Rule of Living*, ed. R. Harvey, EETS OS 106 (London, 1896).
—, *The Fire of Love*, tr. C. Wolters (1972; repr. London, 1988).
—, *The Fire of Love* (London, 1988).
—, *The Incendium amoris*, ed. M. Deanesly (Manchester, 1915).
—, *The Melos amoris*, ed. E. J. F. Arnould (Oxford, 1957).
Rossignol: An Edition and Translation, ed. J. L. Baird and J. R. Kane (Kent, OH, 1978).
The Cloud of Unknowing: And Related Treatises on Contemplative Prayer, Analecta Cartusiana 3, ed. P. Hodgson (Salzburg, 1982).
The Lyfe of Soule, ed. H. Moon, Salzburg Studies in English Literature, Elizabethan and Renaissance Studies 75 (Salzburg, 1978).

The Officium and Miracula of Richard Rolle of Hampole, ed. R. Woolley (London, 1919).
The Poems of the Pearl Manuscript: Pearl, Cleanness, Patience, Sir Gawain and the Green Knight, ed. M. Andrew and R. Waldron (1978; repr. Exeter, 1987).
The Prickynge of Love, ed. H. Kane, Salzburg Studies in English Literature, Elizabethan and Renaissance Studies 92/10 (Salzburg, 1983).
William of St Thierry (Guillaume de St Thierry), *Exposé sur le cantique des cantiques*, SC 82, ed. J.-M. Déchanet (Paris, 1962).
—, *La Contemplation de Dieu. L'Oraison de dom Guillaume*, SC 61, ed. J. Hourlier (Paris, 1959).
—, *Lettres aux frères du Mont-Dieu*, SC 223, ed. J. Déchanet (1976; repr. Paris, 1985).
—, *Meditativae orationes*, tr. M.-M. Davy (Paris, 1934).
—, *Oraisons méditatives*, SC 324, ed. J. Hourlier (Paris, 1985).
—, *The Works of William of St Thierry*, 1, *On Contemplating God, Prayer, Meditations*, tr. Sister Penelope, Cistercian Fathers Series 3 (Shannon, 1971).
—, *The Works of William of St Thierry*, 2, *Exposition on the Song of Songs*, tr. C. Hart, Cistercian Fathers Series 6 (Shannon, 1970).

Secondary Texts

Adams, J. N., *The Latin Sexual Vocabulary* (London, 1982).
Alford, J. A., 'Biblical *Imitatio* in the Writings of Richard Rolle', *ELH*, 40/1 (1973), 1–23.
Allen, H. E., *Writings Ascribed to Richard Rolle, Hermit of Hampole, and Materials for his Biography* (New York, 1927).
Alter, R., *The Art of Biblical Narrative* (London, 1981).
Altfranzösisches Wörterbuch, ed. A. Toblers and E. Lommatzsch (Wiesbaden, 1963).
Astell, A. W., 'Feminine Figurae in the Writings of Richard Rolle: A Register of Growth', *MQ*, 15/3 (1989), 117–24.
—, *The Song of Songs in the Middle Ages* (Ithaca, NY, and London, 1990).
Auerbach, E., *Literary Language and its Public in Late Latin Antiquity and in the Middle Ages* (Princeton, 1965).
Barrett, C., 'The Language of Ecstasy and the Ecstasy of Language', in M. Warner (ed.), *The Bible as Rhetoric: Studies in Biblical Persuasion and Credibility* (London, 1990), 205–21.
Bell, D. N., *The Image and Likeness: The Augustinian Spirituality of William of St Thierry*, Cistercian Studies Series 78 (Kalamazoo, 1984).
Bennett, J. A. W., *Middle English Literature*, ed. and completed by D. Gray (Oxford, 1990).

Benton, J. F., 'Consciousness of Self and of Individuality', in R. L. Benson and G. Constable, with C. D. Lanham (eds.), *Renaissance and Renewal in the Twelfth Century* (1982; repr. Toronto, 1991), 263–95.

Blanpain, J., 'Langage mystique, expression du désir dans les sermons sur le Cantique des Cantiques de Bernard de Clairvaux', *CCist* 36, 1 (1974), 45–68; 36, 3 (1974), 226–47; 37, 3 (1975), 145–66.

Bouwman, G., *Des Julian von Aeclanum Kommentar zu den Propheten Osee, Joel und Amos* (Rome, 1958).

Bouyer, L., *The Christian Mystery from Pagan Myth to Christian Mysticism* (Edinburgh, 1990).

Brésard, L., 'Bernard et Origène commentent le Cantique', *CCist*, 44/2 (1982), 111–30; 44/3 (1982), 183–209; 44/4 (1982), 293–308.

—, 'Bernard et Origène, le symbolisme nuptial dans leurs œuvres sur le Cantique', *Cîteaux*, 36/3–4 (1985), 129–51.

Bruckner, A., *Julian von Eclanum: Sein Leben und seine Lehre* (Leipzig, 1897).

Burrow, J. A., *Medieval Writers and their Work: Middle English Literature and its Background 1100–1500* (Oxford, 1982).

Bynum, C. W., ' " . . . And Woman His Humanity": Female Imagery in the Religious Writing of the Late Middle Ages', in C. W. Bynum, S. Harrell and P. Richman (eds.), *Gender and Religion: On the Complexity of Symbols* (Boston, 1986).

—, *Holy Feast and Holy Fast: The Religious Significance of Food to Medieval Women* (London, 1987).

—, *Jesus as Mother: Studies in the Spirituality of the High Middle Ages* (Berkeley, 1982).

Camille, M., 'The Image and the Self: Unwriting Late Medieval Bodies', in S. Kay and M. Rubin (eds.), *Framing Medieval Bodies* (Manchester, 1994), 62–99.

Carfantan, J. (tr.), *William, Abbot of St Thierry: A Colloquium at the Abbey of St Thierry*, Cistercian Studies Series 94 (Kalamazoo, 1987).

Carrol, T. A., *The Venerable Bede: His Spiritual Teachings* (Washington, DC, 1946).

Carruthers, M., *The Book of Memory: A Study of Memory in Medieval Culture*, Cambridge Studies in Medieval Literature 10 (1990; repr. Cambridge, 1993).

Casey, M., *Athirst for God: Spiritual Desire in Bernard of Clairvaux's Sermons on the Song of Songs*, Cistercian Studies Series 77 (Kalamazoo, 1988).

Châtillon, J., 'De Guillaume de Champeaux à Thomas Gallus: Chronique d'histoire littéraire et doctrinale de l'École de Saint-Victor', *RMAL*, 8 (1952), 139–62, 247–73.

—, 'Les Trois Modes de la contemplation selon Richard de Saint-Victor', *Bulletin de littérature ecclésiastique*, 41 (1940), 3–26.

Chenu, M.-D., *La Théologie au douzième siècle* (Paris, 1966).
Clanchy, M. T., *From Memory to Written Record: England 1066–1307* (1979; repr. Oxford, 1993).
Clark, J. P. H., 'Richard Rolle as a Biblical Commentator', *DR*, 104 (1986), 165–213.
—, 'Richard Rolle: A Theological Re-assessment', *DR*, 100 (1983), 108–39.
Coleman, J., *English Literature in History: Medieval Readers and Writers* (London, 1981).
Constable, G., 'The Popularity of Twelfth-century Spiritual Writers in the Late Middle Ages', in A. Molho and J. A. Tedeschi (eds.), *Renaissance: Studies in Honor of Hans Baron* (Dekalb, IL, 1971), 3–28.
—, 'Twelfth-century Spirituality and the Late Middle Ages', in O. B. Hardison (ed.), *Medieval and Renaissance Studies: Proceedings of the Southeastern Institute of Medieval and Renaissance Studies* (Chapel Hill, NC, 1971), 27–60.
Copeland, R., *Rhetoric, Hermeneutics and Translation in the Middle Ages: Academic Traditions and Vernacular Texts*, Cambridge Studies in Medieval Literature 11 (Cambridge, 1991).
—, 'Richard Rolle and the Rhetorical Theory of the Levels of Style', *MMTE* 3 (1984), 55–80.
Cornelius, R. D., 'The Figurative Castle' (Univ. of Bryn Mawr Ph.D. thesis, 1930).
Curtius, E. R., *La Littérature européenne et le Moyen-Age latin*, 2, tr. J. Bréjoux (Paris, 1956).
Davy, M. M., 'L'Amour de Dieu d'après Guillaume de Saint-Thierry', *RSR*, 18 (1938), 319–46.
Déchanet, J.-M., '*Amor ipse intellectus est:* La Doctrine de l'amour chez Guillaume de Saint-Thierry', *RMAL*, 1 (1945), 349–74.
—, *Guillaume de Saint-Thierry: Aux sources d'une pensée*, Théologie Historique 49 (Paris, 1978).
Delfgaaw, P., 'La Nature et les degrés de l'amour selon S. Bernard', *Saint Bernard théologien*, Analecta sacri ordinis cisterciensis, 9 (1953), 234–52.
Dictionary of Medieval Latin from British Sources, 2, ed. R. E. Latham (Oxford, 1981).
Ellis, R., 'Author(s), Compilers, Scribes and Bible Texts: Did the Cloud-Author Translate *The Twelve Patriarchs?*, *MMTE* 5 (Cambridge, 1992), 193–221.
Emden, A. B., *A Biographical Register of the University of Cambridge to 1500* (Cambridge, 1963).
Engammare, M., *Qu'il me baise des baisiers de sa bouche: Le Cantique des cantiques à la Renaissance, Étude et bibliographie* (Geneva, 1993).
Etymologishes Wörterbuch der Französischen Sprache, ed. E. Gamillsheg (Heidelberg, 1969).
Evans, G. R., *The Mind of St Bernard of Clairvaux* (Oxford, 1983).

Evans, R., 'An Afterword on the Prologue', in J. Wogan-Browne, N. Watson, A. Taylor and R. Evans (eds.), *The Idea of the Vernacular: An Anthology of Middle English Literary Theory 1280–1520*, Exeter Medieval Texts and Studies (Exeter, 1999), 371–8.

Falk, M., *Love Lyrics from the Bible: A Translation and Literary Study of the Song of Songs*, Bible and Literature Series 4 (1976; repr. Sheffield, 1982).

Fischer, B. (ed.), *Novae concordantiae bibliorum sacrorum iuxta vulgatam versionem critice editam*, 2 (Stuttgart-Bad Cannstatt, 1977).

Ford, S. de, 'The Use and Function of Alliteration in the *Melos amoris* of Richard Rolle', *MQ*, 22 (1986), 59–66.

Freyhan, R., 'The Evolution of the Caritas Figure in the Thirteenth and Fourteenth Centuries', *JWCI* (1948–9), 68–86.

Fulton, R., 'Mimetic Devotion, Marian Exegesis, and the Historical Sense of the Song of Songs', *Viator*, 27 (1996), 85–116.

Gabel, J. B., and C. B. Wheeler, *The Bible as Literature: An Introduction* (Oxford, 1986).

Gillespie, V., '*Lukynge in haly bukes*: Lectio in some Late Medieval Spiritual Miscellanies', *Spätmittelalterliche Geistliche Literatur in der Nationalsprache*, Analecta Cartusiana 106/2 (Salzburg, 1984), 1–27.

—, 'Postcards from the Edge: Interpreting the Ineffable in the Middle English Mystics', in P. Boitani and A. Torti (eds.), *Interpretation: Medieval and Modern. The J. A. W. Bennett Memorial Lectures. Eighth Series* (Cambridge, 1993), 137–65.

—, 'Mystic's Foot: Rolle and Affectivity', *MMTE* 2 (1982), 199–230.

—, 'Strange Images of Death: The Passion in Later Medieval English Devotional and Mystical Writing', *Zeit, Tod und Ewigkeit in der Renaissance Literatur*, Analecta Cartusiana 117/3 (Salzburg, 1987), 111–59.

Gilson, E., *The Mystical Theology of St Bernard*, tr. A. H. C. Downes, Cistercian Studies Series 120 (1934; repr. Kalamazoo, 1990).

Goulder, M. D., *The Song of Fourteen Songs*, Journal for the Study of the Old Testament, Supplement Series 36 (Sheffield, 1986).

Guimet, F., '*Caritas ordinata* et *amor discretus* dans la *Théologie trinitaire* de Richard de Saint-Victor', *RMAL*, 4 (1948), 225–36.

Hausherr, I., *The Name of Jesus*, tr. C. Cummings, Cistercian Studies Series 44 (Kalamazoo, 1978).

Hodapp, W. F., 'Richard Rolle's Passion Meditations in the Context of his English Epistles: *Imitatio Christi* and the Three Degrees of Love', *MQ*, 20/3 (1994), 96–104.

Hourlier, J., 'S. Bernard et Guillaume de Saint-Thierry dans le "Liber de amore"', *Saint Bernard théologien*, Analecta sacri ordinis cisterciensis, 9 (1953), 223–33.

Hussey, S. S., 'The Audience for the Middle English Mystics', in M. G.

Sargent (ed.), *De cella in seculum: Religious and Secular Life and Devotion in Late Medieval England* (Cambridge, 1989), 109–22.

Javelet, R., *Image et ressemblance au douzième siècle*, 2 vols. (Paris, 1967).

—, 'Thomas Gallus et Richard de St Victor mystiques', *RTAM*, 29 (1962), 206–33; 30 (1963), 88–121.

Jennings, M., 'Richard Rolle and the Three Degrees of Love', *DR*, 93 (1975), 193–200.

Kallistos of Diokleia, bishop, *The Power of the Name: The Jesus Prayer in Orthodox Spirituality*, Fairacres Publication 43 (1977; repr. Oxford, 1982).

Keel, O., *The Song of Songs: A Continental Commentary*, tr. F. J. Gaiser (Minneapolis, 1994).

Kermode, F., and A. Robert, *The Literary Guide to the Bible* (1987; repr. London, 1997).

Kittay, E. F., *Metaphor: Its Cognitive Force and Linguistic Structure* (1987; repr. Oxford, 1989).

Knowles, D., *The English Mystical Tradition* (1961; repr. London, 1964).

LaCoque, A., *Romance, She Wrote: A Hermeneutical Essay on Song of Songs* (Harrisburg, PA, 1998).

Lakoff, G., *Women, Fire and Dangerous Things: What Categories Reveal about the Mind* (Chicago and London, 1987).

Landy, F., *Paradoxes of Paradise: Identity and Difference in the Song of Songs*, Bible and Literature Series 7 (Sheffield, 1983).

Leclercq, J., 'Aux sources des sermons sur les Cantiques', in J. Leclercq, *Recueil d'études sur Saint Bernard et ses écrits*, 1 (Rome, 1962), 275–320.

Leclercq, J., *Études sur le vocabulaire monastique du Moyen Age*, Studia Anselmiana 48 (Rome, 1961).

—, 'Influence and Noninfluence of Dionysius in the Western Middle Ages', *Pseudo-Dionysius: The Complete Works*, tr. C. Luibheid, The Classics of Western Spirituality (New York, 1987).

—, *L'Amour des lettres et le désir de Dieu: Initiation aux auteurs monastiques du Moyen Age* (1957; repr. Paris, 1990).

—, 'L'Attitude spirituelle de S. Bernard devant la guerre', *CCist*, 1 (1974), 195–225.

—, '*Lectio divina*: Jésus livre et Jésus lecteur', *CCist*, 48/3 (1986), 207–16.

—, 'Aspects littéraires de l'oeuvre de S. Bernard', in J. Leclercq (ed.), *Recueil d'études sur Saint Bernard et ses écrits*, 3 (Rome, 1969), 13–104.

—, 'Mary's Reading of Christ', *Monastic Studies*, 15 (1984), 105–16.

—*Otia monastica: Études sur le vocabulaire de la contemplation au Moyen Age*, Studia Anselmiana 51 (Rome, 1963).

— 'Saint Bernard et Origène d'après un manuscrit de Madrid', in J. Leclercq (ed.), *Recueil d'études sur Saint Bernard et ses écrits*, 2 (Rome, 1966), 373–85.

Lees, R. A., *The Negative Language of the Dionysian School of Mystical Theology: An Approach to the Cloud of Unknowing*, Analecta Cartusiana 107 (Salzburg, 1983).
Ligey, G. M., 'The *Canticum amoris* of Richard Rolle', *Traditio*, 12 (1956), 369–91.
Louth, A., *Denys the Areopagite* (London, 1989).
Lubac, H. de, *Exégèse médiévale: Les Quatre sens de l'Écriture*, 3 vols. (Paris, 1959–64).
McLaughlin, J., 'St Bonaventure and the English Mystics', *S. Bonaventura 1274–1974*, 2 (Rome, 1974), 279–87.
Matter, E. A., *The Voice of my Beloved: The Song of Songs in Western Medieval Christianity* (Philadelphia, 1990).
Mellet, P., *Notes sur le désir de Dieu chez Guillaume de Saint-Thierry* (Notre-Dame de Géronde, Switzerland, 1967).
Minnis, A. J., 'Affection and Imagination in *The Cloud of Unknowing* and Hilton's Scale of Perfection', *Traditio*, 39 (1983), 323–66.
—, 'Langland's Ymaginatif and Late-Medieval Theories of Imagination', *Comparative Criticism*, 3 (1981), 71–103.
—, *Medieval Theory of Authorship: Scholastic Literary Attitudes in the Later Middle Ages* (1984; repr. Aldershot, 1988).
—, 'The Sources of *The Cloud of Unknowing*: A Reconsideration', *MMTE* 2 (1982), 63–75.
—, A. B. Scott (eds.), with the assistance of D. Wallace, *Medieval Literary Theory and Criticism c.1100–c.1375: The Commentary Tradition* (1988; repr. Oxford, 1991).
Miquel, P., *Le Vocabulaire latin de l'expérience spirituelle dans la tradition monastique et canoniale de 1050 à 1250*, Théologie Historique 79 (Paris, 1989).
Morris, C. M., *The Discovery of the Individual, 1050–1200* (London, 1972).
Morse, R., *Truth and Convention in the Middle Ages: Rhetoric, Representation and Reality* (Cambridge, 1991).
Ohly, F., *Hohelied-Studien: Grundzüge einer Geschichte der Hoheliedauslegung des Abendlandes bis zum 1200* (Wiesbaden, 1958).
Oxford Latin Dictionary, ed. P. G. W. Glare (1968; repr. Oxford, 1992).
Pantin, W. A., *The English Church in the Fourteenth Century* (Cambridge, 1955).
Perella, N. J., *The Kiss Sacred and Profane: An Interpretative History of Kiss Symbolism and Related Religio-Erotic Themes* (Berkeley and Los Angeles, 1969).
Pfaff, R. W., *New Liturgical Feasts in Later Medieval England* (Oxford, 1970).
Phillips, S. H., 'Mysticism and Metaphor', *International Journal for the Philosophy of Religion*, 23 (1988), 17–41.

Pietras, H., *L'Amore in Origene*, Studia Ephemerides 'Augustinianum' 28 (Rome, 1988).
Raby, F. J. E., *A History of Christian-Latin Poetry* (Oxford, 1953).
Renevey, D., 'Anglo-Norman and Middle English Translations of the Hymn *Dulcis Iesu Memoria*', in R. Ellis and R. Tixier (eds.), *The Medieval Translator* 5 (Turnhout, 1996), 264–83.
— 'Enclosed Desires: A Study of the Wooing Group', in W. F. Pollard and R. Boenig (eds.), *Mysticism and Spirituality in Medieval England* (Cambridge, 1997), 39–62.
—, 'Encoding and Decoding: Metaphorical Discourse of Love in Richard Rolle's Commentary on the First Verses of the Song of Songs', in R. Ellis and R. Evans (eds.), *The Medieval Translator* 4 (Exeter, 1994), 200–17.
—, 'Margery's Performing Body: The Translation of Late Medieval Discursive Religious Practices', in D. Renevey and C. Whitehead (eds.), *Writing Religious Women: Female Spiritual and Textual Practices* (Cardiff and Toronto, 2000), 197–216.
—, 'Name Above Names: The Devotion to the Name of Jesus from Richard Rolle to Walter Hilton's *Scale of Perfection* I', *MMTE* 6 (1999), 103–21.
—, '*The Name Poured Out*: Margins, Illuminations and Miniatures as Evidence for the Practice of Devotions to the Name of Jesus in Late Medieval England', *The Mystical Tradition and the Carthusians*, Analecta Cartusiana 130/9 (Salzburg, 1996), 127–47.
Riehle, W., *The Middle English Mystics*, tr. B. Standring (London, 1981).
Robillard, J. A., 'Les Six genres de contemplation chez Richard de Saint-Victor et leur origine platonicienne', *Revue des Sciences Philosophiques et Théologiques*, 28 (1939), 229–33.
Ruello, F., 'Statut et rôle de l'*intellectus* et de l'*affectus* dans la *Théologie mystique* de Hughes de Balma', *Kartäusermystik und-mystiker*, Analecta Cartusiana 55/1 (Salzburg, 1981), 1–46.
Schulte, F., 'Das musikalische Element in der Mystik Richard Rolles von Hampole' (Univ. of Bonn thesis, 1951).
Schumacher, M., 'Mysticism in Metaphor', in *S. Bonaventura 1274–1974*, 2, (Rome, 1974), 361–86.
Simon, M., 'Le "Face à Face" dans les méditations de Guillaume de Saint-Thierry', *CCist*, 35/2 (1973), 121–36.
Simpson, J., *Piers Plowman: An Introduction to the B-Text* (London, 1990).
Smalley, B., *The Study of the Bible in the Middle Ages* (1952; repr. Oxford, 1983).
Soskice, J. M., *Metaphor and Religious Language* (1985; repr. Oxford, 1989).
Spicq P. C., *Esquisse d'une histoire de l'exégèse latine au Moyen Age* (Paris, 1944).
Stegmüller, F., *Repertorium biblicum medii aevi*, 11 vols. (Madrid, 1950–1980).

Stock, B., *The Implications of Literacy* (Princeton, 1983).
Stoeckle, B., 'Amor carnis – abusus amoris: Das Verstandnis von der Konkupiszens bei Bernhard von Clairvaux und Aelred von Rieval', *Analecta monastica*, 7, Studia Anselmiana 54 (Rome, 1965), 147–76.
Taylor, C., *Sources of the Self: The Making of the Modern Identity* (Cambridge, 1992).
The Victoria History of the Counties of England, 3, *A History of Yorkshire* (London, 1974).
Turner, D., *Eros and Allegory: Medieval Exegesis of the Song of Songs*, Cistercian Studies Series 156 (Kalamazoo, 1995).
Verdeyen, P., *La Théologie mystique de Guillaume de Saint-Thierry* (Paris, 1990).
—, 'Parole et sacrement chez Guillaume de Saint-Thierry', *CCist*, 49 (1987), 218–28.
Watson, N., *Richard Rolle and the Invention of Authority*, Cambridge Studies in Medieval Literature 13 (Cambridge, 1991).
—, 'Richard Rolle as Elitist and as Popularist: The Case of *Judica me*', in M. G. Sargent (ed.), *De cella in seculum: Religious and Secular Life and Devotion in Late Medieval England* (Cambridge, 1989), 123–44.
—, 'Translation and Self-Canonization in Richard Rolle's *Melos amoris*', in R. Ellis (ed.), *The Medieval Translator: The Theory and Practice of Translation in the Middle Ages* (Cambridge, 1989), 167–80.
Weber, S. A., *Theology and Poetry in the Middle English Lyric: A Study of Sacred History and Aesthetic Form* (Columbus, OH, 1969).
Wenzel, S., *Preachers, Poets, and the Early English Lyric* (Princeton, 1986).
White, H., 'Langland's Ymaginatif, Kynde and *The Benjamin major*', *MA*, 55 (1986), 241–7.
Wilmart, A., 'Le Cantique d'amour de Richard Rolle', *RAM*, 20–1 (1939–40), 131–48.
Wogan-Browne, J., N. Watson, A. Taylor and R. Evans (eds.), *The Idea of the Vernacular: An Anthology of Middle English Literary Theory 1280–1520*, Exeter Medieval Texts and Studies (Exeter, 1999).
Yates, F. A., *The Art of Memory* (London, 1966).
Zimmerman, J. A., *Liturgy as Language of Faith: A Liturgical Methodology in the Mode of Paul Ricoeur's Textual Hermeneutics* (London, 1988).
Zinn, G., Jr., 'Book and Word. The Background of Bonaventure's Use of Symbols', *S. Bonaventura 1274–1974*, 2 (Rome, 1974), 143–69.
—, 'Personification Allegory and Vision of Light in Richard of St Victor's Teaching on Contemplation', *University of Toronto Quarterly*, 46 (1977), 190–214.

Index

Aaron, 15
accubitus, 55
Aelred of Rievaulx, 20, 36
   Speculum caritatis, 36
affectio, 32, 36–8, 48–9, 54, 58–9, 68, 72–3, 75, 78, 111, 123
affectus, 36–7, 42, 48, 56–7, 68, 91
alienatio, 12
Allen, H. E., 66, 106
Ambrose, St, 24
Anselm of Canterbury, St, 42
apophatic theology, 44–5, 50, 111, 114, 120
Aquinas, Thomas, 63
archetype (*figura*), 55
Arnould, E. J. F., 93
Asher, 11
Astell, A. W., 63
auctor, 3, 18, 66–7, 80, 94, 132
auctoritas, 127
audience and readership, 5–6, 22–3, 28–30, 37, 47, 52, 58, 65, 67–8, 70, 78, 80–2, 87, 94, 103–8, 111–12, 116, 120–1, 128, 133, 140, 144, 154
Augustine, St, 1–2, 14, 21, 24–5, 153
   Confessions, 2
   De doctrina christiana, 14
   On Free Will, 2
   On the Trinity, 2
authorial presence, 127

Bala, 11, 13
beatific vision, 2, 22, 40–2, 49, 52–3, 57–8, 100, 104, 118, 120
   face to face, 22, 41–5, 47, 50–53, 55–7, 59, 104, 114–15, 118, 120
Bede, the Venerable, 26, 29
   Allegoria expositio, 26
beloved, 15, 23–4, 30, 35, 58, 77, 86–8, 90–1, 95, 98, 100, 103, 111, 118, 149
Benjamin, 11

Benton, J. F., 151, 153
Bernard of Clairvaux, 4, 16, 20, 23–4, 26–33, 35–8, 40–2, 47, 54, 64, 68, 70, 72, 75, 77, 83, 91, 131, 149, 152
   De diligendo deo, 30, 32, 38
   Sermones super cantica canticorum, 27, 32, 37, 153
Bernard of Portes, 27
Bible, 2, 24–5, 31, 54, 67, 75, 82, 100, 124, 126–7, 146, 150
   Book of Ecclesiastes, 27, 69
   Book of Genesis, 18, 25
   Book of Proverbs, 27
   Exodus, 44–5
   Gospel according to Luke, 85
   Letter to the Ephesians, 15
   Old Testament, 2, 17, 48
   Psalms, 85
   Psalter, 67, 124, 134, 140
   Second Letter to the Corinthians, 113
Blackeney, Guillaume, 64
body, 1, 9–10, 19, 25, 28, 32, 37–8, 46–8, 54, 66, 85, 94, 98, 112, 114, 135, 142–3
Bonaventure, St, 123–4
   Breviloquium, 123
breasts, 3, 22, 28–9, 51, 68, 73–4, 81, 84–6, 89, 135
bride and bridegroom mysticism, 16, 18, 25, 32–4, 42, 45, 47–3, 59, 82, 88, 97, 100–1, 135, 157
   nuptial imagery, 23, 39, 41–2, 48, 57, 90, 100–1
Byntree, William, 64

calor, 67, 107–8, 134
canor, 67, 94, 100–1, 106–8, 112, 114, 134
caritas, 25, 37–40, 51, 54, 56, 67, 76–7, 79, 84, 86–7, 90, 95, 100–1, 109, 111, 115–17, 120–1

Index

Carthusian spirituality, 64
Cassian, John, 24, 143
  Collationes, 24
cataphatic theology, 21, 45, 50, 117
Chaucer, Geoffrey, 136
Christ
  as *arbor vitae*, 98
  as book, 58
  body of, 37, 46, 81, 85
  and the Church, 26–7, 152
  deified, 110
  devotion to, 152
  devotion to the Name of Jesus, 89–91, 100, 130–1, 139, 149
  and elected soul, 27, 34, 100, 117, 136
  in his humanity, 31, 37, 44, 46, 51, 54, 77
  Incarnation of, 43
  as mother, 85–6
  Passion of, 43
  soldiers of, 30
Cloud-author, 20
cognition and language, 18, 30–1, 40, 50, 52, 59, 67, 80, 83–5, 87, 96, 110, 118, 123, 151
commentary practice, 1–2, 4–5, 15, 23–30, 35, 41, 47–9, 53, 59, 64–5, 67–8, 74–6, 80, 82, 85, 87, 90–4, 101–3, 108–9, 118, 120, 124–8, 131–2, 135, 145, 149, 151–3, 157
commentators, 1, 3, 21, 23–6, 30, 32, 35–6, 42–3, 53, 59, 66, 75, 77, 79–80, 91, 151
comparatio, 18
conceptual domain, 78–9, 87–8, 93, 96, 116
confessors, 144
coniungere, 86
consciousness, 4, 12, 30, 50, 63, 81, 96, 113, 118, 123, 125, 131, 133, 148, 150–1
contemplation
  degrees of, 12–14, 17
  ecstasy of, 11, 18–19, 52, 103, 114
  modes of, 12
  work of, 13
contemplative, 5, 15, 28, 31, 38–9, 58, 71, 75, 77, 84, 99, 109, 113, 116–17, 129–30, 145
contemplative activity, 11, 14
contemplative experience, 50, 78, 80, 82, 87, 101, 115, 119, 120, 127–9
contemplative life, 18, 31, 39, 50, 54, 58, 74, 76–7, 83, 99, 101, 106–7, 111, 113, 125, 137, 138
contemplative practice, 4, 107
contemplative process, 13
contemplative state, 5, 70
contemplative system, 4, 77
continuous prayer, 132, 150
conversion, 31, 34, 54, 68, 72, 93, 108, 132–3, 138–9, 144–5
Copeland, R., 86, 96, 122, 131
copulare, 86, 137

Dan, 11
Dante, Alighieri, 124
degrees of love, 5, 32, 36, 38–40, 76, 104, 121–5, 128–9, 131, 138–9, 145, 147, 150
  insatiabilis (fourth degree), 39, 75
  inseparabilis (second degree), 39, 75
  insuperabilis (first degree), 39, 76
  insuperable, 121, 148
  insuperable, inseparable and singular, 148
  singularis (third degree), 39, 75, 89
delectatio carnalis, 69
Denys the Carthusian, 63
dialogic exchange, 153–4
dialogic form, 129
dilatatio mentis, 12
Dina, 11
Dionysian system, 16, 110
dulcor, 67, 79, 107–8, 134

ecstatic experience, 113
effectus, 48, 56
electus, 72, 93, 106, 108–9

Horstmann, K., 66

inventio, 123
Isidore of Seville
  Etymologiae, 128
Issachar, 11

Jacob, 11, 13, 15–16, 42
Javelet, R., 55
Jesus, *see* Christ
John of Genoa, 128
  Catholicon, 127
John Scot Erigena, 43
Jorz, Thomas de, 64
Joseph, 11, 97
jubilation (*jubilatio*), 76, 99, 134, 137

jucunditas, 19
Judah, 11, 16
Julian of Eclanum, 26
   Libellum de amore, 26
Julian of Norwich, 20
justi, 95

Kirkby, Margaret, 141–4
kiss (*osculum*), 3, 19, 30–3, 45–7, 50–2, 56, 74, 78, 81, 83–4, 88–9, 95–8, 100, 137, 145

Langland, William, 20
language
   carnal, 77–8, 84, 99, 120, 145
   figurative, 9, 20, 50, 56, 98, 133, 141
   of love, 3–5, 17, 47, 54–5, 59, 70, 78–9, 85, 87–8, 95, 101, 107, 111, 118–21, 138–9, 149
   mystical, 21
language of interiority, 1–2, 63
language theory, 9, 15, 151
Leah, 11, 16
lectio divina, 24
lectulus floridus, 117
levels of the soul
   animal, rational and spiritual, 11, 52, 54
Levi, 11
lexical terms, 4, 38, 78–9, 82, 96, 98
liber naturae, 152
linguistic competence, 5, 14, 89
linguistic signs, 96, 113
linguistic system, 50, 63, 83, 106, 151
literary competence, 21, 58, 145–6
literary intention, 105
liturgical practice, 135
liturgy, 4, 109, 135, 136
Lombard, Peter, 67
love
   carnal, 3, 29, 31, 58, 76–81, 83, 87, 93, 94, 105, 110–11, 117, 119, 137
   intellectual, 55
   as perfection of letters, 146
lover
   of God, 53, 81, 103
lovers
   carnal, 71, 79, 105–7, 118
   spiritual, 105, 137
Lubac, H. de, 26, 41
lyrics, 4, 73, 122–3, 130, 150

Mary, Virgin, 3, 26, 73, 85, 89
   Assumption of, 85

   as *exemplum*, 30
   as mother, 84–5
masculinization, 54
Matter, E. A., 4, 24, 63, 75, 152
medieval literary theory, 2, 4, 20
   accessus, 28
   causa divina, 28
   causa scribendi, 27, 93
   forma materialis, 93
   inscriptio, 28
   interpres, 33, 48, 67, 127
   materia, 28
   modus agendi, 28
   modus scribendi, 33
   proemium, 93
   prologues, 26, 147, 152
   'type C' prologue, 28
medieval subjectivity, 1, 153
memory (*memoria*), 10, 36
'messager', 67, 127, 144, 154
metaphoric potential, 35
metaphorical discourse, 5, 16–18, 20, 30, 33, 41, 50, 55–6, 58, 69, 78, 80, 93, 96, 110, 116–21, 123, 138, 145, 151
metaphorical meaning, 3, 15, 37, 72, 74, 78–81, 84–5, 99, 101, 121, 145
metaphors, 11, 13, 15, 17–19, 29, 58, 82–4, 87, 96, 100, 114, 117, 139, 149
   and utterance, 15, 29, 83
Migne, J.-P., 63
   Patrologia latina, 63
Minnis, A. J., 2, 124, 157
misogyny, 69, 154
moderni, 115
Moses, 15, 45
Murray, E., 74
music
   of the heart, 149
   musical vocabulary, 94
   spiritual, 94–5
mystical experience, 4, 47, 51, 59, 78–80, 91, 96, 98, 101, 104, 113–14

Naphtali, 11, 13, 18–19
narrative voice, 3, 4, 37, 42–3, 64, 82, 89–90, 111, 126, 128–9, 135–6, 141, 143, 152
nativity, 89
Neo-Platonism, 2, 10, 43, 114, 153
Nicholas of Lyra, 63
nightingale, 101, 150

nun of Yedingham, 125, 129, 131
nuns and anchoresses, 5, 73

obumbratio, 97
oculus mentali, 112
Ohly, F., 63
Old Egyptian love poetry, 25
oleum effusum verse, 88–9
oratio, 92, 124
Origen of Alexandria, 24–6, 34, 44, 49
Ovid, 79
    Ars amatoria, 79

para-mystical phenomena, 116
Paul, St, 12 112–16, 122, 129
performance, 4, 6, 24, 34, 48, 52, 54, 66, 92, 109, 112, 122–5, 127, 150
    as drama, 34, 48–9, 111
persona, 94, 105, 107–8, 122, 125, 138, 144
personification, 11, 84
Petrarch, Francesco, 124
Plotinus, 2
politics of accessibility, 104, 123, 125, 132, 138, 140, 144
Pomerius, Julianus
    De vita contemplativa, 146
postil, 4, 22, 66–7, 74, 92–3, 100, 103, 125, 128
process of interiorization, 78
process of invention, 13
prolegomena, *see* medieval literary theory prologues
Pseudo-Dionysius, 17, 42, 129

quaerere Deum, 32

Rachel, 11, 15–16
radical reflexivity, 1, 6, 9, 47
raptus, 77
ratio, 36, 90
rational soul, 148
rational man, *see* reason
reading process, 2, 9, 16, 23–5, 29–30, 32, 35–8, 47–8, 52, 59, 66, 75, 81, 92, 98, 104, 123, 130, 133–5, 137, 141, 152
reason, 2, 10–15, 17, 19–20, 23, 27, 32, 42, 47, 55, 65, 70, 75, 80, 112, 119
reasoned imagination, 11, 14, 19
recipients, 5, 27, 73, 77, 104, 109, 112, 123–4, 126–33, 135–40, 142–8

religious discourse, 147
reprobi, 92, 106
revelacio, 115
rhetoric, 67, 125, 137
    alliteration, 94
    anaphora, 94
    balance, 94
    eloquium, 94
    inventio, 67
    paranomasia, 105
    prosopopeia, 127
    synaesthesia, 95
    synderesis, 18
    translatio, 13, 18
rhetorical devices, 18, 67, 86
Ricardian system, 12, 16
Richard of St Victor, 4, 7, 9–12, 14–16, 18, 20–1, 27, 29, 35–6, 39, 50, 54, 63, 75–6, 91, 97, 112, 148, 151
    Pseudo-Richard of St Victor, 27, 28–9, 35, 41, 75, 91
    The Four Degrees of Violent Charity (*De IV gradibus violentae charitatis*), 36, 39, 75
    The Mystical Ark (*Benjamin major*), 4, 9, 11, 13, 15–17, 19, 152
    The Twelve Patriarchs (*Benjamin minor*), 9–10, 13, 15–16, 97, 151
Richard Rolle and the Invention of Authority (N. Watson), 66
Rolle, Richard
    Canticum amoris, 72, 88, 149
    Contra amatores mundi, 5, 102–6, 109–10, 120–4, 128, 136–7
    Ego dormio, 124–8, 130–3, 135, 138–40, 144, 147–9, 154
    Emendatio vitae, 109, 124–5, 132–3, 136–41, 144
    English Magnificat, 67
    Incendium amoris, 5, 69, 94, 103–4, 109, 134
    Melos amoris, 5, 66–7, 69, 73, 75, 91–4, 101, 103–4, 109, 114, 116, 122–5, 131–4, 136, 150
    Six Old Testament Canticles, 67
    Super apocalypsim, 67
    Super canticum canticorum, 5, 66–8, 73, 76, 80, 83, 88, 91–4, 101–4, 109, 116, 122–5, 131, 134, 136, 143
    Super psalmum vicesimum, 5
    Super threnos, 67
    The Commandment, 125, 132, 138–9, 144

The Form of Living, 125, 138–40, 142–4, 147–50, 154
Rousseau, J.-J., 1
Ruben, 11
rumination (*ruminatio*), 46, 92, 96
Russell, John, 64

sacra scriptura, 124, 127
sapiencia increata, 111
Scott, A. B., 2, 124, 157
self, 1–6, 11, 16, 18, 20–4, 26–7, 33–5, 37, 40–1, 45, 47, 50, 54, 57–8, 63–4, 66, 71–2, 74, 81, 92, 94, 96–7, 102, 104, 105–7, 109, 113, 120–1, 130, 132, 134, 136–7, 139, 141–2, 146, 151, 157
 and introspection, 2, 91
 and medieval psychology, 36, 40–1
 self-awareness, 134
 self-effacement, 134
 self-examination, 153
 self-fashioning, 21
 self-realization, 11
 self-reflexivity, 152
semantic field, 3, 43, 52–3, 59, 77–80, 82, 84, 137, 141
sensatio, 115, 118
sermo divinus, 29
sexual desire, 72
sexual language, 2
signa, 123
Simeon, 11
similitudes, 13–15
Simon, M., 43
sitting posture, 55, 97
Smalley, B., 2
solitary life, 64, 74, 93, 108, 117, 121, 142–3, 145, 147, 154
song, 23, 28, 31, 34, 48, 51, 54, 72, 77, 93, 95–6, 109, 112–13, 125, 132, 134, 137, 147, 149, 156
Song of Songs, 1–4, 19, 22–3, 25–8, 39–41, 46–8, 52–62, 66–7, 74, 77–8, 84, 86–7, 90, 92, 94, 96–9, 101–2, 106–7, 109, 111, 117, 119–20, 122, 125–8, 131–2, 134–5, 138–9, 146, 148–9, 151–3, 157
 ecclesiastical treatment of the, 3
 Marian interpretation of the, 3
 mystical treatment of the, 3, 82, 86, 91, 152
soul, 2–3, 8–9, 12, 14, 16–19, 24–5, 28–37, 39–51, 53–6, 59, 72, 75–6, 78, 80, 83–6, 88–9, 91, 93, 95–6, 98, 100–1, 110–12, 115, 117–19, 130, 132–3, 135, 138, 145, 147, 149, 152
 as *anima*, 29, 53–4,
 as *animus*, 54
 rational, 11
spiritual adviser, 127, 129
spiritual journey, 34, 51, 103, 133
spiritual love, 30–1, 48, 54, 58, 76, 103, 105, 107, 109–11, 118, 120, 125, 131, 136, 137, 141, 147
spiritual proficiency, 141
spiritus, 45–6, 51–2, 54, 117, 153
Stegmüller, F., 64
sublevatio, 12

Taylor, A., 2
 Sources of the Self, 2
textual strategy, 105–6, 110, 112, 116, 120–1, 128, 132, 144
The Voice of my Beloved (E. A. Matter), 24
Theiner, P. F., 103
timor, 36
transference, 5, 15, 18–19, 49, 72, 77, 80, 109, 128, 149
translation, 20, 49, 80, 94, 96, 108, 114, 122, 124, 126–8, 133, 135, 140, 150
tristitia, 36
tropes, 29, 50, 63, 64
Turner, D., 63

union (*unio*), 11, 16, 18, 21, 23, 34, 41–3, 45, 47, 53, 56, 58–9, 64, 77–8, 90, 95, 110, 118, 145
unitas spiritus, 51–2

Vandenbroucke, F., 93
Verdeyen, P., 49
vernacular theologies, 1
vernacularity, 123, 125, 127
virtus imaginativa, 18, 20
visio, 114–15

Waleys, Thomas, 64
Wallace, D., 124
Watson, N., 66, 92, 94, 104, 124
William of St Thierry, 4, 6, 20, 28, 30, 35, 40, 41, 58, 64, 70, 75, 81, 91, 104, 106, 114, 117, 152–3
 De contemplando Deo, 41–2, 44
 Expositio super canticum canticorum, 41, 46–7

Golden Epistle, 53
Meditativae orationes, 41–3
womb, 84–5
women, 5
women and Rolle, 68–73, 77, 79, 106, 144, 153

work of contemplation 9–11, 16, 21, 97
wound, 37, 83, 85, 99

Zabulon, 11
Zelpha, 11